MUSIC TO·DAY

MUSIC TO-DAY

Its Heritage from the Past, and Legacy to the Future

BY

JOHN FOULDS
Opus 92

AUTHOR OF "EDUCATIONAL ASPECTS OF MUSIC"; "CHALLENGES"; "ANCIENT GREEK MUSIC"; "MODERN MUSICAL PROBLEMS"
(LONDON UNIVERSITY LECTURES)
ETC.

With numerous Musical Illustrations

Noverre Press

First published in 1934

This facsimile reprint published in 2010 by

The Noverre Press
Southwold House
Isington Road
Binsted
Hampshire
GU34 4PH

© 2010 The Noverre Press

ISBN 978-1-906830-31-1

A CIP catalogue record for this book is available from the British Library

CONTENTS

PART ONE

BY WAY OF INTRODUCTION

Apologia—A Clear Vantage-ground—Viewpoints—Musical Patriotism—More Intelligent Listeners—Occult and Overt—The Rationale of Inspiration—The most Important Aspect of Music To-day 13

PART TWO

A SURVEY OF MUSIC AT THE PRESENT TIME

CHAPTER I.—PROBLEMS AND PREJUDICES . . . 25
§ 1. Distrust of Modern Composers 27
§ 2. An Unparalleled Revolution 28
§ 3. New Wine: New Bottles 29
§ 4. Certain Objections 30

CHAPTER II.—A COLLOQUY 33

CHAPTER III.—MODES 41
§ 1. Diatonal Music 41
§ 2. Greek Modes: Gregorian: Major and Minor . . 44
§ 3. Pre-Greek, *i.e.* Early Aryan 44
§ 4. A greatly Extended Modal System . . . 45
§ 5. Atonal Music 56

CHAPTER IV.—QUARTER-TONES 59
§ 1. Whole-tones, Half-tones, Quarter-tones . . 59
§ 2. Quarter-tone Signs 61
§ 3. Aural Possibilities and Vagaries . . . 64

Contents

	PAGE
CHAPTER V.—THE VOICE	66
§ 1. Nature's Perfect Instrument	67
§ 2. Words and Music	67
§ 3. Gregarious Song-impulses	71
§ 4. Accentuation and Quantity	73
CHAPTER VI.—THE ORCHESTRA	75
§ 1. Intimacy with the Orchestra Desirable	75
§ 2. Appreciation of *Timbres*	76
§ 3. Novel Tone-colours	77
§ 4. Some Examples	79
§ 5. Instrumental Discrepancies	86
§ 6. Conducting and Conductors	90
§ 7. Generalities	94
CHAPTER VII.—COLOUR AND MUSIC	97
§ 1. The Pictorial Sense in Musicians	97
§ 2. Seeing and Hearing	99
§ 3. The Remington Colour-organ	100
§ 4. Scriabin and the *Tastiera per Luce*	101
§ 5. Suggested Tables of Correspondences	102
§ 6. Personal Reactions to Sound	103
§ 7. Unity and Diversity	104
CHAPTER VIII.—MUSIC AND SOME PSYCHO-PHYSIOLOGICAL REACTIONS	107
§ 1. Therapeutic Effects of Music	107
§ 2. Women and Music	111
§ 3. Familiarity and Contempt	114
CHAPTER IX.—CERTAIN CONDITIONS TO-DAY IN THE MUSICAL WORLD	123
§ 1. Ways and Means	123
§ 2. 'Light' Music	127
§ 3. A present-day Aberration	132
§ 4. Emancipated Rhythm	136
§ 5. Mechanized Music	140
§ 6. Conclusions of Part Two	150

Contents

PART THREE

TOWARD A MUSICAL ÆSTHETIC

	PAGE
CHAPTER X.—SOURCES OF INSPIRATION	155
§ 1. Musical Æsthetic in a State of Chaos	155
§ 2. Musical Appreciation	156
§ 3. A Septenary Classification	159
§ 4. Genius Defined	161
§ 5. Relatively restricted Range of Music hitherto	163
§ 6. A Five-planal Conception	165
§ 7. Music and Sex	177
§ 8. The Ensouling of Music	179
CHAPTER XI.—QUALITIES OF INSPIRATION	185
§ 1. Of the Vital Principle in Music	186
§ 2. Of the Beautiful in Music	188
§ 3. Of Idealism	190
§ 4. Of Purity in Music	192
§ 5. Of Spirituality in Music	192
§ 6. Of Individuality and Originality	193
§ 7. Of Mysticism and Mystical Inspiration	198
§ 8. Conclusions of Part Three	215

PART FOUR

MODERN MASTERS AT WORK

CHAPTER XII.—GENERALITIES	219
§ 1. Obiter Dicta	219
§ 2. Nationality in Music	220
§ 3. Impressionistic, post-Romantic, neo-Classicist, Verist, Expressionist, etc.	226

Contents

	PAGE
CHAPTER XIII.—A SERIES OF SWIFT VIGNETTES . . .	228

Strauss—Elgar—Stravinsky—Reger—Busoni—Ravel—Wolf—Schönberg—Bartók—Kodály—Falla—Hindemith—Honegger—Milhaud—Poulenc—Szymanowski—A German Group—An American Group—A French Group—An English Group—An Italian Group.

CHAPTER XIV.—A DIGRESSION WITH SOME CONSIDERATION OF THE DUAL WORLD OF MUSIC; HUMAN AND DEVA . . 279

CHAPTER XV.—VIGNETTES CONTINUED 293

Scriabin—Debussy—Delius—MacDowell—Sibelius.

§ 1. A Vignette Tailpiece 324

PART FIVE

NEW VISTAS

CHAPTER XVI.—TECHNICAL 329
 § 1. The Perfect Orchestra 330
 § 2. Counterpoint of *Timbres* 333
 § 3. 'Just' Intonation 333
 § 4. Auralizing Music 336
 § 5. Improved Listeners 339

CHAPTER XVII.—NON-TECHNICAL 341
 § 1. Simplicity—Complexity—Synthetic-Simplicity . 341
 § 2. Orientalities 343
 § 3. Improvisation 345
 § 4. Music and Magic 346
 § 5. 'Nature'-Pitch 347
 § 6. A Synthesis of Arts 349

CHAPTER XVIII.—CONCLUSION 351

INDEX 355

LIST OF MUSICAL ILLUSTRATIONS IN TEXT

		PAGE
1.	*Quartetto Intimo* (Foulds)	33
2.	*Quartetto Intimo* (Foulds)	33
3.	*Suite für Klavier* (Hindemith)	34
4.	Whole-tone Scale	43
5.	Whole-tone System: Free	43
6.	*Dorfmusikanten-Sextett* (Mozart)	43
7.	A Table of 90 Modes	46–47
8.	" Enigmatic Scale ": *Ave Maria* (Verdi)	51
9.	Example of Polytonality	56
10.	Passage in Quarter-Tones (Foulds)	62
11.	Accentuation and Quantity: example	73
12.	*Also Sprach Zarathustra* (Strauss)	79
13.	*Prometheus* (Scriabin)	80
14.	First Symphony (Brahms)	80
15.	Pianoforte Concerto No. 2 (Brahms)	80
16.	*Le Sacre du Printemps* (Stravinsky)	80
17.	*Roi Lear*: Overture (Berlioz)	80
18.	*Song of the High Hills* (Delius)	81
19.	*Die Brautwahl* (Busoni)	81
20.	*Tosca* (Puccini)	81
21.	*Le Sacre du Printemps* (Stravinsky)	82
22.	*Don Juan* (Strauss)	82
23.	*Dynamic Triptych* (Foulds)	83
24.	*Also Sprach Zarathustra* (Strauss)	83
25.	Example of Instrumental *Timbres*	84
26.	*Pacific 231* (Honegger)	84

List of Musical Illustrations in Text

	PAGE
27. *A World Requiem* (Foulds)	85
28. Example of Percussion *tutti*	85
29. Piano-Quartet (Schumann)	116
30. Double-Concerto: violins (Bach)	116
31. *Variations* (Elgar)	116
32. *Meistersinger*: Overture (Wagner)	117
33. (A) Jazz rhythm	136
(B) *Bolero* (Ravel)	136
(C) *Dynamic Triptych* (Foulds)	136
(D) String-Quartet No. 2 (Bartók)	137
(E) An Indian *Tala*	137
34. *Symphonie Pathétique* (Tchaikovsky)	138
35. *The Perfect Fool* (Holst)	138
36. Quartet: Finale (Foulds)	139
37. String-Quartet (Bartók)	255
38. Pianoforte Concerto No. 2 (Bartók)	256
39. A Fanfare	264
40. *March: Suite für Klavier* (Hindemith)	264
41. *Pastoral Symphony* (Vaughan Williams)	275
42. *Variazioni senza Tema* (Malipiero)	278
43. *Symphonie Fantastique* (Berlioz)	286
44. *La Damnation de Faust* (Berlioz)	287
45. Pianoforte Sonata No. 8 (Scriabin)	298
46. *L'Après-midi d'un Faune* (Debussy)	306
47. Symphony No. 8 (Sibelius)	322
48. *En Saga* (Sibelius)	322
49. Three Mantras from *Avatara* (Foulds)	335
50. *Gurre-Lieder* (Schönberg)	337
51. 'Promethean' chord (Scriabin)	342

PART ONE
BY WAY OF INTRODUCTION

BY WAY OF INTRODUCTION

Apologia—A Clear Vantage-ground—Viewpoints—Musical Patriotism—More Intelligent Listeners—Occult and Overt—The Rationale of Inspiration—The Most Important Aspect of Music To-day.

THERE would need to be reasons given, it seems, why a composer should lay aside the tools and methods of his art and enter the domain of the psychologist, the musicologist, the æsthetician. And he would be a temerarious fellow indeed who should do so at all, lacking a conviction that he had a unique, even though but a small contribution to make. For, in the nature of things, if he have devoted his life to his art—the goddess of which is assuredly a jealous goddess—he must needs be lacking in the particularized knowledge and appositeness of expression exhibited by the specialist in these domains.

Possessed of such a conviction, however, his contribution should owe little to speculative, studiously tentative or nebulously theoretical excursions into their realms, but almost everything to an extended practical acquaintance with the world of music, both on its creative and interpretative sides.

Beyond doubt there is obscurity in the minds of many about various technical questions which arise concerning the music of our day; beyond doubt also there are fascinating problems connected with psychological and psychical aspects of the art which are rarely explored; equally beyond doubt there is a demand for enlightenment of the obscurity surrounding these questions on the part of a large number of persons—perhaps a larger number than ever before in our history.

The composer who is really a creative artist ought, *ipso facto*, to be in a position to offer information upon the rationale of inspiration, about which no musicologist, however learned, can speak at first hand. The practising artist should likewise be able to speak from a unique position upon the interesting question of reactions to music on the part of performers and audience alike. As to matters of æsthetic—the branch of music of widest and most general interest, but one which is in a condition of almost complete chaos at the present time—if he be in a position to indicate even cursorily and tentatively a schematization which seems to cover the facts as we meet them, and thus to assist in the formation of a more reliable and penetrating evaluation of music than that to which we have been accustomed in the recent past, he may be held to have justified his excursion into 'fresh fields and pastures new.' And, at the least, he shall have obtained for himself the refreshment that results from a change of activity during a lacuna betwixt two major efforts in his own, more proper, sphere of labour.

It is proposed to offer neither an historical review of music, nor a series of gossipy 'personal paragraphs' about the daily doings of the fashionable musicians of the moment. A large and rapidly increasing musical public has arisen in recent years which desires neither type of book. It includes numbers of keen, young, ardent music-lovers who are avid of information of a certain clearly defined character. For since the time of Haydn and Mozart, when the average amateur was well able to bear his part in performances of the masters' works, a cleavage has gradually become

By Way of Introduction

apparent between the amateur and the professional performer—a hiatus which cannot be bridged. Such demands are made nowaday upon the technique of performers that no one who has not devoted a lifetime to the task of acquiring such a technique can hope to deal at all adequately, even on the merely digital side, with the extraordinary difficulties of, say, a Prokoviev violin concerto, or a Ravel piano piece. Since the advent of pianola, gramophone and radio, however, millions are able to listen to modern masterpieces and thus the hiatus spoken of above may be narrowed appreciably (if not indeed completely spanned) in the realms of æsthetic—of evaluation and appreciation.

What is so arresting in the attitude of these new music-lovers, whether one observes them in such differing venues as Berlin, Vienna, Paris, Rome, New York, or London, is their real desire to be able to respond to the composer (an attitude enormously stimulating to the creative artist), and their interest in the finest and highest. There is no denying, however, that they need help and guidance amid the perplexing artistic problems of to-day, when pretentious mediocrity is so rife, and meretricious dilettantism raises its voice as loudly as—more loudly indeed than—genuine artistry.

If then, having noted the principal problems which face us (Part I): we make a brief study of the more unusual of the technical devices which seem to baffle so many of our potential modern music-lovers, showing how these have developed logically from the past (Part II): if, further, we attempt to erect for their guidance some clearly defined and logical musical æsthetic, however incomplete—some kind of musical touchstone so to say, to which they may refer their own, often somewhat vague impressions, and upon which they may base their own judgments (Part III): following this, if we make practical application of such æsthetic principles by an estimate of the more outstanding composers of our day, referring them and their works, however tentatively, swiftly and cursorily, to the various categories postulated (Part IV): and if, finally, we permit ourselves a glimpse of the possibilities which lie in the future (Part V): we shall have covered the ground proposed.

More familiar with the written note than the written word, I am not likely either to underrate the difficulties or to be over-sanguine of complete success.

There is, however, it seems, a dearth of works of the present scope and type by practical musicians; quite 90 per cent of writing about music, musicians and musical affairs emanating from the pens of various kinds of onlookers—onlookers who may indeed ' see most of the game,' but who sometimes draw strange conclusions therefrom, or, more frequently still, raise problems and leave them for their readers to solve.

So that, although one may not altogether endorse Arnold Bennett's dictum: "The least critical word of the most prejudiced and ignorant creative artist is more valuable than whole volumes writ by dilettanti of measureless refinement and erudition": one may still believe that a creative artist of extended experience, having contacted many of the richest personalities in the musical world of our day, and setting himself honestly to put forward his reactions, conclusions and prognostications, can hardly fail to be stimulating and may be helpful.[1]

[1] "The question should be fairly stated, how far a man can be an adequate, or even a good . . . though inadequate critic of poetry, who is not a poet, at least *in posse*." Coleridge, *Anima Poetæ*.

By Way of Introduction

From what viewpoint, then, could such a survey be taken with some degree, at least, of impartiality?

It is now some thirty years ago that my master, Hans Richter, told us at a small luncheon party that he once heard Brahms say: "for the next great forward step in music, to England look." An interesting discussion followed for several musicians of discernment were present. Adolf Brodsky made perhaps the most striking contribution in something like these words: "Because England has at present no uninterrupted and well-knit stylistic traditions like Germany, Italy, Russia and France, the English have therefore the freer musical minds, the clearer vantage-ground from which they may survey the surrounding musical world and the more virgin soil from which may spring the next lusty sapling, as Brahms seems to have prophesied." Brahms spoke, of course, of composers, and time only can prove or disprove his prophecy. Brodsky's comment upon it, however, is surely germane to our present subject also. For nowhere should it be more easily possible to keep the mind free from narrow national musical prejudice than in England. Indeed many of the books by our musicologists prove this to be so, and for the very reason given by Brodsky.

Following the war, a period of somewhat exaggerated musical patriotism ensued. All countries participated. The author had best say at once that it is an attitude with which he has little sympathy. There are a number of persons in the musical world who look for the salvation of a country's music to the intensification of its national characteristics, and would base a new national music upon its old folk-

Music To-day

songs. Frankly, I am not of these. The time is past and will not return. Interest in folk-music from an archæological and ethnological point of view, and the greatest delight in its characteristic and perennial beauty, will, let us hope, never die. But for present-day composers and protagonists to concentrate upon such, or any other narrow nationalistic phenomena, goes clean against the main evolutionary trend of the art. Only out of a new realization of world-wide emotional-mental solidarity—even sodality—can the real music of the future be born.[1]

It may be objected that these problems are the business of composers themselves rather than for the general music-loving reader. This is not so, however, for the music-lover as he progresses, is meeting, and will meet, just the same problems the composer has faced at previous stages in his own progress. It is a difference of degree, not of kind. As the music-lover grows in power of appreciation and assimilation, so he approaches more and more nearly the state of the composer *when the latter is exercising his ratiocinative* (not his creative) *function*. More than once has the remark been made that we do not want more creative artists or interpreters either, the world being full of them—good, bad and mediocre; but we do want more discerning and intelligent listeners. Ridiculous though it be to desire a diminution of creative urge in an art that is already stifled beneath a mass of material lacking just this quality of inspiration; it is incontrovertible that a more penetrating and logical public judgment on the art would help greatly in separating the wheat from the chaff in the music of our day; a discriminatory function never before so necessary.

[1] Cf. p. 220 *et seq.*

By Way of Introduction

All serious artists desire to see evidence of a keener and better-balanced public judgment. Indeed it is imperative that this should be something like commensurate with the gigantic increase of interest which is so noticeable a feature of life to-day. To creative artists above all it is an urgent necessity (their work jumping less readily to the eye and ear than that of interpretative artists). For it is certain that there never was a time when so much crude and tentative work received the encomiums that only productions of the most gifted intellects deserve.

We must therefore, for all of the above-mentioned reasons, foster a more intelligent discernment in this matter, and it is toward this end, and toward an elucidation of some of the many and diverse problems which face the music-lover to-day, that I offer these studies. I make no pretence of being entirely impartial or completely unbiassed—which of us is?—at least I have indicated what my standpoint will be, and clearly foreshadowed (when I spoke of inspirational and allied psychic faculties), that some attention will be given to a much neglected branch of musical study. Such neglect is of course quite understandable because of the paucity of first-hand experience available. But it is a self-imposed condition that the great bulk of information and speculation along these lines which is offered in the following pages shall rest upon experience obtained at first hand.

Difficulties beset both the chronicler and the student of these as yet largely occult aspects of the art. As might have been expected, musicians as a whole are less interested in such questions, even when closely related to their art, than any other type of creative workers. And the main reason is not far to seek. For the technique of the art of music, both upon its creative and interpretative sides, is so exceedingly complex as almost to invite a measure of concentration out of all proportion to its real importance. No composition would be worth performing or listening to which displayed merely technical skill, even though of a high order; all experience of music pointing to one salient fact, namely, that technique without inspiration is powerless to preserve a work of art. A truism, of course. Yet, will it be believed that in the hundreds of schools, colleges and academies of music, whence thousands of budding composers debouch annually upon an unsympathetic world, no attention whatever, so far as I am aware, is paid to what I may call the rationale of inspiration.

You cannot teach inspiration it will be said; still less can you learn it. I do not assert that you can do either. I do say study it. And there is a great deal more data available than is commonly supposed. For it is almost impossible to find a sympathetic and even fairly exhaustive biography of our great composers that does not contain a number of highly suggestive facts appertaining to this aspect—the dynamics of their inspiration: suggestive, that is to say, to one who is concentrating for the moment upon their inspirational as distinct from their technical activities. (As to which of these is the more important, hear, for example, the opinion of the Italian composer Malipiero[1]: "Every real work of art subordinates the mere technique to the animating idea.")

One reason for the instinctive dislike of this and allied subjects which so many people betray, is the indubitable fact that once we leave the realms of the technical and objective, and attempt to deal with those subtler subjective states whence all that is loftiest and most enduring in our art emanates, we immediately become suspect as converts to the ranks of those from whose pens gush dogmatic assertion, unclear thinking, pseudo-pontifical pronouncements and vague sentimental generalities, like water from a fountain.

[1] In his pamphlet *The Orchestra*.

By Way of Introduction

Alas that in so few cases is it a Fountain of Life. The prolific issue of such works, however, at least indicates a demand. It also suggests to the student that behind such demand lies a degree of potential belief which should certainly not be abused, but (so far as statement of fact, correlation of experience and comparison of data can do so), encouraged and fostered. And the paucity of such information from the viewpoint of the music student is appalling.

Now once the artist has contacted his source of inspiration and is clothing such inspiration in a physical expression for the delectation of his fellow-men, he is concerned primarily with the *effects* of his work. I do not mean the amount of applause he earns by his composition or his performance. That is comparatively easy to achieve and soon palls. What does interest him is the degree and quality of inner response he obtains from his listeners. Music, perhaps the loftiest of the arts in origin,[1] is the most severely practical in its mode of presentation. One chord out of tune; one progression incompletely cognized, realized and externalized, and the edifice you have been building up is instantly shattered, the mood dissipated, and the total effect nullified. That is what I mean by saying that the practising artist is concerned with the effects of his work. This being so, he is, I believe (contrary to what is generally supposed), peculiarly well equipped to investigate just such problems as these. Instead of being the nebulous, dreamy, unstable creature of the romantic novelists of last century, he is, in reality, pre-eminently the type of person who is best able to bring down remote and rarefied thought-vibrations and give them cogent physical expression.

Almost all the great composers (it is sure to occur to readers) managed without making any study of the occult laws which operate through the sound-art. Of what use then is this branch of our study?

It is, of course, true that genius can accomplish all;

[1] Cf. p. 105.

much more, in any case, than can be attained by sheer learning. It is equally true, however, that human progress takes the form of concentrating upon, and rendering overt, the workings of natural law which were formerly occult. Not to digress into instances of what everyone knows, I refrain from giving examples of physicists 'discovering' what occultists have long before predicated. "Many a truth which was formerly occult is now overt." But the *methods* of the scientist, painstaking, accurate and wonderfully patient, are worthy of the sincerest form of flattery, and could/should be applied to this branch of our subject with marvellous results. For I confidently assert that no composer has yet realized the potentialities of a single musical tone. I speak of what I know. And I have seen a far greater effect produced by a single note of a certain *timbre*, than by whole symphonies comprising uncountable thousands of notes: good symphonies too, and beautifully played.

It will be understood that I am not speaking here of æsthetic values, or of effects upon the mentality of listeners, but of what I can only call magical effects. And by magic—it is a word the use of which here is sure to be misunderstood by some—I mean a change in the vibration of a listener effected by means whose manner of operation is at present unknown. Music-lovers, at any rate, should not jib at this word, for all music is designed to effect a change of some sort in some part or other of the hearer's make-up. Nor is there anything dangerous, unethical, immoral, or subversive of good, in this aspect of music. Alas that there should be need, even in the twentieth century, to say this.

The occult power of sound is at the same time the most important and the most neglected of the many and varied aspects of music to-day.

PART TWO
A SURVEY OF MUSIC AT THE PRESENT TIME

CHAPTER ONE: PROBLEMS AND PREJUDICES

*Distrust of Modern Composers—An Unparalleled Revolution
—New Wine: New Bottles—Certain Objections.*

THERE is, clearly apparent in the world of to-day, a more widespread interest in music than ever before. It has been a swift *crescendo* indeed, and appears to continue with increased rapidity. No one will quarrel with it—no musician certainly—except it be as to the quality of perception, the power of discrimination and the general level of æsthetic judgment shown forth. Here an important consideration arises. For, side by side with this enormous expansion of interest, there has grown and is still growing a certain distrust of all progressive composers; a habit of discounting in advance any work by a composer who is not content to purvey stereotyped emotional stimulant *via* the old-established melodic and harmonic routes. It is an attitude more frequently met with, as far as my experience goes, in England and Italy than in France, America, or Germany; and more noticeable among cultured than among the comparatively uninformed listeners of all the nations; the latter having of course fewer sophistications to surmount and fewer preconceptions to overcome.

With the vast majority of listeners, music goes in at one ear and out at the other, missing the brain *en route*.

Of the modicum whose brain is also acting, many will reach the conclusion that because a work is clever, it is only clever.

Music To-day

Remains a tiny fraction—those who, well knowing that cleverness is almost a *sine qua non* in modern music, would wish to penetrate through complexity of statement to simplicity of ideation. And this is the type which the serious artist is desirous of seeing greatly increased. It is a question, however much one may dislike the word, of education. The 'masses' are, without doubt, musical. The musical faculty is deeply rooted and widely spread among them, and indescribable joys await them when their latent powers of assimilation and evaluation are fostered. Their perceptive faculties should not be overlaid with masses of 'facts' relative to 'form,' pulse, and the like tiny facets of the technique of the art; subjects dear to certain types of teachers of 'musical appreciation'; but *educated*. (From *educo*—to draw out.)

Obviously it is the emotional response which should first be cultivated. Debussy told us in the *Revue Blanche* that in acting as its music-critic he would concentrate rather upon the emotional significance than the construction of works. "This will surely be held to be of greater importance than the game of dissecting them as though they were curious pieces of mechanism. Men in general forget that as children they were forbidden to dismember their playthings."

There are to-day many splendid old musicians whose knowledge of the great composers from Bach to Brahms is quite extensive. They cannot bear, because they simply cannot understand, anything since Strauss' *Heldenleben*. On the other hand considerable numbers of young people are undoubtedly ready to spring forward with the 'new' musicians, could only the hiatus between 'old' and 'new' be elucidated for them on its technical side. These people do not look for mere amusement, still less will they agree to be bored; what they really want is to learn something about modern music, and many of them display a lively intellectual curiosity which certainly deserves to be fostered.

§ 1. DISTRUST OF MODERN COMPOSERS

Meanwhile distrust, misvaluation and contempt are undoubtedly met with on all sides. One frequently hears from concert-goers such remarks as: " I don't like this modern stuff at all. Don't understand it "; " Why is it so full of discords? " " A hideous cacophony! " " Where are the melodies? " " I think the composer is just ' pulling our legs.' " These and many other misconceptions will be dealt with as we proceed, but this last charge of wilful levity must be controverted at once. For perhaps never before in the history of music were so many serious-minded composers at work on the major problems of their art. (There is, it is true, a note of the sardonic, the bitter-comic finger-to-nose, the satirical, in modern music;[1] a note which has not been sounded before. But this is quite another matter). What is encouraging about these and similar queries (that is, when they are not jejune to the point of inanity) is that they proceed, not from philistines, conservatives ingrain, ' diehards,' or apostles of the *status in quo*, but from open-minded persons who are really desirous of understanding.

Their doubt, distrust, dislike and utter misvaluation of modern music, is shot through with a curious fascination. They cannot ignore it. They feel there is a wondrous thrill to be had of it, could they but effect a re-orientation

[1] For example, in the music of Lord Berners.

in their own musical make-up at all commensurate with that which has taken place recently in the art. They are 'musical' people. By heredity and environment alike they are music-lovers, but their ability to respond is dependent upon their ability to understand in some measure the language in which the composer's ideations are being conveyed to them. A considerable majority I am convinced are fully capable of appreciating his message, could they but understand the *words* (melody, harmony, counterpoint, etc.), in which he is addressing them.

§ 2. AN UNPARALLELED REVOLUTION

Such difficulties are in no way surprising when one reflects that since about the year 1900 a revolution has occurred in the art without parallel in the whole of its modern history. So vast has been the distance traversed in a short thirty years that a music-lover well able to understand (I do not say able properly to evaluate) all the music written up to the end of last century, finds himself utterly unable to comprehend that of our day. Not only is he unable to realize what is being talked about; he cannot even understand what is being said. In other words; being quite incapable of understanding the language, he cannot penetrate to the thought, of which the word is a mere vehicle of expression. More explicitly; the technique of music through and by which the composer expresses his ideations, has changed so completely that it presents a kind of barrier, instead of a conduit, between our listener and his goal. Thus he becomes annoyed and exasperated, and frequently feels that he is facing problems incapable of solution and living amid conditions of utter musical chaos.

New Wine: New Bottles

It is impossible and should be unnecessary for him to study closely for himself all the lines of development of all the composers of all nationalities on their technical as well as expressional sides. This is a lifetime study. There is every reason, however, why a *résumé* of such study should be placed before him as clearly and succinctly as possible.

§ 3. NEW WINE: NEW BOTTLES

One of the first questions that arises in his mind is this: " Why should the composer—assuming that he has something to say—express himself in words we do not understand? What is wrong with the old vocabulary? " This is something like the question that torments the minds of certain purists over the so-called ' Americanization ' of English. Where the well-known word or phrase is inadequate to express the thought, or—and this is important —where a familiar thought can be better expressed by its means, then the use of a newly coined word or phrase is completely justified. As James Joyce said, if I understood him rightly; his so-called ' new ' words and phrases convey impressions which are not always possible of representation by ready-made ones. And if it be objected that such new words and phrases do not convey clear thought-concepts, the obvious rejoinder is that they do convey other and subtler impressions than thought-concepts, impressions which can be communicated in no other way. If this be so, the end must justify the means.

Similarly: when a composer finds his ideations utterly incommunicable by way of long-accepted melodic-turns, familiar chord-progressions, stereotyped rhythmic formulæ or banal vocal-instrumental *timbres,* he is forced to invent new ones through which, and through which only, it is possible to communicate them with even approximate truth.

§ 4. CERTAIN OBJECTIONS

Two objections arise which had better be met at once. Firstly: that the means of expression, melodic, harmonic, rhythmic, etc., which were available about the end of last century, are perfectly adequate to express any thought or mood the composer may desire to convey to us.

None can really know this but the composer. An analogy may help. The Bach technique was not adequate for Brahms, nor that of Mozart for Tchaikovsky; nor was Beethoven's for Berlioz, Weber's for Wagner, Palestrina's for Malipiero, Rameau's for Debussy nor Wagner's for Strauss. Purposely coupled together here are the names of a master and an admirer—master in his turn. It is true that the change is vastly greater and has been more cataclysmic between the period of, say, Brahms and Schönberg, than between any of the previously named. It has been, I repeat, a revolution. And after revolutions do we not expect the old order to be changed? It may be taken as a fact that the old harmonic, melodic, and rhythmic formulæ, are *not* capable of expressing many of the moods, thoughts, or inspirations which, inexhaustible as Nature herself, abide in the womb of the universal consciousness as ideations, until some pioneer of musical thought, raising his consciousness to a point at which he can contact them, plucks them forth for our delectation. Freshness of statement commensurate with that of the ideation becomes a necessity to the single-minded creative artist.

Second objection: that an enormous mass of music is

Certain Objections

produced annually which is nothing more than an adroit re-presentation of quite familiar thoughts dressed out in a new-looking garb.

This is true. More's the pity. Nothing can excuse such a proceeding; for unless a composer has 'something to say' he should remain silent. Alas, this is an age when we suffer terribly from what 'Dr' Josef Holbrooke has correctly diagnosed as "verbal diarrhœa." But it is not only of the musical world that this is true. In the world of politics, of finance; in domestic circles, in business; in sciences [1] and arts; in the gigantic literary world of to-day, there is vastly more talking than thinking, more thought than cognizance; [2] and enormously more of ratiocinative than of creative activity. In spite, however, of the heavy spate of merely cerebral compositions which threaten to inundate the musical world, no open-minded and impartial student will deny that we have a great deal of music nowadays which is honestly attempting to explore new realms of the super-normal, and is forced to couch its message in equally unfamiliar terms.

Other objections to the 'new' music, and these by far the greater in number and weight, result from the natural lethargy of humanity in general rather than from any real antipathy. People in the mass love to wallow in the familiar.[3] How often has not any professional musician

---

[1] Dr Wheeler of the British Medical Association : "The best word I can find for this pedantic verbiage is the American word 'hokum.' It epitomizes admirably all this obscurantist jargon. In the professional archæology of to-day 'hokum' is on the increase, and the same is true in other branches of science."

[2] Take a simple illustration of the difference. Having the faculty known as 'fixed pitch' I sing, for example, a middle C. I *know* it is C. No amount of thought can achieve this result, just as no argument can controvert it. This is knowledge; cognition: as distinct from thought; ratiocination.

[3] Cf. Familiarity and Contempt, p. 114.

been requested to " play/sing us something we know." Truly, inertia is the greatest enemy of the onward-pressing spirit in the artist. The too, too solid flesh, the frigid mind, the torpid heart . . . this ineluctable physical.[1]

From suchlike depressing considerations, which have perhaps beset the creative thinker since the beginning of time, let us betake ourselves to the more invigorating air of a concrete musical example, whose pros and cons may be discussed, and value considered, *qua* music and that alone.

[1] And yet, in Busoni's noble words : However deeply rooted in the human nature are inertia and attachment to the habitual; equally characteristic of all that has life, are energy and opposition to the existing order.

CHAPTER TWO: A COLLOQUY

HERE are three short pieces of music which, a mere thirty years ago, would have been counted utterly unintelligible. Such is not the case to-day.

Music To-day

Whatever may be thought of their æsthetic value, emotional effect or spiritual significance (if any), the musical thought and presentation offer no difficulties to one whose musical mentality is approximately up to date. A good musician of the year 1900, for instance, might ask: In what key are these pieces? Surely you cannot have satisfactory music without a key. To which the typical musician of to-day might reply: The first one is in no key; without fixed tonality; atonal. The second is in several different keys simultaneously; polytonal: and its effect, to my ear, is quite satisfactory in spite of this absence of the old-fashioned fixed tonality.

MUSICIAN OF FORMER TIMES: Do you tell me that it is possible to hear and to disentangle music played in different keys simultaneously?

MUSICIAN OF TO-DAY: Most certainly I do. The human ear is, we are told, a more highly evolved organ than the eye [1] and is perfectly easily capable of this small feat. What is at fault is not your ear, which probably receives and

[1] Cf. Jules Combarieu: *Music, Laws and Evolution*. The function of the ear.

A Colloquy

reports quite correctly, but your musical intelligence which is insufficiently trained.[1]

MUSICIAN OF FORMER TIMES: But there is not a single chord which I know and can recognize. I doubt if there is one I have ever heard before.

MUSICIAN OF TO-DAY: Quite so. Why should there be? If a composer is serving up merely a *réchauffé* of old, already digested thoughts, then the old, already digested chords, progressions, rhythms and other *clichés* will serve his turn. Should he, however, have the felicity to contact, in some moment of Dionysiac ardour, an unfamiliar vibration, a hitherto unexpressed ideation, some remote echo of far-off archetypes, he must perforce, in his attempt adequately to body it forth, create new chords, progressions, melodic lines, *timbres*, and a thousand and one other means of expression which shall be commensurate with the thing to be expressed. I am far from suggesting that *only* new methods—new harmonies, odd *timbres* and so on—should be employed. Indeed, I believe that even the good old common chord has, as yet, far from yielded up its last ounce of dynamic, and that the whole tendency will be toward producing equal or greater effects by immeasurably simpler means than are usual at present.[2] But I deprecate the all too common attitude of condemnation of new methods because of their newness. Their aptness as vehicles

---

[1] An illustration from the sister art of painting may help here. As a youth I was out sketching one day with Yeend King, A.R.A., who after a short while strolled across to look at the boy's work. " What colour are those tree-trunks ? " he asked. " Black, against the blue sky," was the answer. Whereupon the master produced his own sketch showing tree-trunks scrumbled with the most lovely blues, purples and richest brown-pinks: which colours, the boy, upon a re-examination of the scene, saw to be perfectly accurate. The intelligence, not the eye had been at fault.

[2] Cf. p. 341. Simplicity—Complexity—Synthetic-Simplicity.

Music To-day

of expression should be our first consideration; our second, the value of the thought which they express.

Musician of Former Times: But there is no time-signature, although, thank heaven for small mercies, the composer does vouchsafe a bar-line now and again.

Musician of To-day: I will refrain from giving a dissertation upon pulse, accent, rhythm and the like. Moreover, these may be found in various text-books. The rhythm is as free as the tonality, and the bar-lines are merely an aid to swift comprehension. Recollect what Schumann said: He who shakes off the tyranny of time and delivers us from it will, as far as one can see, give back freedom to Music.[1]

Musician of Former Times: I'm afraid, however, that with the best will in the world I receive no impression of melody. Surely there can be no fine music without melody. Is there melody in this music, or has the composer, like so many moderns, apparently repudiated melody altogether as one of his sources of appeal?

Musician of To-day: I am glad you used the word 'apparently.' Lack of melody is a charge that has constantly been brought against new music, as well in the past as in more recent, and indeed present times. A new melodic idiom not immediately recognizable is always denied. We may well be tired of the old story of Fétis and his inability to discern any melody in the *Tannhäuser* overture. None the less do we see to-day quite as amazing instances of the failure to recognize as a melody, one that is not couched in some old-fashioned and threadbare idiom. By alteration of a note here and there, the addition of a few easily recognizable chords, and by cramming the result into one

[1] *Neue Zeitschrift für Musik.*

A Colloquy

of the old lilting doggerel 'rhythms,' each of these lines of melody could be rendered amenable to the meanest musical intelligence.

MUSICIAN OF FORMER TIMES: Well then, granting that these are veritable melodies, I see that at one point there are several of them running simultaneously. Surely it is not possible to follow each one clearly at the same time.

MUSICIAN OF TO-DAY: It is true that people vary greatly in their power thus to follow several counterpoints. (It happens that I myself can do it, and can therefore vouch for the possibility. Upon the other hand I can only play one game of chess at a time, and that badly, whereas Capablanca, I understand, can play twenty games simultaneously. It is a faculty which persons possess, as I say, in varying degrees, but it is capable of development.) Were it otherwise, however, this would still be no valid argument against the use of such a device. Wagnerites may still be met with who cannot separate in their consciousness the three simultaneous themes at the end of the *Meistersinger* overture. Tovey, in his valuable " Companion to '*Die Kunst der Fuge*,' " argues that to complain that we cannot attend to all three themes at once is like arguing that no picture ought to be larger than a postage stamp because that is fully as large an area as the eye's centre of clear vision can comprise.

MUSICIAN OF FORMER TIMES: Of what significance then are these strange devices in the first excerpt, some of which resemble an exiguous sharp, others, a two-storied flat?

MUSICIAN OF TO-DAY: These signs indicate that the succeeding notes are to be sharpened or flattened, respectively, by one-quarter of a tone.

Music To-day

MUSICIAN OF FORMER TIMES: But you don't seriously suggest that such small intervals can be detected and recognized by the human ear. Many professional musicians, even some singers, frequently demonstrate that they cannot reproduce even half-tone intervals accurately.

MUSICIAN OF TO-DAY: That is no concern of ours. You might as soundly argue that because I cannot be trusted to drive safely at a faster speed than thirty miles per hour, nobody should be allowed to exceed that speed.

You may accept it as a fact that music-lovers can readily distinguish intervals of a quarter-tone, and that the professional orchestral player can detect much finer degrees even than these. Why, therefore, should they not be used by composers if and when their thoughts demand such subtleties of expression?

MUSICIAN OF FORMER TIMES: To take a broader issue, one not of technical detail but of difficulty of appreciation. I feel certain that nothing will ever convince me that there is any beauty or real value in, for instance, the first of these quotations.

MUSICIAN OF TO-DAY: You would be well advised to beware of conclusions so wide-reaching and so rigid as this. A well-known Brahms lover, a man of middle-age, used formerly to inveigh against this master bitterly and at length upon every opportunity. And, mark this, there was reason in his criticisms. No master is perfect, and Brahms is eminently vulnerable from several angles. What has happened to our friend meanwhile is that his power of appreciation of the beauties, subtleties and grandeurs in this composer's works has increased so greatly that he has become more or less reconciled to the imperfections. And he is incalculably to the good, on balance.

A Colloquy

MUSICIAN OF FORMER TIMES: Is that not merely an example of a natural change of view that often accompanies the attainment of mature years?

MUSICIAN OF TO-DAY: There is, of course, something in that, but not much. What has really happened is an increase in his understanding, and therefore in his powers of appreciation, rather than a diminution of his critical faculty.

But, to revert to our specific question; it has often happened in my experience that a discord which seemed at first to be unbearably harsh—seemed indeed to have been flung into the texture as hurtfully as possible, of malice *prepense*—has afterwards proved, when carefully assayed, to be capable of giving real delight to the listener. I will go so far as to say that if you will take the third quotation to your piano and play it over and over until it is reasonably familiar, you will gradually come to recognize (in greater or lesser degree according to your temperament) its almost hypnotic effect. And if you possess the dual faculty of sympathetic-nervous as well as cerebro-spinal response you will become aware of being gradually yet inexorably urged toward a state of consciousness unlike any you have previously experienced.

MUSICIAN OF FORMER TIMES: Suppose, then, I admit that I desire to enjoy and understand more of this new music, what would be the procedure you would recommend?

MUSICIAN OF TO-DAY: I would wish first of all to put you *au fait* of the technical devices, some of which prevent your understanding *what* the composer is saying; second, to furnish you with a series of æsthetic standards by reference to which you may be able more clearly to comprehend what he is writing *about*.

Music To-day

MUSICIAN OF FORMER TIMES: Well, although interesting, it is all rather confusing; and it still remains more comfortable, even if not so stimulating, to listen to the old-fashioned music; and I still wish that composers would say what they have to say in terms which I can understand.

MUSICIAN OF TO-DAY: To all objections brought against the iconoclastic methods of the modern composer, Berlioz' words may be opposed—words as true to-day and as necessary as when he uttered them in 1862:[1] Music nowaday, in her vigorous youth, is free, is emancipated and can do what she pleases. Many old rules have no longer any vogue; they were made by unreflecting minds, or by lovers of routine for other lovers of routine. New needs of the mind, of the heart, and of the sense of hearing, make necessary new endeavours and, in some cases, the breaking of ancient laws.

[1] *À travers Chants.*

Chapter Three: Modes

Diatonal Music—Greek Modes: Gregorian: Major and Minor—Pre-Greek, i.e. Early Aryan—A Greatly Extended Modal System—Atonal Music.

§ 1. DIATONAL MUSIC

A COMPOSER of our day who has a deep and wide range of ideas to express—a mobile fancy, a keen sensibility and a lambent inspiration—may well find himself forced not only to use every technical device which has hitherto been evolved, but also to evolve new ones. So be only that the new technical devices are as fitted to their ideas as the old, they should be equally welcome. But they must arise from an imperative inner impulsion to utter something which cannot be as well said in the old words. Mere newness of technical methods, mere tricks, may tickle the palate momentarily, but they cannot hold the attention for long.

Now some of his ideas will be expressible by melodic, others by harmonic means; some by contrapuntal, others by unilinear means; some in diatonic, others in atonic terms. The composer who limits himself to any one of these 'pairs of opposites' is thereby limiting his range of expression. It is for this reason that I find myself in disagreement with those who aver that the end toward which *all* expansions converge is pure chromaticism. Valuable though it be to have command over a free chromaticism, it should be realized that by its use only a comparatively

Music To-day

restricted field of experience can be expressed. It is but a part of the technical equipment of a composer, which to be anything like complete must include equal mastery of diatonal, including modal, means. Expansion, not contraction of our means of expression is the *desideratum*. Contrast the mainly diatonic *Meistersinger* with the almost entirely chromatic *Tristan*, and one sees a great master concentrating upon either at will, and with equal appositeness. A typical composer of our day will certainly have attained freedom from 'key-consciousness'; will be, that is to say, able to express quite easily and naturally in atonal terms those of his thoughts which need statement in such terms. And it is not too much to say that, conversely, any composer of to-day who cannot express those of his ideas which demand it, in atonal terms, is making less than full use of the technique available. (It is as if a motorist of to-day should confine himself voluntarily and permanently to a hand-starting device, and refuse to use a self-starter; a *reductio ad absurdum*.)

Not all his ideas, however, can be adequately expressed by use of atonal methods. Some of them will still ask for the stabilizing influence of a keynote by reference to which only can their message be conveyed. Thus we have two main categories into one or other of which all our music falls: Diatonal; based upon scales or modes having reference to a keynote: Atonal; without reference to any scale or mode, or keynote. The chromatic scale is not, of course, a mode at all, but cf. Section 5 as to one of its modern derivatives, Polytonality.

In Section 4 of the present chapter will be found some remarks upon the absence of a dominant in modal music, a characteristic which inheres in whole-tone writing. The

Diatonal Music

whole-tone system to which Debussy was so addicted cannot properly be considered as either scale or mode. A mode exists by reference to a tonic and in lesser degree to a dominant, and no mode would seem to be satisfactory, as such, lacking these. The whole-tone system is either based on three blocks of chords,

when it is allied to the Diatonic system, or it is treated quite freely and becomes, in fact, Atonal.

Learned discussions as to whether Debussy invented the whole-tone 'scale' or copied the idea from a colleague, fall rather flat when we remember that Mozart used it *as a joke*:[1]

and that it is really an ancient Eastern 'scale.'

[1] In his *Dorfmusikanten-Sextett*.

Music To-day

Let us examine a little more closely certain aspects of the Diatonal system.

§ 2. GREEK MODES: GREGORIAN: MAJOR AND MINOR

It has long been the custom among musical pundits to point back to Greece and to the Greek modes as a starting-point for investigation along these lines. It is a method I deprecate for reasons which will presently appear. If, however, we state the facts as succinctly as possible it comes to this: that the Greeks were used to employ some fifteen modes, also a chromatic and enharmonic system beside the diatonic. About the year 600, in the time of St Gregory the Great, some fourteen were chosen as being considered, we may imagine, the most suitable for use in church ritual. From these fourteen modes the composers of sæcular music gradually, as time passed, fixed upon two as being adequate to their needs, and these two—our major and minor—have sufficed, and have done so admirably, all through the splendid period in Western music which contains the names of Bach, Handel, Haydn, Mozart, Beethoven, Schubert, Schumann, Mendelssohn, Brahms, Wagner, Verdi, Franck, and all their contemporaries. In a word, all the music known to the average listener from say 1700 to 1900 is written in either the 'major' or the 'minor' mode. An occasional use of one of the Greek modes[1] is such a rarity as not to controvert this statement.

§ 3. PRE-GREEK, *i.e.* EARLY ARYAN

So much for modal records stretching back as far as ancient Greece. But the world has rapidly grown smaller

[1] *E.g.* Beethoven's use of the so-called Lydian mode in opus 132.

A Greatly Extended Modal System

of recent years, bringing the 'immemorial' East, and some at any rate of its culture, more nearly home to the Western consciousness. And it is now seen that behind the restricted two-modal system of the Bach-Strauss epoch; behind the fourteen-modal church music of the Gregorian period; behind the fifteen-modal system of the Greeks, looms the splendid, ancient musical tradition of India— India, the cradle of the Aryan race; mother of its languages, musical as well as verbal—beautifully and logically constructed upon its seventy-two modes. Tempting though it be we must not digress into an examination of this grand musical system,[1] though I will record my view that we have as much to learn from it as to add to it.

§ 4. A GREATLY EXTENDED MODAL SYSTEM

What is germane to our present argument is that we can descry, behind the seventy-two-modal system of India a still more extended one—a system, namely of ninety modes, a table of which will be found on pp. 46 and 47. This table is culled from the foreword to a work called *Essais sur des Modes*,[2] which continues:—

> Between the harmonic system of yesterday, and that of to-day, there is a gap which many music-lovers, both amateur and professional, find some difficulty in bridging. While able to understand and appreciate the older harmonic system they are utterly unable to grasp much of the music of the modernists. One important reason for this is that the 'old' music makes use of only two modes,

---

[1] But cf. p. 343 *et seq.*

[2] *Essays in the Modes*: six pianoforte pieces, with a foreword upon the ninety modes, certain of which are exemplified in this Vol. I. (Maurice Senart, Paris, 1926.)

A TABLE OF NINETY MODES

Music To-day

major and minor, while much modern music is written in a 'free' manner. There is a definite hiatus in the minds of many students between the old and the new, and the writer has often been consulted by pupils and others as to how they may fill in this gap with knowledge and practice. He therefore offers the present work as a contribution to an elucidation of one aspect of the question.

These essays [written for pianoforte] should be practised and dwelt upon in the mind until each of the modes exemplified therein seems to the student as 'natural' (as in truth it is) as the major and minor of the past 200 years. . . .

Should there be truth behind the writer's claim it would appear worthy of study. For, having posited two main categories into one or other of which all our music falls—diatonic, and atonic—what a gigantic extension of the first would this appear to be, and what potentialities it would seem to open up. Even a cursory examination of (*and practice in*) these modes reveals an illimitable vista, which, stretching back beyond the ancient Indian system, also points forward to unexplored regions whose possibilities we can but dimly guess at. For *each one of these ninety modes is as valuable in its own way as the major and minor of the era recently ended;* each is as characteristic as these; and each is capable of expressing certain states of consciousness, certain ranges of vibration, which are incommunicable by any other means at present known to us.[1]

It will be observed that every mode in this table contains an invariable dominant in addition to the tonic. Modes

[1] This I am aware is an immense claim to make, and may I fear sound magistral, even pontifical, to those who have not experimented and tested over a number of years, as the author has. The proof is in their own hands.

A Greatly Extended Modal System

exist by reason of the relation of their component notes to a tonic, and in only slightly lesser degree (to my ear) by the stabilizing influence of the dominant. Once this latter is withdrawn or tampered with (*i.e.* either flattened or sharpened), the mode, *as such*, completely disintegrates. It is in just this quality of concentration that the value of modes inheres. If their purity be not guarded and their particular and unique qualities preserved, their extraordinary potency, by contrast with chromatic and atonal systems, is seriously vitiated.

Why Busoni suggests 'trying' his proposed scales against chords which contain notes foreign to the mode to be exemplified, is a mystery to all who have realized that the power of mode resides in its utter purity. Chaos and anarchy lie that way. The same charge might be brought against many musicians, even against masters, who happen not to have laid hold of this important truth. Indeed, so great a musician as Brahms, when he puts his hand to accompaniments to old modal songs, is not above reproach from this point of view. Frankly, he quite spoils them for any musical intelligence which is at all evolved along these lines. Many instances might be adduced in support of this view. One, relevant to a melody which is likely to be known by all readers may be mentioned before resuming our main study. The so-called 'Londonderry Air' has, of recent years, been harmonized and dis-'arranged' by innumerable musicians. Yet however admirable these transcriptions may be in respect of adroit instrumentation and telling presentation, they almost all suffer heavily under examination of their harmonization from the standpoint taken up here. This is a plain diatonic tune with more than a hint of pentatonic derivations: not a chromatic note in the whole of it.[1] Yet a great proportion of these musicians have surrounded it with a viscous chromatic slime which not only obstructs its free flow, but renders it completely obnoxious to anyone who has the first faint beginnings of appreciation of propriety of modal style and intrinsic purity.

The chromaticism of Spohr's harmonic style, whether you merely tolerate or actively dislike it (of course you cannot love it), at least conforms with that of his melodic line; but these bastardized accompaniments of modal or diatonic melodies by chromatic harmonies do nothing of the sort. I suppose the unintentional sponsor of this malmarriage of diatonal melody with chromatic harmony was Grieg. In certain cases, and to a limited extent, it is, no doubt, inoffensive. In the case mentioned above it is positively hurtful. And in every case of modal melody, the addition of chromatic harmonies—even the employment of a single note which does not inhere in the mode itself— is a discount off its true beauty and power and is therefore a violation of any ear and mind which are, in this respect, cultured.

Again I repeat that I advocate this enormously extended modal system only as one item in our musical equipment, and in order to retain it at its highest potentiality, purity (in the sense in which I have used the word here) is essential. Perhaps it is because he vitiated his mode on the only occasion he used one (*i.e.* excepting, of course, the major and minor), that Verdi found no immediate followers along this path. In his *Ave Maria*[2] he makes use of a mode[3] (that which

---

[1] Although I have seen the lowest of the low lay their sticky hands on the sixth bar and sharpen the dominant to force it to conform with the unspeakable vulgarity of their ' harmonization.'

[2] First performance, Paris, 1898.

[3] Which he calls an ' enigmatic ' scale.

A Greatly Extended Modal System

appears as III M of our table) in an impure form. He sharpens his dominant.

It is true also that he does not seem to have at all assimilated even this confused form of the mode. He is thinking along traditional lines and applying to his thought, as it were, a scheme which forces it into a strange garment. It is the expression only which savours of novelty; the basic thought is not new.

Some musicians find a difficulty in defining Atonality and arrive at the conclusion that all forward movement ends in pure chromaticism. There is a danger here; source of a great deal of the present confusion about modern music. All—composers, performers, and music-lovers alike, should learn to walk before they attempt to run. I have spoken of two distinct kinds of music. Modal, having reference to a tonic; Atonal, bearing no such reference. To be of greatest value these ought, I am convinced, to be kept independent in the mind. Just so the painter refrains from mixing on the same palette oil-colour and tempera.

When we concentrate for a sufficient length of time upon one of these very potent modes, without admitting a single note outside the mode under immediate scrutiny, we become aware of their extremely exclusive behaviour. So much so that once the basic vibration of any particular mode is really established, the introduction of any note which is foreign to it produces an almost unbearably discordant effect. Hence, in the work already mentioned [1] each essay

[1] as well as in a movement from the same composer's *Dynamic Triptych* and other of his works

confines itself absolutely to the notes of its own mode and admits none other.

Although, in the work referred to on p. 45, I have written an example in each of these modes, and have given them separate titles such as: Exotic, Ingenuous, Strophic, Introversive, Military, Prismic; it should not be thought that I identify the modes themselves with the moods indicated, but only these particular examples. For if a mode *in itself* expressed a mood, the value of creative effort would be negatived. A mode would already be a work of art, instead of being but one of the many implements of the artist.

Now it might seem that having fought for harmonic freedom through the centuries as it were, and having at long last achieved it—for the typical composer of our day is completely emancipated so far as key-consciousness is concerned—such voluntary submission to the mere eight notes of any mode as that mentioned above, is a retrograde step indeed. We know, however, that much ' free ' music affects us not at all, so that freedom is not, in itself, a quality which inevitably produces the desired results. If we can also demonstrate that voluntary and temporary acceptance of the 'tyranny of Mode' brings enormously increased and concentrated power, the apparent sacrifice is clearly worth while.

It may appear to be a backward step. But all progress is said to be cyclic; look back but far enough and you perceive the vantage-ground whence the next forward-step may be taken.

I would like to see a movement among musicians somewhat analogous to the pre-Raphaelite movement among painters in the nineteenth century. This would take the form of a pre-Bach revival. Bach has ' come again ' of late, and we should be grateful for that, but a closer study

A Greatly Extended Modal System

of, and assimilation of the methods of those composers whose work and tendencies were epitomized by Palestrina, would do much toward clearing the ground for the next step forward. Just as Bakst found that the ideal of the Russian decorative school of painters was to be discerned in a tiny work of Fra Angelico; so a composer may yet arise who will vision a new musical world through the inspiration of Palestrina.

As to the simplicity (from one point of view) of this modal approach, we must remember that simplicity is no more a quality to be eschewed than is complexity one to be cultivated. The greatest art is always that which makes its effect by the simplest means. Which does not at all imply that it costs its creator less sweat of brow than intricate and involved work. Quite contrary is the fact.[1] Therefore, having once assured ourselves that the apparent simplicity of this modal device is not that of inanity, but of unusual refinement, we may add it to our musical equipment without *arrière pensée* upon that score.

That journeyman musicians may seize upon this, or indeed upon any apparently novel device, to produce a new-sounding jingle to tickle jaded ears, is quite possible. It has always been possible and is an objection no more applicable to this use of modes than to any other technical contrivance in the art.

Exploiters are many—explorers, rare.[2]

The moment we discern the mainspring of a piece of music to be a mere intellectual device, its magical spell is broken. And it is a startling commentary on the state of music and musical evaluation to-day that such an enormous

---

[1] Cf. p. 341. Simplicity—Complexity—Synthetic-Simplicity.
[2] "Yea, forsooth, and verily, the imitative shall inherit the earth."

Music To-day

proportion of works, having no deeper source of inspiration than this exploitation of technical jimcrackery, should so often be awarded the encomiums which ought to be reserved for the profoundest discoveries in the art.

This extension of modal technique then, if it be adopted at all—and there are signs of a number of composers adding it to their equipment—may be abused like any other of our technical devices. But we (composers I mean) do not theorize first and compose afterward to suit those theories [1]; but in externalizing ideations for the edification first of ourselves and afterward of those who care to listen, the *last* thing that happens is the arrangement of our means of expression into a system.

Many modern composers have assuredly felt their way forward until they have arrived at a medium of expression which seems to them as adequate an idiom as they can possibly attain to. They have found then that, particularly upon its harmonic side, their technique included many newnesses which were eminently capable of being erected into a system. Several have succumbed, and I will admit being tempted some years ago to publish outlines of a new harmonic system of my own. A wise friend advised against this. " In doing so," he said, " you would only be helping to close doors; the exact opposite of what you really wish to do." Then I noticed that more than one of my pupils were actually beginning to box themselves up in the system I had evolved; or were beginning to trick themselves out in garments that really only fitted my sole self. The group of modes about which we are concerned here is, however, no such system within which one may remain boxed up. I only suggest it as one of many new avenues

---
[1] That is; as a rule: Schönberg is, however, suspect. But Cf.

A Greatly Extended Modal System

along which to approach the adytum. And I have found in a fairly extensive practice that, subject to the reservations already made, its effect is always one of liberation and added inspiration.

The pertinent question is somewhere asked by Malipiero as to why Palestrina never repeated himself (as do the composers since his day), and his reason is: Because Palestrina did not confine himself to the 'major and minor' modes.

Traces of one sort or other of modal influences are quite frequently met with in modern music, but most listeners are so totally unfamiliar with modal thought as to be quite unable to dissect out these passages from chromatic, atonal, or polytonal surroundings, and the whole appears to them to be an inconsequent, illogical *olla podrida*, no moment of which is their musical intelligence really able to grip. In a recent series of definitions of musical terms, designed ostensibly for persons without previous musical training, H. Farjeon says about modes: "These two modes [*i.e.* the major and minor] are by far the most important," and so they are, in the sense that almost all the music one hears is written in them. In the sense of being the most important in sheer musical value in present-day compositions this would not apply and I reiterate boldly, after an intensive as well as extended study of them, that *each* of the ninety modes shown on pp. 46–47 is equally valuable; and that the eighty-eight modes which are other than our old major and minor, are equally 'important' with 'these two.'

Quite contrary to this great extension of the modal system are the efforts of one Oscar Esplá who elects to compose all his music in *one* mode. The one to which he has chosen to limit himself somewhat resembles No. II O of our table. But, inasmuch as he flattens the dominant he completely destroys the virility of even the one mode of his choice. Mention should also be made here of the labours of Josef Hauer, who has erected into a system a modal grouping in forty-four (Greek) *tropes*. These *tropes* are, he believes, destined to replace the traditional modes. Again one traces a backward glance as far as Greece—no farther.[1] His dodecaphonic studies over, his system completed, he seems to have lapsed into as *sentimentalisch* a type of actual composition as ever brought tear to the cheek of a *gnädiges fräulein*; for his work *Wandlungen* certainly proves that he does not practise what he preaches.

§ 5. ATONAL MUSIC

Entirely the opposite of these modes which are so closely related to their tonic, is ATONALITY, a style of composing without reference to any mode (scale) or tonic. It has resulted from Polytonality in something like the following manner:

[1] A tendency deplored in Section 2, p. 44 *Greek Modes*.

Atonal Music

Above, we have a group of phrases played simultaneously. Each stands in its own clearly discernible key as indicated. The ear can perfectly well distinguish them, even separate them; but the musical intelligence refuses to accept any one key as that to which the whole may be referred. Further, at no moment may this music, considered vertically, be said to be in any one key. Considered in its totality it is without key, although its constituent parts, read horizontally, strictly obey the old key system. It had been but a short step from a congeries of themes all in the same key, to the above state of affairs, though it had taken a long time to accomplish. The next step was the very short one of composing music without reference, in any of its parts, to either mode (scale) or tonic. *Voilà!* Emancipation was achieved. Pure atonality ensued—complete negation of the tonic. In this type of music no note bears relation to any one bass, no chord to a root, but all notes have their value reciprocally because of their relation to each other. (Anyone specially interested in this new departure might consult the various textbooks, or, better still, study the music which makes use of atonality.)

This was a real addition to our means of expression and its use is most certainly justified on occasion. I cannot, however, do other than deprecate its constant use, throughout every one of their works, by its votaries. Just as, above, I deprecated the constant use of modal, to the exclusion of other systems; just as I advocated only the occasional use, when appropriate to the ' thing to be expressed,' of quartertones; just so I feel that the range of ideations which may adequately be expressed by the atonal system is so restricted, so narrow and so *précieux*, that its use to the exclusion of other systems is a veritable misuse. And if the persistent atonalist assert that this system *is* the appropriate expression of all the heights and depths his consciousness is able to contact, I can only make the rejoinder that he is no great traveller.

Upon studying atonal works by composers of French, German, English, Russian, Italian, Belgian, American, Spanish, Indian and other origins, an interesting point emerges, namely, that the music seems to have entirely lost its nationalistic character. The orchestration of the Frenchman and the Indian shows traces, perhaps, to an experienced musician, but even the orchestration of the others gives no such indication, and the actual ' thought-stuff ' in all cases is remarkable in its sameness. A forward glance along these lines seems to show clearly enough that music is rapidly attaining, if indeed it has not already achieved, the status of a world-speech.

Atonality is then a firmly established system, and is a necessary item in the technique of any representative composer of our day. No music-lover who desires to get to grips with modern music—sympathetic grips *videlicet*—will dismiss as a wilful aberration a device which has been accepted, endorsed and practised by many of the foremost creative minds in music to-day.

CHAPTER FOUR: QUARTER-TONES

*Whole-tones, Half-tones, Quarter-tones—Quarter-tone Signs
—Aural Possibilities and Vagaries.*

IN the year 1898 I had tentatively experimented in a string-quartet,[1] with smaller divisions than usual of the intervals of our scale, *i.e.* quarter-tones. Having proved in performance their practicability and their capability of expressing certain psychological states in a manner incommunicable by any other means known to musicians, I definitely adopted them as an item in my composing technique.

§ 1. WHOLE-TONES, HALF-TONES, QUARTER-TONES

By no means inclined to exploit this new feature for its own sake, I refrained from its further use until (in 1912), having set myself to paraphrase in music the sensations received from certain pictures, I again found it necessary to call upon this item in my musical vocabulary. A picture by Brunet in the Salon had greatly impressed me; a 'Colombine.' On the technical side it was a superb essay in ultra-chromaticism, and in my attempt adequately to render in music the effect made by this picture I was forced over the old borderlines and produced a piece described as a 'Study in Whole-tones, Half-tones and Quarter-tones.'[2]

It must be understood that the quarter-tone as here used has nothing whatever to do with those 'micro-

[1] Programme of which bears this date.
[2] No. 2 of *Music-Pictures*. (Queen's Hall 1912, Hallé Concerts 1913.)

tones'[1] with which Eastern musicians are wont to embellish their modal melodies. It is an indigenous growth, natural offspring of the Bach equal-tempered scale, having no relation therefore to 'natural tuning' of the scale, or 'just intonation', to which we shall turn our attention in Chapter XVI. In our Western music a moment arrived when freedom of harmony and modulation could only be achieved by a mathematical division of the octave into twelve equal parts: Bach stabilized this, as everyone knows, in *Das Wohltemperirte Klavier*. Quarter-tones, as used in the above-mentioned and in other more recent works, are divisions of these twelve equally spaced semi-tones into equal parts—as nearly equal, that is to say, as the ear will ordinarily register—*i.e.* into quarter-tones. In the book referred to in the footnote on p. 60, also in *A Dictionary of Modern Music and Musicians* (1924), and in the *Encyclopædia Britannica* (1929), as well as in various fugitive articles, I am accused of using 'third-tones': ('tertia-tones'). These are errors. The use of quarter-tones as above described is my only 'offence' in this branch of music.

Smaller intervals than quarter-tones are certainly impracticable with our present instruments, and here is the test of which a practising artist will never lose sight. Now

---

[1] The addition of this word to our musical terms must be ascribed to Maud MacCarthy, whose labours in bringing Indian music to the Western world have not yet been adequately recognized. Her singing of twenty-three notes (srûtis) within the octave is, by the way, a complete refutation of the argument that the quarter-tone is too small an interval for practical purposes. Scholes remarks that an illustration, in public, of the twenty-three notes within the octave was perfectly satisfactorily sung by this artist, as he checked both the starting and finishing notes on his piano and found them to be correct. (*Listener's History of Music.* Vol. III). Now it is very much more difficult to sing intervals so small as this, than merely to distinguish them by ear, and the above facts ought to dispose of a good deal of reluctance on the part of certain persons to allow of the possible use of quarter-tones in practical musical affairs.

Quarter-tone Signs

it has been ascertained by scientific measurement that any good violinist of our splendid orchestras of to-day tunes his instrument to the tenth of a tone before he is satisfied that it is what he would call 'in tune.' A practical composer needs no further proof of the practicability of this quarter-tonal device, so far as the power of the human ear is concerned. Of the instruments at our everyday disposal, only the strings and the voice can make use of this device, but its employment will surely extend in many other directions.

Facetious friends may assert roundly that they have heard quarter-tones all their lives, from the fiddle strings and larynxes of their musical friends, who produced them without any difficulty whatever . . . by accident! Very likely. Does this affect our argument? Columbus discovered America without in the least intending to, by a sort of accident; which does not prevent us of the twentieth century voyaging thither by design.

§ 2. QUARTER-TONE SIGNS

This new device of the quarter-tone necessitated the invention of a new series of signs. The quarter-sharp sign, it was felt, should somehow resemble the ordinary sharp without confusion being possible between it and the sign for double-sharp. Similarly, the quarter-flat, while showing some affinity with the familiar flat, should be distinct from the double-flat sign. The following were adopted and have been used in many works:

The sign ♯ sharpens the succeeding note one quarter of a tone.

The sign ♭ flattens the succeeding note one quarter of a tone.

Music To-day

Here is a typical instance where the use of quarter-tones conveys a mood-picture which seemed to the composer, rightly or wrongly, not to be exactly communicable by any other means:

I have recently made a close study of a work written throughout in quarter-tones; a string-quartet by Alois Hába, opus 7. Several points emerged from this scrutiny. In the first place there is scarcely a single bar in any of the four parts throughout the work in which this device is not employed. So far as my understanding can penetrate no new ideations are offered us in the work. The effect there-

Quarter-tone Signs

fore is somewhat as if a poet should retell the old, old story of Cinderella in words every one of which should contain a 'th.' Or as if a *chef* should flavour every course from *hors d'œuvre* to coffee with lobster.

Speaking generally, it certainly seems that a work of anything like extended scope and range of expression would need a far wider technical treatment. Were we to employ the whole of our technical resources in a work of any length, they would be inadequate to represent a tithe of the variety and glory that may be contacted in the inner realms of man's consciousness, and which it is the composer's privilege to transcribe in physical-plane terms for our edification and delight.

Upon the technical side a practical objection cannot fail to arise. For the signs adopted by this composer— ♭ for quarter-sharp and ↄ for quarter-flat—are unnecessarily confusing to the eye, even after prolonged acquaintance with them; the former having all the appearance of an ordinary flat sign whose stem had failed to print quite clearly along about one third of its length. At any rate the eye and the intelligence accept it at once as an ordinary flat sign and dire confusion results.

There are rumours also of a Mexican composer and others elsewhere who are said to be using this device and, in my view, for the reasons already given, the time will certainly come when its acceptance as a 'legitimate' means of musical expression and its adoption into our all-too-small musical vocabulary will be a *fait accompli*.

Again it seems necessary to repeat that, as we saw when discussing Modes, any demi-semi composer might seize upon this device of quarter-tones and exploit it for the sake of any cheap notoriety he might obtain because of its superficial newness. No real artist would countenance such a procedure. But it would be a deadening philosophy indeed that should proscribe a valuable device because it is possible of abuse. Besides, no artist of discernment could be deceived into believing that the newness had been forced upon such a composer by inner compulsion to express. To others of less experience or power of discernment certain remarks in a later section devoted to considerations of æsthetic may be of help.

§ 3. AURAL POSSIBILITIES AND VAGARIES

We have instanced the power of the good orchestral violinist to perceive intervals a great deal smaller than the quarter-tone, but it must be admitted that the gift varies greatly in different individuals. So gifted a musician as Stokowski admits having to concentrate most carefully in order to co-relate these small intervals. And in the nature of things there will be many who will be totally unable to do so.

Indeed *I believe there is as much tone-deafness as colour-blindness in the world.*

But the ear will improve as has the eye. (Time was, we are told, when only three colours were perceptible in the rainbow). And even as it stands to-day, the ear is usually far in advance of the musical intelligence.

Cases such as one I came across recently of a man hearing every musical sound too sharp—technically known as *hyperacusis*—or another, where a man heard at a different pitch the one ear from the other; these, thank heaven, are rare cases and perhaps of more interest to *medico* than *musico*. In this connection the case of Bruckner may be recalled. I was present at a rehearsal in Vienna where the

Aural Possibilities and Vagaries

full symphony orchestra included ten double-basses. Not one note of these, so he declared emphatically, could the composer hear, below the D just under the bass-clef stave. At the same time his sense of intonation was rarely developed and his appreciation of balance of *timbres* decidedly beyond the normal. At the other end of the scale discrepancies are also frequently to be noticed. Not everyone can hear the extremely high note of the bat-squeak. Increasing numbers, I have noticed, are becoming able to hear upper partials, harmonics resulting from a struck or sustained low bass note. Fewer, however, far fewer it seems to me, are able to detect the resultant tones *below* a given chord. These are so clearly apparent to some composers that there is a distinct danger of leaving out the lower parts of the harmony altogether and trusting to the discernment of the listener. I suppose not one listener in ten thousand would fail to ' realize ' the major third at the end of those Palestrina movements which finish with a bare fifth upon the tonic. But the realization of resultant basses from chords only the upper parts of which are given, demands a degree of apperception not at all common in this country or Germany or Italy, whatever may be the case in France where my friend Georges Migot seems to be working somewhat along these lines.

All which considerations, however, are beside the question of the practicability or otherwise of quarter-tonal music, which I have proved, at least to my own satisfaction, to be a common-sensible technical forward-step, and one, moreover, which is readily discernible and assimilable by the average ' musical ' ear and intelligence of to-day.

CHAPTER FIVE: THE VOICE

Nature's Perfect Instrument—Words and Music—Gregarious Song-impulses—Accentuation and Quantity.

WE belong to a period when the orchestra has attained in many ways, a superiority over the voice. This is due in the main to the fact that the great German masters since Bach have largely concentrated upon instrumental art, have entrusted many of their greatest and most monumental inspirations to the orchestra, and have thus stimulated instrumentalists, instrument makers, and succeeding composers also to devote an enormous amount of attention to it.

These masters certainly altered the state of affairs between the time of William Byrd, 'Father of English Music' who wrote in 1588, that "there is no music for instruments comparable with that made by human voices, when the same are well sorted and ordered," and that of Schumann, who declared: "All my life I have put vocal music on a lower level than instrumental." (This however did not prevent the composition of about one hundred songs in what he called his 'song year'; 1840).

It is possible that Time will bring the full circle, and restore—upon a higher general level—the pre-eminence which nature would seem to have planned for the human voice. The time is not yet.

Many music-lovers indeed have become so obsessed by the fascination of instrumental *timbres* that they roundly declare their preference for these to vocal ones.

Nature's Perfect Instrument

§ 1. NATURE'S PERFECT INSTRUMENT

But the voice is Nature's perfect instrument, however badly we may perform upon it, and the pendulum will again swing in its direction.

How far the choral art lags behind the orchestral, even in England which rightly prides itself upon its splendid choral bodies, was well instanced some years ago when one of our finest choirs essayed a performance of an unaccompanied Choral Symphony of Bantock. The result was chaotic. The realization of pitch, both positive and comparative, was completely lost after but a few bars. *Finesse* of part leading, of nuance and dynamics, would have disgraced the ordinary café band, and any conception of totality of impression or homogeneity of rendering was conspicuous by its absence. Now Bantock well knows how to write for the voice, so that no indictment could be brought against the composer upon this score. But in this country there are twenty orchestras which could well cope with an instrumental symphony of tantamount difficulty: whereas it is doubtful whether in the whole world a choir exists which could do equal justice to the work under consideration.

§ 2. WORDS AND MUSIC

Some of the choicest inspirations of our finest composers have been imperishably enshrined in the song form. Some of the most cherished music the world has produced; from the homeliest cradle-side lullaby—from the working-songs of reapers, fishermen, harvesters, up to the grandest art-songs of Schubert, Schumann, Wolf, Brahms and all the others. There is something indescribably *intime* about a simple sentiment set to appropriate music and sung by a sympathetic artist.

Yet I venture to say boldly that a perfect wedding between finest poetry and finest music is an impossibility. This is not the 'sour grapes' attitude of one who has tried hard and failed, for, if it does not sound too vain, I have a warm corner in my heart for certain pieces of my own in this form. But where a poet has scaled the heights and has found the perfect expression for his ideation, the greatest musician ever born can do no other than rob him of many of his most valuable and beautiful characteristics, even though he add others of his own. Similarly, no poet could fit out adequately with words a great purely musical inspiration. Attempts have been made to enhance Keats' *Nightingale* ode. *Quelle horreur!* Where poetry has attained such sublimity as this it becomes an impertinence for anyone to manhandle it in any way whatsoever. *Per contra*, when Leonora appears in the prison house all we need to know is that she is voicing her undying love: when Isolde sings her divine swan-song we need no words at all.

There are many who maintain, and not without good reason, that the silent kinema was potentially if not actually a higher art-form than the 'talkie'; that, given a sufficiently coherent plot interpreted by competent actors, the imagination was stimulated, set free and allowed to soar in a way that is only prevented by the addition of the spoken word. Some such line of thought occurs to one in connection with the question of words to music. Many an opera having a comprehensible plot (not all have, as we well know) has been more completely enjoyed when sung in a language not one word of which was understood. Certain songs depend

Words and Music

for their 'message,' it is true, upon the words; others not at all. This being so the wedding of music with words is not always such a happy affair as many suppose.

A nation's language may be a fascinating and delightful as well as an informative subject for study. Philological, ethnological and many socially significant considerations arise, and it is only too easy, when the attention is focussed upon these, to fail to realize that the most valuable ideas transcend their expression; in other words, an ideation is of greater value than even the most adroit presentation of it. No doubt something is missed by those who cannot read Homer in the original, Dante in the Italian, Goethe in the German, Cervantes in the Spanish, Shakespeare in the English, Kalidasa in the Sanskrit; but what is missed is undeniably the lesser part, and the essential greatness of these Over-men shines out clear in any even moderately adequate translation.

W. B. Yeats and I discussed this question of music to poems more than once, some years ago, and I sympathized quite sincerely with the poet's conclusion that no musician of all those who had made the attempt had been able to enhance his poems; but that in every case (so I understood him) the effect of the songs was appreciably less than would have been the case had the poems been beautifully declaimed without music.

Many interesting questions of diction, stress, quantity, rhyme, and so on were discussed, upon all of which the poet's views were profoundly interesting to a musician. What appears to be the heart of the matter is this:

It would seem that when the words are homely, narrative, or descriptive (of emotional or scenic import), music may enhance the effect; but that when the poet attains a height of real creative ' raptus ' and finds commensurate expression for this in words, such a unity of presentation with conception is achieved by him that the fitting of music to such a poem becomes not merely redundant but actually hurtful. I cannot develop this idea until we have studied, in the Section on Æsthetic, a scheme which will clarify the reader's thought on these matters, after which further allusion will be made to it.[1] Taking the matter where it stands, however, we may notice a growing tendency to use the voice apart from words, employing its more purely musical qualities upon various vocables—vowels principally—in conjunction with instrumental *ensemble*.

The so-called *vocalises* of various composers, and the frequent employment of a chorus in this way simply because of its *timbre*-values—these are pregnant indications to a modern music-lover. There is, of course, nothing new in this idea; it is a perfectly natural and logical extension of the *Hallelujah-* and *Amen*-chorus sort of thing, where the former gave a general basic notion of praise and the latter of finality; the words bearing not even an onomatopœic value.

Mahler, Scriabin, Delius, Debussy, Holst, Medtner, Sibelius, Satie, Duparc and many more have used and are using the voice in this manner. And its potentialities in the way of contrasted *timbres*, enchanting *nuances*, and magical combinations either with other voices or with orchestral instruments, are illimitable. But note that these are only potentialities at present. From the point of view of the creative musician, the human voice, despite the efforts of legions of voice-producers and professors of *bel canto* methods and the like, is to-day the least fully exploited of

[1] Cf. p. 350.

Gregarious Song-impulses

all our music-making instruments. More of this in our final chapters.

At both ends of the scale; alike at its most purely musical and where it most nearly approaches speech, as well as in a *rapprochement* between the two, lie many possibilities which have never yet been faced.

That I do not consider the last-mentioned problem incapable of solution may be inferred from the attempt in *The Reed Player*[1] to make satisfactory use of this device. It is marked to be rendered *parlando musicale* throughout, but when the poetic fervour is at its most lyrical pitch, actual notes are printed; at its least, merely *tempo* indications. Between these two limits lies scope for all those unexplored subtleties which inhere in the most magical and potent of all musical instruments—the human voice.

§ 3. GREGARIOUS SONG-IMPULSES

In Teutonic, and particularly in English-speaking countries where the organization of large groups and the recognition of what is called the 'team-spirit' has been fostered for so long, the amassing of large choral bodies has followed as a matter of course. From this results the pre-eminence of English choral singing.

There is, however, another and more popular aspect of this gregarious instinct which has more than once been exploited. Noticing that every activity that draws together bodies of men in the fraternity of any common impulse chooses the sung melody as the most natural and effective means of expressing the consciousness of spiritual sodality: noticing also that nothing else whatever produces a unifying

[1] Op. 51, No. 5 (Curwen).

effect so swiftly upon such large numbers of persons; political, religious, and military leaders have vigorously encouraged it. For they know that speeches, sermons or addresses are far less effective for their ends than is communal song; far less powerful, less unifying and less stimulating. During the recent upheaval when more and larger groups of men were massed than ever before, there was a universal impulse toward vocal expression.

Since then this impulse has crystallized (in England chiefly) into a definite and widespread activity known as Community Singing, and although in some cases ridiculous words and inane music are used as the vehicle of expression, the whole activity presents certain features of interest to the music-student.

It becomes clear that song stands *facile princeps* as the social art, and that it is the only one that can be employed by a large number of technically untaught persons at the same instant and in the same manner.

As an experience it can be indescribably moving; and to hear 100,000 people all singing a fine tune and all inspired by the same emotional urge is to enlarge a musician's sense of the inner power of his art.

Yet it can be unutterably banal. And to hear, as I once did, upwards of 100,000 men drearily wailing in unison something about 'Light amid th' encircling gloom,' on a foggy London afternoon at a *football match*, was rather too much for my risibility.

But the idea is capable of still greater expansion, and one can conceive of the possibility of truly colossal results along these lines in the future.

Accentuation and Quantity

§ 4. ACCENTUATION AND QUANTITY

Composers have improved greatly of recent years in the matter of intelligent treatment of accentuation and word stress. Time was when words had to fit in as best they could to an adamantine melody. The old hymn: '*Er* . . . bide with me' is a fair sample of the kind of thing that used to be tolerated; and, not to mince words, almost all the 'great masters' were as great sinners in this respect as anyone else.

In more recent times, Hugo Wolf, so far as my knowledge of German can carry me, very seldom erred in this way—our own Arthur Sullivan, I believe, never.

Still it is surprising to come across cases even to-day of blundering in this matter by composers who exhibit the utmost adroitness in other ways.

It is all very well for a comic song composer to make merry with his words to the tune of:

> *I* want . . . to *BE* happy
> *But* I . . . won't *BE* happy
> *Till* I . . . 've made *YOU* happy
> *Too*.

It is quite another matter when we find a work claiming serious attention containing such things as:

Hiccups in the middle of a word are apt to be associated with a too intensive devotion to Bacchic joys.

In addition to the extended use of the voice apart from words, as a purely musical 'instrument' in 'art' music, further hints will be found when we come to study the therapeutic effects of music [1]; the ease with which it can cope with quarter-tones, just intonation,[2] and other more subtle divisions of the octave than our tempered scale; and particularly the potentialities which its use exposes in those domains where the musician meets the scientist; the artist, the philosopher; the idealist, the materialist.[3]

[1] PART TWO, Chapter VIII, p. 107.
[2] PART FIVE, Chapter XVI, p. 333.
[3] Cf. CONCLUSION, p. 351.

CHAPTER SIX: THE ORCHESTRA

Intimacy with the Orchestra Desirable—Appreciation of Timbres—*Novel Tone-colours—Some Examples—Instrumental Discrepancies—Conducting and Conductors—Generalities.*

At the present time we are witnessing a distinct decline in opera, not only in this country but in other countries also where it has hitherto flourished exceedingly. Interest in great choral activities is also held to be markedly on the decline. And it may well be asked in what branch of music is centred the increasing interest we have already noticed.

To a certain extent, no doubt, chamber music is receiving greater attention than formerly, but it is chiefly and most markedly upon orchestras and orchestral concerts that the young music-lovers of to-day are concentrating their attention. And this is easily understandable; for the modern symphony orchestra with its hundred instrumentalists is by far the grandest, most subtle, most varied and characteristic instrument known to us at present. Moreover, it is an instrument, familiarity with which does not breed contempt, intolerance, or even satiation.

§ 1. INTIMACY WITH THE ORCHESTRA DESIRABLE

I have often wished that those multitudes of ardent young enthusiasts one sees at the principal orchestral concerts in the capital cities of the world could once make the experience of sitting *in* an orchestra. True, from this position the balance of the orchestration is out of strict proportion, the dynamic is distorted, the attention focussed on parts instead of the whole, and the sum total of the composer's intention hardly graspable unless one already has the full score 'in one's head.' Still, speaking from experience, it may be said that a strange thrill is obtainable in this way which is not to be paralleled. An extraordinary effect of mystery—contrary to what might have been expected—is experienced by anyone situated in the heart of an orchestra, or say, by the side of the conductor. The contrasted *timbres* are more sharply differentiated. The solo phrases seem to be more intensely vitalized. The *ambience* or aura of the orchestra, a very real and noticeable phenomenon, is clearly realized (and in this matter one orchestra will differ from another in a surprising degree). The sheer physical exhilaration of a *tutti fortissimo*, which none but a decadent would deride, can nowhere else be experienced in such intensity;[1] whilst the differing distances from which the various group-sounds reach one can lend a real charm unobtainable when one is seated in the auditorium at a distance and hears the whole orchestra *en masse*. Such an experience is not, of course, within the bounds of the practical, and is merely mentioned here as a sidelight of some interest.

§ 2. APPRECIATION OF 'TIMBRES'

A more penetrating evaluation of *timbres*—of contrasting qualities of tone-colour, in the orchestra as well as in all other fields of music, is eminently desirable. *Timbre* being one of the most dynamic and magic-making constituents of

---

[1] A well-known young actress once explained to me why she did not care for orchestral concerts. "The orchestra is never anything like loud enough," was her comment.

the sound-art, I marvel that so little attention, comparatively speaking, is paid to it. Professional musicians of standing, no less than dilettanti, are culpable in this matter. It is a question of innate faculty, plus attention, resulting in increased refinement. Once any real degree of perception is attained to; once the ear becomes at all highly sensitive and responsive, our delight in true and beautiful *timbres* and consequently our potential enjoyment of fine music increases a hundred-fold. It is a quality the possession of which on the part of the listeners is greatly desired by all serious composers, for, lacking it, an audience is unable to enjoy not to say accurately to evaluate many of their choicest moments. I am not inveighing here against mere loudness and extolling mere subtlety and suchlike virtues of sensitivity. It is not amount of tone but quality that is the *desideratum*. And it is true that no ear which can claim any degree of real refinement in this direction can regard as other than vulgar, commonplace, and obnoxious such bastardized intruments as the hundred-and-one contraptions with which attempts are made upon the market; noise-emitters whose fitting place is either the wide-open spaces or the underworld.

§ 3. NOVEL TONE-COLOURS

At the same time it should be recognized that the craving for new shades of tone-colour and new *timbres* (as evinced chiefly in jazz orchestras and the like), indicates a real and deep-seated need and one that ought not to be left to the purveyors of trick-music to supply. The mere fact that the majority of instruments evolved to meet this demand are bad instruments, capable of producing only inferior qualities of tone, debased and vulgar in *timbre* and unsatisfactory of manipulation, by no means justifies us in assuming that the 'classic' orchestra includes at the present day all the types and varieties of tone-colour which are desirable. I think, on the contrary, that our range of types is really extraordinarily narrow and restricted, and that the craving for an extension of our very limited gamut of *timbres* is quite healthy and eminently desirable and ought to be (will be) met as time goes on. From this point of view it is distinctly unfortunate that the power to discriminate between pure and impure—therefore between satisfactory and unsatisfactory—*qualities of tone* is one of the least developed of our musical faculties at the present time. Were it at all equal to our ability to perceive correctness of intonation, for example, such instruments as the cornet, euphonium, concertina, reed-organ, saxophone, and most of the new 'music'-making devices of our day would be far less amiably regarded than is the case, and we would, in fact, be compelled to search out improvements in this respect in order to bring them into line with what would be an imperative demand.

Familiar as one may be with every department and device in the modern symphony orchestra and greatly as one may admire it as a magnificent instrument, it would be a grave mistake to imagine that the limit has been reached in this matter of variety of tone colour. A far greater range of expression should be possible, and will be when our palette of colours is increased. This should be done by the addition of 'true' colours however, and it is here that one deplores the lack of anything like unanimity and any widespread or deeply penetrative discrimination of *timbre*-values—even among professional musicians.

Some Examples

§ 4. SOME EXAMPLES

The opinion already expressed as to the subtlety, variety and grandeur of the orchestra may be supplemented for the benefit of readers who may not be familiar with its constitution. (Berlioz' book on the subject, a little out of date as regards certain technical matters, remains the most interesting of all for the music-lover; and the most stimulating. Strauss has amplified and brought it up-to-date in a masterly way. Forsyth has a fully informative book upon orchestration, among the best of its kind in any language; especially upon the technical side.)

An appreciation of *timbre* will be found to be one of the most fruitful sources of delight to the amateur, and he should embrace every occasion of learning to detect instantly not only the various characteristics of the instruments, but to recognize the variety of expression each instrument can achieve within its own range.

The protean characteristics of the string family, as being very much more familiar to the average music-lover than those of the other instruments, hardly call for special examples in a brief review. It is not so with wind and brass, many tone-qualities of these instruments escaping the notice of the inexperienced listener—to his great loss.

The flute may indeed sound vertiginous: [1]

[1] *Also sprach Zarathustra;* Strauss.

it can also magically enchant you with Syrinx voice: [1]

and though nobility and grandeur may seem to be beyond its powers, in what other terms can we describe [2]

His little piccolo brother is not always condemned to the task of shrilly emphasizing the top line in the orchestral *tutti*; he too, given the chance, will raise a melodious voice: [3]

Bass flute will speak in tones you shall hear from none other: [4]

No instrument can be more poignant in passages which speak of desolation or melancholy than the oboe, and no composer has surpassed Berlioz in this use of it: [5]

[1] *Prometheus*; Scriabin.   [2] First Symphony. *Finale*; Brahms.
[3] *Pianoforte Concerto*; Brahms, op. 83.
[4] *Le Sacre du Printemps*; Igor Stravinsky.   [5] *Roi Lear*, Overture.

Some Examples

With the highly individualized English horn many can be eloquent; few indeed so magical as Delius:[1]

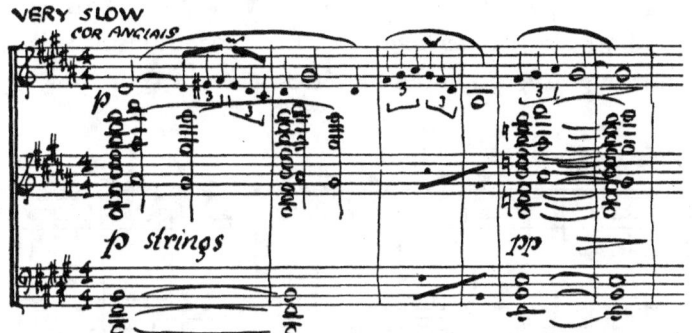

The clarinet has long been the darling of the 'tune-with-accompaniment-for-strings' type of composer. Almost every amateur's score shows instances of suave sentimentalities of this pattern. Busoni can however enchant you with its *chalumeau* tones in irresistible fashion:[2]

'Charm' is a word that few would be prepared to use regarding the bassoon; yet Puccini can achieve it:[3]

[1] *A Song of the High Hills.*   [2] *Die Brautwahl: Pezzo Mistico.*
[3] *Tosca*, Act III, toward the end.

Music To-day

The value of the bassoon in passages of *macabre* import has long been known. And Berlioz' superb use of four in his *Faust* is perhaps only paralleled by Wagner's writing for four horns in *Meistersinger*. A fine modern instance is the following 'Evocation des Ancêtres':[1]

and in a similar connection everybody who has once heard it will recall the double-bassoon *solo* in Paul Dukas' *L'Apprenti Sorcier*.

Perhaps no one since Wagner has used the horns so well as he has done in *Meistersinger*; a feast of instruction and delight to all. Strauss has splendidly followed, and, even in the early *Don Juan*, conceived an effect which, little as you may admire the melody itself, is tremendously arresting:

A peculiarly threatening effect which has nothing to do with the oh-so-familiar 'stopped' sounds is sometimes

[1] In *Le Sacre du Printemps*; Stravinsky.

Some Examples

produced by this group, and as it is somewhat rare I append a few bars:

Who, that has once heard it, will ever forget the blazing splendour of that trumpet whose voice assails the high heaven:[1]

Mutes modify the trumpet-tone in varying degree according to the material used, as well as other factors. By use of *papier-mâché* mutes of a certain pattern I found it possible to obtain a tone which perfectly corresponded with the flute *timbre*, and made a ravishing colour-*ensemble* in the following passage:

[1] In *Also sprach Zarathustra*; Strauss.

Trombones are not condemned to the everlasting task of thundering out unison melodies in the Tannhäuser overture tradition, or even *pp* themes as in that often-quoted and unforgettable passage in Schubert's C major symphony. They also can show an agile turn if necessary:[1]

A unique employment of different kinds of drums to mark out a counterpoint of rhythms may be of sufficient interest to quote. The theme was reiterated at a quick *tempo* by violins, etc. Simultaneously it was given out at half-speed by other instruments, at quarter-speed by others, and at one sixteenth by still others. The last (the slowest moving) were reinforced by bass drum; the slightly faster moving, by *timpani*; the next group by tenor drum; and the most rapidly moving group by side drum:

[1] As in *Pacific 231*; Honegger.

Some Examples

We might fittingly conclude these desultory remarks on instrumental characteristics with a *recherché* example for harp, piano, celesta and *batterie* only:

in which the varying indications of dynamic (as *f* for Celesta and Harp, *p* for Xylophone, *ppp* for Timpani) with the intention of securing a definite balance in the total result, will be noticed.

Many of our present-day composers are extremely adroit in their orchestration. A few no doubt are less so; but really clumsy orchestration may be said to be a thing of the past.

§ 5. INSTRUMENTAL DISCREPANCIES

I have heard some surprising effects resulting from the lack of unanimity in *timbre*-evaluation already remarked upon, although there has been a rapid improvement noticeable in recent years. Ponderous and tremendously portentous German trombones resemble elephants in a boudoir when they are dealing with the delicate accompaniment-stuff of the Italian operatic school, which was intended, of course, for the more agile and subtle valve-trombones. Oboes of the 'pommer' quality of tone, still occasionally to be heard in Germany, are capable of throwing utterly out of balance any modern wood-wind effects. What is to be done however when Mendelssohn, familiar with the raucous *timbre* of this type of oboe, uses it as a third trumpet?

Again, it was a common practice of Schubert (and his contemporaries) to eke out his two horns with two bassoons [1] in four-part harmony. Now the bassoon is the bass instrument of the oboe family. But so intent have been both players and conductors upon producing instruments capable of fulfilling the duties of deputy horns, so to say, that the German bassoons of to-day, forsaking their true family, have

---

[1] Cf. *e.g.* the beginning of the slow movement in his B minor Symphony (*Unvollendet*).

Instrumental Discrepancies

become a sort of wooden horn and have, to really sensitive ears, lost more than they have gained.[1] It would have been just as sensible to 'improve' the oboe into a better deputy-trumpet by rendering its tone louder and more raucous. Happily, it has progressed in a contrary direction. French, Belgian, and some English bassoons retain the true, slightly more reedy, certainly more sympathetic quality which allies the instrument to its true double-reed oboe family, and it may be imagined to what discrepancies this gives rise when German works are performed by French orchestras, or *vice versa*. Worse still are the results when two bassoonists in the same orchestra use, the one a French type, the other a German type of instrument. The latter are impeccable in intonation and possess great flexibility in execution; which qualities however, admirable and desirable though they be, hardly compensate for the loss of those which are so noticeable a feature of the best French and Belgian instruments.

Horns are still a problem from this point of view, the German instrument being more agile and capable of a far more powerful *forte* than the French horn. I have heard the impressive horn theme in the *finale* of Brahms' first symphony, which should sound like a 'voice from the dead,' played with a veiled, mellifluous tone scarce to be heard above the *pianissimo* of the accompanying strings. Shall we sacrifice the power and assertiveness of the type of instrument demanded by many modern composers, for the glamorous, poetic, French instrument written for and expected by Berlioz, Debussy and a great many others?

Trumpets offer another unsolved problem. Nowaday the small C trumpet is ubiquitous throughout the world and composers are compelled perforce to write for it. Thus

[1] Cf. New Vistas (technical) p. 331, *in re* a desirable attitude in this matter.

they obtain at any rate the result they expect. It is far other with most of the 'classics'; and to hear, as we so frequently do nowaday, parts which were written for the noble and powerful instrument in F played upon the much lighter and more delicate instrument in C is not always edifying.

I have already mentioned the grand sonority of the German trombones which are not approached in this respect by any other. At times I regret the almost complete disappearance of the noble bass instrument in G whose use by Schubert in such a unique and personal way, alone almost justifies its retention. The world-wide popularity of Wagner with his characteristic scoring for the brass, succeeded in imposing his types of instrument upon large orchestras everywhere. The advent of the new French school with their demand for more delicate *timbres* from oboe, English horn, bassoon, French horn; and their preference for a lighter type of trombone tone and for the smaller and more delicate trumpet in C, has of course affected many orchestras and composers.

The best orchestras perform prodigies. In conjunction with the great conductors, they offer feasts of gorgeous beauty and banquets of sheer delight. All the same, the above indictment must stand, even though no remedy can be suggested. And I am sure at least, that the unique features of the *timbre* of each of the families in the grand orchestral *ensemble* should be carefully preserved.[1] I am reminded, in this connection, of an occasion when the principal viola player in a celebrated orchestra acquired at great cost a beautiful old instrument by Gasparo di Salo. Proud of his purchase, he showed it to the famous conductor-in-

---

[1] Cf. p. 331.

Instrumental Discrepancies

charge with the enthusiastic remarks: "It is a wonderful instrument, in splendid preservation, rather large to handle, but of a tone! Magnificent! Sounds like a 'cello." To which came the dry rejoinder, "I prefer a viola that sounds like a *viola*."

A keen ear, and one that is accustomed to evaluating tone-qualities, can readily discern two types of violoncello. Some are really basses. (The violoncello is, of course, the natural bass instrument of the string family; the *double*-bass being what its name implies.) Other 'cellos are really of baritone quality and most modern soloists use instruments of this type. One sometimes hears 'cellists in string quartets using the baritone-type 'cello, and here it is definitely less satisfactory, for its real bass quality is needed in almost every movement of every work. Which is but another instance of how extraordinarily casual are even some professional musicians regarding this very important question of *timbre*.

Tubas may often be noticed which seem to be guessing whether to be bass or contrabass. In some orchestras I have recently seen the player change from a smaller tuba (presumably one in F) to the magnificently sonorous large instrument (I supposed the one in B B Flat) for different works, and in many cases this expedient is fully justified. Percussion instruments vary a good deal in different countries, *timpani* however remaining fairly constant. The quality of the *glockenspiel* varies between a mere tinkling knock, and a resounding metallic clang.

During the lifetime of the writer it has been interesting to notice the gradual levelling-up of orchestras throughout the world in this matter of tone-values. Nowaday, the amenities of travel being so much greater, tours of the celebrated conductors and orchestras are more frequent than formerly, and as a result this levelling-up is more nearly a *fait accompli*. Still, the discrepancies particularized in this section remain, and are a real barrier to the rapid dissemination of certain types of highly organized modern compositions throughout the world. Worse still, they militate against the rapid spread of a modern composer's works. If his delicate horn-effects come out properly in Paris or London, they may be too prominent in Berlin. If his trombones achieve their desired nobility and impressiveness in Vienna, they may be almost unheard in a Roman presentation. A gong-note of first importance to his tone-scheme, and one upon which the dramatic effect of a tone-poem may depend, can sound like the signal of Doom in certain orchestras; like a dropped thimble in others I could name.

The position has now become such that if we suppose a programme containing a massive Wagner or Strauss number, a Schubert or Mendelssohn symphony, a typical Berlioz, Debussy, Bizet or Chabrier piece; and a modern work of Delius, Stravinsky, Bloch, or Respighi; none of these will be likely to achieve a perfect presentation from the point of view of fidelity to the composers' demands as to *timbre* and balance of tone-qualities.

It should be realized that the composer depends upon a degree of uniformity in this matter of tone values for many of his finest effects, and that therefore its importance in disseminating works throughout the world cannot be exaggerated.

§ 6. CONDUCTING AND CONDUCTORS

One of the musical phenomena of the age is the rise to eminence, pre-eminence, of the *Chef-d'orchestre*, the *Dirigent*,

Conducting and Conductors

the Conductor. It is really not so long ago that the function of starting the orchestra, giving certain broad indications and so on, devolved upon the principal first violin player; leader as we sometimes miscall him.

With the old types of music this system was apparently well able to cope. At any time since Spohr it would have been impracticable and we cannot imagine an orchestra attempting the commencement of Schumann's *Manfred* overture, for example, under such conditions. Almost all typically modern works would be impossible; and in a recent case, when half the orchestra and half the chorus maintained a 4/4 rhythm against the 7/4 of the rest, chaos would quickly have resulted without a firm indication by the conductor of four beats with the left hand and seven with the right.

The conductor is, of course, much more than a mere *tempo*-indicator. But so anxious are some of the younger aspirants to demonstrate this, that they seem to have forgotten that after all (or rather, *before* all) it is necessary to be able to beat a steady *tempo*. I have seen several of recent years who lack the ability to conduct four bars without unintentional deviation. Similarly, many young pianists debilitate everything they attempt by constant use of a decadent Chopinesque *rubato*. Ability to walk steadily at will must be felt to be inherent in a conductor's style before we can accept his deviations as intentional; apart altogether from the correctness or desirability of such deviations. Particularly in Wagner and some moderns is this ability to continue a *tempo* without deviation of greatest importance; and for the *tempo* to stagger about all over the place in the epileptic manner we can sometimes notice is to vitiate some of their grandest moments.

Music To-day

The orchestral player is an exemplar of the team-spirit *in excelsis*. He sinks to a position of humblest subordination or rises to a personal asseveration of compelling power at a glance from the conductor, at a hint of an inflexion of the *bâton* in his direction. And the 'give and take' between player and player and between the different departments of an orchestra is of a subtlety hard to exaggerate. In the splendid orchestra of my youthful experience, first clarinet, a soulful Italian, and first bassoon, a passionate Frenchman, were continually at daggers drawn . . . in the green room. In the concert-room they would duet divinely—would whisper you " as gently as any sucking dove " in the many lovely passages of Mozart, Beethoven, Schubert, which ask for such playing. In the *finale* of Beethoven's Violin Concerto Joachim would willingly subordinate his *roulades*, his variations and decorations, the while ' papa ' Lalande would raise his poignant bassoon-voice in lamentation the most soul-searching.

All great conductors must possess what is commonly called a 'magnetic personality'; for the first necessity, granted a sufficiency of technical skill, is for a conductor to unify his orchestra. Von Bülow is always spoken of with awe by 'old pro's' regarding his almost hypnotic power in this respect. Nikisch also.

An old 'cellist once told me of his experience with Wagner in the historic Philharmonic concerts which the master conducted in London in 1855. " Beyond question here was a man inspired, but what he wanted we could not make out. He did not inspire *us* for we could not seem to understand either his music or himself." It was a different matter when the master handed over the *bâton* to Hans Richter. Here was no gulf fixed between creative artist and his

Conducting and Conductors

interpreters, but an interpreter-in-chief co-operating closely with willing *confrères*. His eye flashed fire, the fire of contagious inspiration, and lighted up every member of his orchestra. Hence the necessity as he used to say, for the conductor to " have the score in his head, not his head in the score." Every really great conductor has been able first of all to impose his magnetism on his orchestra. Mahler added this gift to his great organising ability and, of course, his profound musicianship.

In this respect no two equally great conductors were more dissimilar than Richter and Toscanini. The former at his best was wont to enlarge his field of magnetism in a marvellous way, seeming to include the whole audience in his emotional sweep. Toscanini remains apparently more self-contained, and forces the audience to contribute its quota of emotion-possibility which he then moulds in a way that can only be described as quasi-hypnotic. Richter might be said to carry the whole audience with him; Toscanini to attract the whole audience *to* him. He is probably the greatest of living conductors. The possession of an unusually retentive musical memory is one of his most useful assets. When we consider that he conducts all concert works and almost all operas from memory, and adds modern works to his repertoire apparently *ad libitum*, there is room for sheer amazement at the vitality of this highly specialized gift in a man of his years. It is, admittedly, a gift of somewhat lesser importance than his purely musical talents, but there is no doubt that the possession of it does set free his other gifts and liberate his remarkably complete musical personality to an extent that might not be possible otherwise. His memory is proverbial and I have seen none put the gift to greater use than he. M. Albert Wolff of the Concerts Lamoureux, and our own Sir Thomas Beecham are also copiously endowed by Nature in this way.

The question of the necessity or the importance of playing or conducting from memory has always been a subject of discussion among musicians. Speaking from experience in both capacities, I should say that there is a point below which the extra anxiety involved in the effort to render a work from memory is a distinct handicap: that musicians in this category (including—I say it kindly—many of our recitalists) ought to use the printed copy without the slightest hesitation. Beyond that point, that is to say where the memorizing of a work has been completely achieved and its recollection has become largely a subconscious operation, the gain is enormous. In the case of a conductor with the " score in his head " the advantage is incomputable. Lucky indeed is the musician who possesses this faculty, though it should be remembered that many of our greatest (exactly as with actors) are not remarkable in just this way.

§ 7. GENERALITIES

Just as with certain painters of former times who were more concerned with line and balance of design than with colour in their pictures; so with certain composers and their orchestral ' colours.' Many works ask for a greater degree of attention upon their construction than their instrumentation. In modern times, however, colour is so highly valued as making instantaneous appeal, that many works have resulted which depend almost wholly upon this element—works from which a power of construction and an architectonic sense are conspicuously absent. The orchestra being capable of practically inexhaustible variety of tone com-

Generalities

binations, it is not surprising that some composers have been glamoured by this factor, and have been tempted to bestow more attention upon it than upon other, equally important, factors. Still, the progress, especially since Brahms and Franck, has been marked.

Contrast the massive scoring of so many passages in later 'classics' with the Debussy-Stravinsky-Scriabin type of work where orchestral *timbres* are detached the one from the other and the characteristics of each instrument exhibited in their purity. When the full palette of colours is used all the time (as in thousands of orchestral works) regardless of the fact that only certain colours are really needed, the ear is debauched. Painters realized long before musicians in general, that in a great many cases only a limited range of colours was needed for certain pictures, and the full effect of the artist's idea was expressed within that range. Composers are increasingly realizing and practising a like selectivity.

How far the average person of the audience revels in the orchestral concert performance as a spectacle, and how ready he (or she) would be to accept it as equally enjoyable if screens were interposed between orchestra and audience, is perhaps not such a moot point as some would think. We can easily imagine what certain conductors would say to the suggestion.

It has however been tried, and certain good results noted.

Bearing in mind then the subtleties, varied characteristics and potentialities of the modern orchestra, it is not surprising that the present generation of music-lovers are concentrating a good deal of their attention upon it and (even as at present

Music To-day

constituted and despite those small ineptitudes and discrepancies to which attention has been directed in this chapter) are finding its wealth of delight-giving possibilities as shown by its great proponents to be virtually endless, and its store of enchantments inexhaustible.

CHAPTER SEVEN: COLOUR AND MUSIC

*The Pictorial Sense in Musicians—Seeing and Hearing—
The Remington Colour-organ—Scriabin and the* Tastiera
per Luce—*Suggested Tables of Correspondences—
Personal Reactions to Sound—Unity and Diversity.*

No survey of musical thought and activity in our day, however cursory, could claim to have covered the ground at all adequately if it failed to give some consideration at least to the very intriguing question of the association of Music with Colour.

§ 1. THE PICTORIAL SENSE IN MUSICIANS

It is platitudinous to say that a close correspondence exists between the pictorial and the musical sense for it has often been noted. Heine declared that when he heard music performed his inner faculties at once translated it in terms of line, mass and colour, into a picture. Upon hearing Paganini play the violin he 'saw' a veritable moving picture, the story of which he narrates inimitably in the *Florentine Nights*.[1] *Per contra*, Beethoven in the Pastoral Symphony, despite what he may himself say as to its being 'more an expression of emotions than portraiture,' does

[1] Which, amusingly enough, the writer composed into a violin and piano piece many years ago: *Rhapsodie nach Heine*. Thus you have the full circle. A musical composition; a performance of it; this visualized by the poet as a moving picture; the picture described by him as a story; and lastly, the story retranslated into music. We do not know, by the way, which Paganini piece it was that wrought so potently upon Heine.

actually attempt to translate *sights* into music. He may imitate the sound of the rumbling thunder; he also paraphrases the flashes of lightning. Not content with copying the call of the cuckoo he will show you unmistakably, just before the finale, blue sky after the storm. This has been inveighed against as bad art.

The same charge was brought against Vivaldi long ago, as it has been against Strauss in our day. Great master of the dramatic, the emotional in music (think for a moment of *Salome*), he will step aside from some of his highest flights to imitate sheep bleating and such like apparent puerilities (*Don Quixote*); and in many of his works he betrays his interest in this purely superficial aspect of tonal imitation. Closer to our subject is the fact that several composers (Mussorgsky and others) have been inspired by pictures to record their sensations in music.[1] Such instances could be multiplied greatly without however throwing any light on our investigation, for they do not in themselves indicate any necessarily real correlation between Colour and Sound. They indicate that pictures may have the power to inspire a composer, by repercussion as it were: nothing more. They might indeed be dismissed from serious consideration as mere *jeux d'esprit* had we not a mass of evidence of the correspondence under consideration which is much more cogent than this. Vague analogies do not interest us. What we would wish to know is this: *does any real correspondence between colour and sound, in fact, exist? If so, what is it?*

[1] My own groups of *Music-Pictures* (*e.g.* those for orchestra, op. 33, Queen's Hall, 1912) were the results of this type of dual reaction.

Seeing and Hearing

§ 2. SEEING AND HEARING

We constantly notice an interchange between these two orders of sensation, and a correspondence between the two arts of which they are the media which some have thought to be an inartistic confusion between them. However wrong such confusion may seem from a purely artistic point of view, it does testify to an instinct which surely has its origin in a natural analogy. Schaunard's 'Symphony in Blue' in Murger's *La Vie de Bohème* indicates what was a very frequent subject of discussion in artistic circles in Paris in the early years of the nineteenth century: Whistler's 'Symphony in White' and many other pictures also. There are many persons who always associate sound with colour and *vice versa*. Among my own personal friends and acquaintances quite a number are endowed with this faculty, and I am by no means prepared to dismiss the idea of the reality of such correspondence, because their experiences do not tally. Numbers of physicists, doctors, philosophers and others, in all parts of the world, are giving attention to this question; are making experiments, correlating evidence and tabulating results which go far toward substantiating the claims of occultists made centuries ago— claims that an exact correspondence between colour and sound is a fact in Nature.[1]

Many philosophers from Aristotle onwards have recognized the possibility. Of workers in our day the names of Drs. Graham Bell (*Photophone* 1880), Maclean, Fournier d'Albe (*Optophone*), de Forest (*Audion*), Edison (*Kineto-*

[1] They go, of course, far beyond this and postulate a series of correspondences which embrace Colour—Sound—Form—Vowels—Psychological States—Elements, etc.

phone), occur to the mind, and any student sufficiently interested to 'pursue truth' along this line will find an enormous amount of information available right up to and including the Baird *Television* apparatus of to-day. To the scientific type of mind the real interest is in obtaining a mechanical apparatus by which light can be transmuted into musical sound. One may see such a machine in the music hall nowaday and very interesting it is.

§ 3. THE REMINGTON COLOUR-ORGAN

The most striking development along these lines, so far as most musicians are concerned, was achieved by G. W. Remington who constructed a colour-keyboard, playing upon which in the manner of a piano-keyboard, not sounds were elicited for the delectation of the ear, but colours were projected upon a screen. No doubt charming tints resulted. This was a purely arbitrary correspondence however—how arbitrary will be gathered when we find that the whole series of correspondences were changed *en bloc* to agree with a change of key. The thing was, in short, nothing more than an ingenious toy, and had nothing whatever to do with the reality which we have predicated.

It should be mentioned in fairness that so far as I know it never claimed to have; but it is none the less subversive of true progress in this matter that such a superficial and in a sense trivial piece of mechanism should have attained such notoriety, and in doing so should have side-tracked a good many serious students who might otherwise have made valuable contributions to this branch of musical philosophy. There may have been no pretence, as I have said, that the colours produced *really* corresponded with

Scriabin and the 'Tastiera per Luce'

the notes which produced them, but to offer this instrument to the musical world was rather like offering to a student of anatomy a mechanical mouse to study. Its interest, relatively, was scarcely more than that.

To an artist the interest in this subject is quite other, and beginning in modern times with the musicians Rameau and Grétry (who said that the scale of human emotions was common to that of colour and of sound, and that "purple red indicates anger, a paler red accompanies shyness," etc.[1]), he studies a more subtle and yet a more practical interchange between them.[2]

§ 4. SCRIABIN AND THE 'TASTIERA PER LUCE'

Remington's instrument was adopted and actually used by Scriabin in his *Prometheus*, a Symphony of Sound and Colour, in the score of which it appears as *Tastiera per Luce*; and although he disagreed with the arrangement of the Remington Colour-scale and adapted one of his own to the instrument, he appears to have accepted the arbitrary and fundamentally untrue method of adjustment already commented on. This appears the more singular since Scriabin was himself a young occultist and must have known that he was using a mere plaything. Possibly he regarded even this as worth while in drawing attention to a neglected side of his art. Another, and perhaps truer reason may be found in Section 7 of this chapter, and in Section 6 of Chapter XVII in our Fifth Part. Rimsky-

[1] Many people, and increasing numbers it would appear, possess this faculty of 'seeing' auric disturbances in terms of colour. Though analogous, even this does not quite touch the point at issue.

[2] Cf. Dr D. D. Jameson, *Colour Music*; J. D. Macdonald, *Sound and Colour*; F. J. Hughes, *Harmonics of Tones and Colours*; J. B. Allen, *Scales in Music and Colours*; G. W. Remington, *The Art of Mobile Colour*.

Korsakov also drew up a scheme of 'correspondences' which is as arbitrary as that of Scriabin whilst differing from it in detail. Thus there exist discrepancies and contradictions even amongst those who are prepared to agree as to the existence of a correspondence of some sort.

§ 5. SUGGESTED TABLES OF CORRESPONDENCES

The truth is that musical sounds do not give rise to colours *upon the physical plane* at all; consequently all correspondences which have been observed to exist between sound and colour, and the multitudinous and well-authenticated records of such observations, are due to a use of psychic faculty.

The 'colour-hearing' sense is widespread, and such a serious investigator as Ortmann arrives at the conclusion that it must be classed as a non-auditory response. It is clearly a non-visual one. It is then psychic, and is designated 'synæsthesia.' But a close study of the use of such faculty —surprisingly widespread as it is in this age of increased and increasing sensitivity—shows that it is but an extension of our normal physical faculties and one we would do well to investigate still more seriously than hitherto. Artists, creative artists especially, ought to give it the most serious attention, for along this line will be found solutions of many of their otherwise insoluble problems. In this at least, Scriabin was right.

Unfortunately, at the present time it is the bringing over of psychic impressions undistorted into the brain that is the least developed and least reliable aspect of the faculty. And it is its unreliability that has caused the discrepancies in the various reports of the correspondence between sound and colour.

Personal Reactions to Sound

One of the first of modern occultists to put this information in clear tabular form was Mme. Blavatsky, whose *Secret Doctrine* contains the following:

C—Red: D—Orange: E—Yellow: F—Green: G—Blue: A—Indigo: B—Violet.

A number of psychics (one of whom is mentioned by Cyril Scott in his *Philosophy of Modernism*) confirm this table of correspondences. Others, however, do not: hence arise the discrepancies spoken of above. Scriabin's table was different. Rimsky-Korsakov's different again, though not in every detail. But such discrepancies between the reports of investigators, irritating though they be, cannot be held to vitiate the basic fact itself. Nor, in recognizing the unreliability of such reports, should we impugn their sincerity or even their relative truth.

These divergencies arise because, whilst the observations themselves may be perfectly accurate, certain conditions have been entirely left out of account: conditions which are vital to the results.

§ 6. PERSONAL REACTIONS TO SOUND

Before, therefore, I could agree to any *ex parte* statement as to such a note definitely producing such a colour, I would require fairly extensive data. For, so far as my observations have extended, the colour resulting from any note played or sung varies according to these several conditions:

First: the *pitch* of the note whose results are under observation.[1]

---

[1] Obviously the resulting colour depends upon pitch; if not, the whole theory falls to the ground.

Music To-day

Second: with what *timbre* it is produced.[1]

Third: upon what 'plane' or 'sub-plane' of Nature such result is observed.[2]

Each and all of these conditions govern the result—and vitally. How, therefore, can we bring ourselves to accept such sweeping assertions as those spoken of above? No painter would be prepared to accept the bald statement that, for example, 'the sea is blue.' He would wish to know whether Pacific, Mediterranean, Atlantic, were in question; whether a morning or evening sky, sunny or cloudy, and many other details all of which affect the question. Finally he would go only so far as to agree that a certain ocean, under a certain sky, *might* appear blue. Similarly, a series of collateral facts condition the results from any given note of music and thus any dogmatic pronouncement that 'C corresponds to Red; A to Indigo' and the like, will need a certain amount of qualification.

Such considerations are, however, of very little weight against one of my most cherished convictions. For I know that such a correspondence does in fact exist. But I have a shuddering detestation of the glib, ready-made, tables-of-correspondences into which certain persons desire to cram the Universe—the Cosmos; tabulations which appear so pat, and which yet explain so little.

§ 7. UNITY AND DIVERSITY

Such an exact and invariable correspondence then, I have satisfied myself, does exist; invariable that is to say, given similar conditions. But the root of the matter lies deeper

---

[1] Changed *timbre* produces changed colour.

[2] The same musical sound gives rise to different colours upon the different 'planes.' Cf. diagram, p. 159.

Unity and Diversity

far than this, and any degree of real appreciation of it throws a flood of light upon some of the most suggestive, even though partially abortive, efforts of several men of genius.

From a scrap of occult lore I cull the following:

In the beginning is the Sound. This [as it becomes manifested and moves in obedience to the laws of vibration which affect everything in the Cosmos] **gives rise to the basic forms** [resulting in the so-called Platonic solids upon which our world is founded]. **The primal light of the universe playing in the interstices between these forms gives rise to the phenomenon which you call 'colour.'**

If we were able to accept this bald statement as a working hypothesis we might deduce from it certain conclusions which would irradiate our present problem. As first: it would show how a real correspondence between sound, form, and colour might come about. Also: how these in their turn give rise to other correspondences, as those between elements, psychological states, colours and vowel sounds; musical tones and various nerve-centres or plexuses in the human body; the therapeutic effects resulting from these, and a whole range of hitherto unsuspected correspondences of the most illuminating character.

Finally, it would throw light upon one of the profoundest facts which genius demonstrates. Few people can understand the power which the man of genius possesses of comprehending a subject in essence without the laborious processes of learning it in detail. He is able to perceive the ideation as a Unity, one and indivisible. It is only the restatement of this ideation in the mundane world which of necessity takes on diversity of expression. Hence arise

Music To-day

those attempts at a synthetic presentation of the Arts, a consideration of which we shall more readily comprehend after we have systematized our thinking along these lines in "A Septenary Classification,"[1] and which we therefore defer to a later section concerning "A Synthesis of the Arts."[2]

[1] P. 159.
[2] P. 349.

CHAPTER EIGHT: MUSIC AND SOME PYSCHO-PHYSIOLOGICAL REACTIONS

Therapeutic Effects of Music—Women and Music—Familiarity and Contempt.

§ 1. THERAPEUTIC EFFECTS OF MUSIC

IN conversation with a learned psychologist some years ago, I heard, without much surprise, the following dictum: "In the main, you musicians are too fiercely concentred on the narrowest aspects of your art. The great majority of you give all your attention to the merely entertaining aspects of music; the remainder (your 'highbrows') are intent on its technical, artistic, or even spiritual qualities, and in one or other of these categories can be placed all musicians save perhaps one or two. You agree?" I was bound to. Of course it is so. Among our other limitations (Nietzsche said that musicians think less than other artists; Carlyle, that we talk too much), too narrow a view of the possibilities of the sound art, and too great attention upon its purely artistic aspects—these are indictments to which we must undoubtedly plead guilty.

Now sound is one of the great forces of Nature, like heat, light, electricity; and to restrict the application of its potentialities to mere amusement for leisure moments is as shortsighted as to use, say, electricity for lighting purposes only. Moreover we are apt to forget that other kingdoms of Nature as well as the human kingdom are profoundly affected by music and react to it in a degree that we ought more carefully to note. We know, for example, what effect it can make in the mineral kingdom. Many of us have taken part in the old experiment of shattering tumblers or gas globes by first ascertaining the note to which they respond, their keynote, so to say, and sustaining this note with increasing intensity until it overcomes the force of cohesion between the physical particles, and they are violently disrupted. One has 'assisted' in several other very instructive experiments along analogous lines which carry real lessons for all music-lovers.

Again, as to the vegetable kingdom, we have the word of such an authority as Sir Jagadîsh Bose, regarding the power of sound in stimulating or retarding the growth of plant life. He has demonstrated the power of organized sound (music), to quicken plant growth enormously, as also to force back the vital forces, thus causing the plant to fade, to wilt, ultimately to die.

In relation to the lower animal kingdom too, we possess in music a very powerful force—though one that is at present scarcely at all exploited. Snakes, lizards and scorpions respond sensitively; monkeys still more readily. Horses will move in step to a rhythm, cows will yield an increased quantity of milk under the influence of music. As to dogs—many are the stories, both short and 'tall,' about the reactions of our friends' animals to various composers' work!

So much then for the effects of music in the mineral, vegetable and lower animal kingdoms. But there can be no doubt that the potentialities of music in relation to the psycho-physiological make-up of man are only now beginning to be intelligently studied, and, as yet, scarcely applied at all.

Therapeutic Effects of Music

A volume could easily be filled with records of physiological effects produced upon listeners by music; from Pythagoras, Plato and Aristotle onward (including Paracelsus and the Alchemists), to the great French and German physicists and the recent inspiring labours of American researchers. Interesting, indeed absorbing as are many of these records, it is not my intention to proceed to catalogue and discuss them here. I mention them because they tend in two distinct directions, at both of which we ought to glance: first, the physiological effects; second, the psychic effects; both being important aspects of the art of musical therapy.

For one of the uses of music, at present merely latent but as I think destined to bulk very largely in the future growth of the race, is as an agent in the art of healing. We are at the very infancy at present of this type of work. Everyone knows, to be sure, that a lullaby can soothe, a rhythmic dance tune 'tickle the toes,' a rousing march stimulate ardour in many people. During the war the sedative effects of music were employed in many hospitals, albeit in a very tentative and quite unscientific manner: but the results all indicated that these effects, when transmitted by the auditory nerve to the whole nervous system, induced a salutary reaction in the morbid part of the organism.

What we have not realized up till now is that these tentative experiments in the therapeutical uses of sound, though true as far as they go, are mere dabblings in an ocean of tremendous possibilities, and are capable of almost infinite extension, of exact tabulation, of really scientific application, and of the most far-reaching and permanently re-creative results. And this not only in nervous, or similar functional disorders as might be supposed, but in the restoration of health in cases even of organic disease. I have myself been a witness of this, and I shall be surprised if we do not hear of some astonishing revelations along similar lines in the immediate future. At a recent Music Teaching Course at Oxford a speaker declared that " in the near future when democracy on the whole realizes the value of music-making of the right type, when people have things wrong with their nerves or *even* with their bodies, they will go to the rhythmiticians and the musicians in order to be cured in their mind and body." It is the 'even' in this quotation to which I have drawn attention, for the vast majority of people, whilst being ready to admit the possibility of music effecting cures or at least alleviation in cases of deranged nerves, etc., would utterly scout the notion of physical cures by its means. Yet, having witnessed the above-mentioned remarkable cure of an unquestionably physical affection, which I confess surprised me greatly, I mentioned it to a friendly M.D. So far from scoffing, he remarked: " Just what I would have expected. Music being a physical vibration must produce, perforce, physical results—in this case definitely harmonizing and curative ones." Being unable, for obvious reasons, to approach this question purely scientifically, I can do no more, and may do no less, than record plainly that I have myself been witness of many and beneficial results obtained by applying various musical tones, sung at 'nature' pitch,[1] to the various physical nerve-centres (as the Sacral, Solar, Cardiac and other plexuses) *to which they correspond.*

This therapy is as yet in its infancy but, I am assured, rapid progress is being made; and the time is perhaps not far distant when the musician, working in conjunction with

---

[1] Nature-pitch, cf. p. 347.

the medical man, will be called upon to supply the dynamic of his art in this direction and for this purpose.

§ 2. WOMEN AND MUSIC

The emancipation of women in the Western world is a phenomenon practically coeval with the musical revolution, and presents certain points of interest in conjunction with it. The unthinking would have us allocate to the male the warlike, the super-active and all those avocations which call for physical strength, endurance and force, and to the female those demanding conservation, preservation and the like. The question is not so simple as this and really involves many collateral subjects into which this is not the proper place, even if one possessed the detailed knowledge, to probe. The recent concentration upon—some would say exaggeration of—the virile qualities of the male and the more passive ones of the female, under the Fascist and Nazi *régimes*, will be recognized as a progressive or a retrogressive step, according to the point of view. Certainly what happened during the war years seemed to open up possibilities for women in the realms of music such as had not occurred before. That they have, upon the whole, signally failed to increase their influence in both creative and interpretative fields of the art is a conclusion at which most people have long since arrived. Exceptions do nothing to shake the conclusion long held by many specialists, that women are comparatively impotent as creative artists.

An illuminating theory which came my way some time ago, which may assist thought upon this subject, and which I therefore give for what it is worth, is this: that the male is polarized as to physical—positive; emotional—

Music To-day

negative; mental—positive. The female is contrarily polarized, physical—negative; emotional—positive; mental—negative.

A study of these comparisons—these oppositions—and a recognition of some of the conclusions to which they would lead us, is none of our business here: but as they would apply to the question under immediate discussion they are certainly of some interest. For even when we remember the dictum laid down recently by Norman Haire that such phenomena as 100 per cent feminine or masculine persons simply do not exist—even when we have made every possible allowance for variations from the normal in either direction—we are still faced with the incontrovertible fact of (and innumerable instances of) the woman 'inspiring' the man: particularly the creative artist.

It is the balancing of a man's nature, the 'tuning' of it, the aligning of the physical, emotional and mental, and the still 'higher' 'bodies,' that is the function so frequently performed by woman, and it is easy to see, by reference to our theory, how this might take place. Commonly referred to in some such phrase as: 'her love inspired him,' it might be nearer the truth to say 'her propinquity intuned him.'

Quite frequently it happens, even to the greatest composer, that amid the cares and worries of our mortal life the *Hamsa*[1] of his inspiration wearies, its pinions flag, flight is no longer possible, and it sinks to earth temporarily exhausted. A lack of free-flowing *Prâna*[2] in one or other of his 'bodies,' or, perhaps more frequently, the temporary disalignment of these bodies is often the cause of the

---

[1] In Oriental imagery the *Hamsa* (Swan) is symbolical of Man's inspired Imagination, or exalted mystical experience.

[2] A name for the universal life when specialized for the support of the separated organism.

breakdown of his inspiration. In such a state, and indeed in many another, nothing is more stimulating than the support of a woman's love; and it is the natural result of this maternal, this cherishing influence—negative where he is positive, immensely prodigal where he is lacking—that the harmonious alignment erstwhile disrupted is now restored in him and his *Hamsa* once more spreads its wings and takes flight for 'eyries far remote and loftiest spheres intangible.' The love affair is not then itself the source of his inspiration, but is the means of attuning him, of re-polarizing his bodies, so that he may once more contact the sources from which he has temporarily been divorced.

Love between the sexes is thus one of the most potent means of inducing this condition of 'raptus,' but it is not the only one—perhaps it is not even so important, so indispensable an ingredient in the artist's life as has been commonly supposed. And were we in possession of a greater amount of intimate data than we can expect to be at this, the end (let us hope) of an absurdly puritanical epoch, we would certainly be able to fortify the above line of argument in a more scientific manner by reference to, and instance of specific cases.

I have yet to meet the woman musician whose response to fine music is equal to man's upon the physical plane (which includes the brain!) or the mental; whereas she is, as a rule, more swiftly moved to purely emotional reactions than he. Upon the creative side woman labours under the dual handicap of being (according to the above theory) negative upon the higher mental levels as well as upon the physical. There may be, there are, exceptions; but these are very few and comparatively unconvincing. I am inclined to believe that 'above' the levels spoken of here the differentiation between the polarization of the sexes—perhaps the phenomenon of sex altogether, as we conceive of it—disappears. But it is a region and a state of consciousness so rarely attained to in the present stage of our evolution that further speculation would serve little or no purpose.

Somewhat obscure though the foregoing may appear, its logicality will become increasingly apparent as we proceed: especially so when we enter the highly involved field of musical æsthetic.[1]

Analagous though it be to the subject of the present section, we had better postpone until I have laid before the reader, in our Third Part, certain considerations which will/should help to clarify thought on the matter, some observations on Music and Sex.[2]

§ 3. FAMILIARITY AND CONTEMPT

A problem which constantly confronts the practising musician — the concert-promoter, programme-arranger, music-teacher and so on—is that which may be summarized under the above heading. For one of the most important of the many factors which affect our estimate of the value of a musical work, and one which also affects profoundly our enjoyment, lies in the constant flux between familiarity and contempt.

This is a strangely neglected aspect of the art but one of such importance that some consideration of it must not be omitted in a review of conditions in the world of music to-day.

Familiarity is the first necessity for the musically un-

---

[1] P. 155 et seq. Cf. also, Mystical Inspiration, p. 198.
[2] P. 177.

Familiarity and Contempt

evolved, and it is a factor so potent that everything which departs from the accustomed is felt to be disagreeable, if not indeed grotesque. Because strange, it is in a high degree unpleasant. To the highly evolved musical intelligence nothing can be so irksome as continued repetitions of a piece of music which he knows from A to Z, upon the expressional as well as the technical side: for it is not easy for the adept to recall the days of his musical innocence. Between these two extremes lies the whole musical world, and, bearing this in mind, the problems which confront composer, performer, conductor, and concert promoter, are many and various. It is just as absurd for the experienced concert-goer or critic to say he is tired of the *Symphonie Pathétique* (as well he may be) and that it ought to be ' given a rest,' as for the tyro to demand constant repetitions of works he has heard before; of ' things he knows.' The majority of persons listen to music quite passively. When, however, listening to music is active and not passive there are two mental operations involved, viz., expectation and recollection. Both imply a certain degree of familiarity, and the readiness with which familiarity is attained to varies greatly.

Familiarity is in itself a pleasant feeling. Involving as it does the recognition-thrill, it is part of the equipment of the composer, and, upon the æsthetic side, one of his most potent devices. The familiar, however, is never allowed by the fine artist to pass over into the trite; banality is abhorrent to him. He enriches the familiar with such a wealth of collateral attributes as to ensure continued discovery of new beauties and subtleties which are not to be grasped upon a first hearing. And yet its first and obvious appeal must be great enough to engage the unwavering attention. It is upon this rock that many a barque hopefully christened 'Success' is wrecked.

The simplest way in which composers give us the pleasure of the recognition-thrill is by use of the device known as the sequence. Here again, upon the speed with which we recognize the formula depends our enjoyment of the repetitions. When Schumann writes:[1]

thus repeating his formula sequentially three times, there will be those who only dimly begin to realize the formula at its third presentation; there are others to whom three statements are too much. This is at the root of the dislike some people feel for Handel and Bach. They cannot bear:[2]

Four repetitions seem irksome to them—even vapid. Similarly when Elgar (a persistent 'sequentialist') tells them three times over that[3]

even though the orchestration be varied, their vital interest weakens.

Some persons do react in this way and it is as well to

---

[1] In the *Pianoforte Quartet*.   [2] Bach: *Double Concerto*.
[3] Elgar: *Enigma Variations*.

Familiarity and Contempt

know it. My Italian godfather threw up his hands, and rolled his great eyes in Mephistophelean hatred of:[1]

" Wagner writes egzercises," he roared.

These are not real indictments of course, for one may ' listen ' with other parts of one's nature besides the brain.

Still there is this much truth behind them, that the sequence is frequently " the last refuge of the destitute composer." And perhaps nowhere is this manufacturer's device more clearly to be noted in any great composer's work than in the finale of Debussy's string quartet. In this movement (and in certain other works also) he has developed to a painful extent the bad habit of saying everything twice over. I do not refer to repetitions of long sections like those in the first movements of classical symphonies, nor to re-statements of long phrases or extended sections: still less to those frequent reiterations of rhythmic formulæ which are so commonly met with in modern music whose effect is intended to be *mantric*.[2] I refer to the immediate repetition of scraps whose import is not so weighty nor their presentation so recondite that the most mediocre modern musical intelligence cannot assimilate them with consummate ease. This movement of Debussy's consists of some 350 bars. The fifth is repeated in the sixth: eleven in twelve: fifteen in sixteen: seventeen in eighteen: nineteen in twenty:

---

[1] *Die Meistersinger;* Overture. Wagner.

[2] A *mantra* is a short rhythmic arrangement either of words or musical sounds of an evocative nature, which, when constantly repeated—in conformity with laws not generally known but as definite as a mathematical formula—set going causes which produce predicable results.

Music To-day

twenty-one in twenty-two: twenty-three in twenty-four: thirty-one and -two in thirty-three and -four: thirty-nine and forty in forty-one and -two: fifty-nine and sixty in sixty-one and -two: eighty-six and -seven in eighty-eight and -nine: ninety-eight to 101 in 102 to 105: 110 and 111 in 112 and 113: 114 and 115 in 116 and 117: 123 in 124: 137 in 138: 139 in 140: 157 to 160 in 161 to 164: 175 and 176 in 177 and 178: 202 to 204 in 205 to 207: 208 and 209 in 210 and 211: 212 in 213: 214 in 215: 220 in 221: 222 in 223: 228 in 229: 244 and 245 in 246 and 247: 252 and 253 in 254 and 255: 260 and 261 in 262 and 263: 322 in 323, 324 and 325: 341 and 342 in 343 and 344: 349 in 350 and 351. All these are absolutely accurate repetitions, not mere resemblances.

Although always bored inexpressibly by this movement, even I had not quite realized until I compiled the above list for the benefit of readers, to what an extent the composer had allowed this insidious trick to obsess him. Debussy worshippers and those who bow down to a great name will look for some occult and deeply portentous significance in this device. If they be at the same time intelligent and candid, they will not find it. For this is one of the most inane movements that ever came from the pen (not to say brain or inspiration) of a great composer.

Taking now a slightly larger view of the question: repetitions of whole melodies unaltered, or with no fresh treatment, may result in added pleasure or in boredom according to the musical intelligence of the listener. Few serious composers of our day, appealing to the average trained musical understanding, would care to do this. And it is significant that the old custom of repeating the whole of the first portion (the Statement) of the great works of the

Familiarity and Contempt

'classic' period in Sonata form, even though such repeat is clearly indicated by the composer, has largely fallen into disuse. It is felt that one hearing of the principal themes has been sufficient for us to be able to recognize them, even in metamorphosis, during the subsequent 'working-out' section. This, as we have shown, is not always the case.

Complete restatements of a melody can rarely be tolerated by an intelligent listener unless they be presented differently so that his intellectual as well as sensuous response is evoked. *E.g.*, Walter's *Preislied* in *Die Meistersinger*, where, as also in many cases of songs, the alteration of the words, verse by verse, also affords some alleviation.

A far more subtle use of the recognition-thrill and a much more conscious exploitation of its evocative powers—one of the most powerful emotional effects in the whole gamut of the musical art—is made by modern composers. It is rarely met with in the 'classics.' An early instance is that of Berlioz' *Symphonie Fantastique* where the *idée fixe* is represented by a theme which appears in contrasted and diversified surroundings throughout the work. And although it is perhaps the least successful device employed in that astounding composition—which was, after all, but the work of a boy—there is clear evidence of the value this composer put upon it, and a foretaste of the indescribably affecting use he was to put it to in subsequent works. Even nowaday—a hard-bit, salted, tough old 'pro.,' I cannot hear the *cor anglais* 'recollection' of the Marguerite melody in his *Faust* without being completely overcome.

The French, as might have been expected, are adepts at suggestion without overstatement. There is a superb moment of this character in Saint-Saëns' *La Fiancée du Timbalier*. The regiment is returning from the wars. She eagerly scrutinises the ranks of the passing soldiers for the face of her lover. . . . He is not there. . . . The regiment passes! . . . We can imagine with how heavy a hand certain composers would paint her grief, exhibit her agony, expose her tortured heart. The Frenchman leaves all this to your imagination, but your imagination vivified and keyed up to incandescence. For what you do hear is the gay *insouciance* of the opening military march dying away in the distance: and, believe me, it is ' of a poignance.'

I well know that Saint-Saëns is not one of the Olympians: but *à chaque saint sa chandelle*.

Schumann just glimpsed the idea. Brahms also, at the end of his Third Symphony. Liszt had dabbled with it—not oversuccessfully as it seems to me. But Wagner uses it with tremendous mastery; and the utter tragedy embodied in the *Trauermarsch* of *Götterdämmerung*, however much it affect the listener in other ways, will be missed by all who cannot put at the master's disposal a store-house of recollections of its themes as they have imposed themselves on him in the previous scenes of the mighty trilogy. By the time we reach César Franck there is distinct danger of the device being used as a work-a-day expedient—of " the trick being made for the sake of the trick, and not for the sake of the Game "—and there is more than one modern symphonic work in which it is abused to such an extent that it ceases completely to retain any evocative virtue.

Another aspect of the *lutte* between familiarity and contempt is the oft-debated question how far your enjoyment is increased or the reverse by knowing exactly what comes next. Discussing this question with a friend of my boyhood—recalling the thrills and ecstasies of our first acquaintance with the great ' classics ' and the possibility of

Familiarity and Contempt

re-capturing those virgin thrills—" Ah no " said he, " it is not by raking among the embers of those brave old days that memory can give us back the key of our lost Paradises."

In Mussolini's play *Napoleon* occurs the following scene: A peasant describes the battle of Waterloo as he watches it through a telescope. Upon this a reviewer commented: " Since we know what happened at Waterloo, no sort of thrill came from that scene." You see the notion. We are robbed of our enjoyment because we know what is going to happen. Is this really so, however? There may be a modicum of truth in it with regard to quite ephemeral pieces depending almost entirely for their effect on turns of plot or surprise endings such as, for example, in so many of O. Henry's stories. It cannot be so in the case of a work of high art.

I must have conducted or performed in Beethoven's *C minor* Symphony at least fifty times, besides studying the score as a youth until I knew it by heart. And I admittedly reached saturation-point long ago. Was it impossible for me henceforward ever again to be thrilled by that work? Certainly, replies the cynic. But the answer is not quite so simple. For I played the work over to a keen young musician, pointed out a great many beauties of the score, revealed some of the power of thought behind its form, and then took him to a performance. He was inexpressibly moved, *and so was I!* The re-orientation in my point of view had given me a new hearing and a fresh heart, and had reinforced from a quaint angle the old platitude about the immortality of great work. There is besides, another unrecognized fact which has a direct bearing on this question, to which I refer in a section upon the Ensouling of Music.[1]

[1] P. 179, *et seq.*

Music To-day

It is surely time for the tyro to cease gibing at those who love and, in a measure understand, lofty works, as 'highbrows'; equally should the experienced cease from sneering at the musically less-evolved. It seems constantly to be necessary to remind ourselves that music-lovers in general are bound to be at various stages of evolution in the art, from neophyte to adept, and that the one state is no more to be deprecated than the other extolled. It is no more right to sneer at the babe for lack of erudition than to suspect the musical *illuminati* of posing.

We have noticed the case of those, who, long familiar with music couched in the 'old' terms of melody, harmony, and counterpoint, find it impossible to overcome their preconceptions and approach the 'new music' with an open mind. It has been interesting to notice many instances of a converse tendency. Many lovers of literature and painting, who cared very little for music formerly, are susceptible to the 'new music' in a way which surprises those who have hitherto dismissed them as unmusical. They are, in many cases, persons of unemotional type, more readily responsive to intellectual than emotional stimuli. The 'old' music being directed toward that part of their nature which is irresponsive, they have been regarded as unmusical. But the new music, in several of its aspects, is directed toward other parts of our make-up, and this is one of the reasons of its success with the formerly insusceptible.

Chapter Nine: Certain Conditions To-day in the Musical World

Ways and Means—'Light' Music—A Present-day Aberration—Emancipated Rhythm—Mechanized Music—Conclusions of Part Two.

As, in accordance with our declared plan, a good deal of attention is given in this book to matters technical, theoretical, controversial, as well as to speculative questions and those tentative æsthetical evaluations which a consideration of musical matters commonly connotes, the present chapter, apart from any intrinsic value which its attitude toward important practical musical affairs may possess, will help us to maintain balance and orientation and will bring us face to face with certain facets of present-day musical activities which may have escaped the notice of many music-lovers.

§ 1. Ways and Means

Consider for a moment the plight of the serious composer in this country; he who, without other means of obtaining a livelihood, is 'called' (as professed religionists would say) to this way of life. There are those who opine that no serious composer should depend upon this gift for a livelihood. Some day (in Stevenson's words), "when the butcher is knocking at the door, he may be tempted, he may be obliged, to turn out and sell a slovenly piece of work." Suppose he have no other resources whatsoever—and the case is not merely hypothetical—what shall he do? He is a highly specialized being; has spent we will say all his life in the service of his art. It is only natural therefore that if he ascend to heights unreached by the average person he will be more or less out of our ken; and if he translate his inner experience in commensurate technical terms he will be telling us of unfamiliar worlds in totally unfamiliar words. Despite all argument to the contrary, he cannot be, and will not readily be understood by the average listener, even though his works are constantly performed. He is, in fact, indulging in one of the most expensive of hobbies. Money has scarcely any influence on his activity, because he is aware that, no matter how well he succeed, the chances are a million to one against any appreciable monetary reward. The hope of making money by his art will not spur him on, for there is no hope. The moment his ecstasy is over and the precious idea committed to paper, the inevitable reaction sets in and he remembers that he himself is the one (and the only one) believer in the truth and beauty of his inspiration. None heeds; none cares. As for payment! This can be had for something *tangible*, for dis-'arranging' a piece, for copying, but for creative ideas, no! Do you remember Mozart modestly asking one ducat for each of three new Concertos, and pathetically adding "who could get them even *copied* for a ducat?" Even to this day payment for 'arrangers,' who are after all but second-hand dealers, is out of all proportion to that for creators. There seems to be a natural conspiracy to deprecate, even to negate, creative endeavour, and to exalt mere hack-work. And to-day many a composer could exclaim with Blake: "I find on all hands great objections to my doing anything but the mere drudgery of business, and intimations that if I do not

Ways and Means

confine myself to this, I shall not live. . . . Why this [his devotion to his artistic ideals] should be made an objection to me, while drunkenness, lewdness, gluttony and even idleness itself, do not hurt other men, let Satan himself explain."

Happy the Wagners and Schönbergs of the world who possess also the gift of attracting converts to their cause; happy the Shaws who are such adroit self-publicity agents. But there are others.

Even if by some extraordinary means he manages to bring his works to actual performance, he enters a field already choked with such a plethora of inane lucubrations that the poor public (lacking in any case any marked degree of real discrimination, as we have so often deplored in these pages) has little chance of according him a just measure of appreciation. But even when by some miracle he does get his work direct to them, and, *mirabile dictu*, they do faintly perceive some lucent gleam of the burning fire of his music, and *do* demonstrate in no uncertain terms their joy and their delight, so powerful are the forces arrayed against him that if he be a free-lance—if he belong to no coterie, clique or claque, no college or academy, no school, faction or 'set' —his success is as a vesta-flame extinguished by the wind and its tangible results, particularly in this country—nil.

Happy Sibelius subsidized by a discerning Fatherland.

Civilization, even in the Western world, is growing old enough to be able to profit by its experiences. We have starved enough of our Chattertons and Francis Thompsons, our Mozarts and Schuberts, to death; and enough of our Berlioz' to unproductiveness. What Verdi 'might have produced' had he lived on after his 88th year may provide highly-spiced food for speculation to your arm-chair musicologist; what Berlioz *would* have done had he had a few paltry thousands of francs he has told us in burning words in the *Memoires*. And, what concerns your active artist still more nearly is the question of the price of his next meal. Only moneyed men can afford to practise serious composition nowaday. Have they then a monopoly of talent? If not, can we afford to leave the existence of the remainder to mere chance? Disturbing and discomforting questions, these.[1]

A similar state of affairs obtains, of course, in other worlds than the musical. However, there are signs that in certain directions we are waking up. Quite recently we realized that it was absurd that the government of this Empire should be left to only those who happened to be men of independent means. We now remunerate those who are elected to office, so that all, of whatever private financial status, may devote the best of their talents to this important activity. Speed the day when we shall behave in some such way to those creative artists who happen to need it.

Meanwhile several courses are open to our composer. First: he may turn out vulgar music (for which there *is* a demand) and publish it under a pseudonym. I am told that many of them do. It must be a horrible experience, and it must lead to an early death . . . of their real inspiration. Second: he may turn his hand to the composition of music which he does not pretend to have contacted in his highest flights—simple stuff to be 'understanded of the people,' and told in words (harmonies, rhythms, etc.) with which the people are familiar. I see nothing at all derogatory in

---

[1] Bernard Shaw writing about a living composer of this type said: He will perhaps endure starvation, to which of course all serious composers are accustomed.

his doing this. So be it is not foul, vulgar, degrading stuff such as that mentioned above, it will do no harm to the listener nor to his own creative gift. Sibelius, for example, has done an enormous amount of this kind of music. And so did Beethoven, Schubert, Mozart, and many more. Fond though one may be of the finest and highest in literature one is not always in the mood for Sir Thomas Browne, Milton, Browning; one can surely without shame indulge one's appetite for Leblanc, Edgar Wallace, O. Henry. Similarly in music. It must fairly often be the case that even a genuine music-lover is not inclined to exert as much musical intelligence as is demanded by a Brahms, a Reger, or a Schönberg. Is his only alternative to be a decadent jazz tune or some such trash? may he not listen with enjoyment to good music of the above description?

§ 2. 'LIGHT' MUSIC

But a habit has recently arisen in certain circles, especially in England, of referring to all music that belongs to this type in contumelious terms as 'light music.' The contradictions and absurdities that arise through the use and misuse of this inane term are endless. Worse still, in the minds of those who like to 'praise with faint damns' in order the more effectually to damn, the scornful relegation of any work to the category of 'light' music is a shibboleth the more dangerous because it is also misleading: and none the less misleading because it is also silly. You do not sneer at Bach the Olympian because he occasionally descended from the heights and wrote dances which were more easily comprehensible by 'the man in the street' than, for example, *Die Kunst der Fuge*. And it should be remembered that he,

Music To-day

unlike our hypothetical composer, was permanently engaged to do his best work: Palestrina also;—happy men. Beethoven's Scottish and German dances and his earnest attempt at 'popular' music with the *Battle Symphony* (*Rule Britannia!*) *Schlacht bei Vittoria,* prove that he also was not above addressing himself to the less evolved among the musical intelligences of his day. Schubert occasionally descended to the level of the Viennese street-ballad. Brahms made his first, and perhaps even to this day his widest successes with pseudo-Hungarian popular tune arrangements.[1] Sibelius perpetrated a *Valse triste,* Ravel a *Bolero,* Rimsky-Korsakov a *Chanson Hindou.*[2]

Many modern composers, starved of the recognition due to their serious works, are driven to seek the pabulum which is to a certain extent necessary to their well-being (they are human like the rest of us, strange to say), by writing some music of a frankly 'popular' nature. They are in good company as has already been noted above. What should not be forgotten is that they do not thereby automatically put themselves outside the pale of serious consideration; and to dismiss them in this categorical way would be as sensible as to speak of Sibelius and Elgar as 'light' composers because of *Valse Triste* and *Salut d'Amour.*

Some modern composers 'in their hours of ease' turn their hands to folk-music, and for some totally inexplicable and completely illogical reason this will escape the opprobrious epithet, 'light.' The composer will even earn encomiums which will react favourably upon his general reputation, and will perhaps even cover the occasional

---

[1] Some of these, long supposed to be authentic Hungarian tunes, are now accepted as original.

[2] Which is about as 'Indian' as a Chopin *Nocturne,* but very little more so.

'Light' Music

introduction of one of his major works to an audience predisposed in his favour. The opposite has happened in the case of Ravel who at the height of his fame has written his egregious *Bolero*—a great 'popular' success. Poulenc has adopted a curious idiom in most of his work: a Mozartian ingenuousness of melody and harmony seasoned with modernities in about equal proportions. The naïveté of the former makes immediate appeal to the non-educated listener whose musical point of view is about 150 years behind the times, whilst the novelties in the latter deceive all who, whilst favourably disposed toward the new music, have not sufficient sheer musical erudition to pierce the deception. A hotch-potch of styles results from this attempt to make the best of both worlds.[1]

Strauss is particularly adroit at finding specious pretexts for the introduction of 'light' music in many of even his major works. In his early suite *Aus Italien* the Neapolitan folk-element is his excuse: in *Till Eulenspiegel* his hero's plebeian origin and natural reactions as narrated in the old story: in *Don Quixote* the antics of the ubiquitous Sancho Panza provide the peg on which he will hang the most homely and banal of his tunes. And rightly so. The dance in *Also sprach Zarathustra*, the baby-in-the-bath episode in the *Symphonia Domestica*, the Baptist's music in *Salome* and many other instances jump to the mind in this connection. But it is in *Rosenkavalier* that this kind of adroitness reaches its apotheosis. For here you have an entire opera based upon a subject which cries out for waltzes, whose charms, whilst strictly in keeping with the libretto, are appreciable by the meanest musical intelligence. These are not accidents. Varese, the Italian-American composer,

[1] Cf. p. 270.

once told me that he asked Strauss his reason for introducing such a commonplace melody at the end of one of his works. The answer was, " Oh, that is just a little *bonne bouche* for the crowd. Make 'em feel happy." Quite frankly *ad captandum vulgus*.

Now I hope I shall not be misunderstood to be inveighing against the composers or works just referred to. Not at all. What type of work a composer chooses to write is entirely his own concern. What I have said does amount to a protest against the invidious and false relegation into one category or the other, of composers who include *both* types of works in their range. We have seen that many of those whom the world has agreed to call great, have written both types of work, and their greatness is not at all assailable because of their divagations into less rarefied realms. There should be an end of this nonsense. It is sufficiently difficult for any musician to retain his artistic integrity amid the welter of commercial interests in which we exist nowaday. When the whole of the vast mass of untrained public, plus certain very powerful commercial interests connected with music, unite in applauding, encouraging and paying handsomely for ephemeral and merely tittilating rubbish, it is regrettable indeed that anyone who really knows better should lend his voice to the chorus. And if, by frequent and thoughtless use of a silly *cliché*, the artist's efforts to put forward his serious major works are even slightly hampered, it is all to the bad.

Oh that a breath of the fresh air of commonsense could be wafted across the still puritanical and slightly fœtid atmosphere of certain ' musical ' circles in this country; that Rossini's famous dictum that " there are only two kinds of music, good and bad," could penetrate their epidermis of

'Light' Music

musical *snobbisme*: that they might realize that there are bad as well as good oratorios, symphonies, operas; good as well as bad comic songs and jazz tunes; and that a horizontal line above which all is 'highbrow' and *comme il faut*, and below which all is 'lowbrow' and *mousse*, is barbarous and quite intolerable.

The last means open to our composer is to orchestrate, arrange, or disarrange other people's work for a special market. As might be imagined, this hack work is usually far more lucrative than mere composition and is a job of work that many even among the great composers have had to turn their hands to. An English composer well known to me was turning out a series of such pieces of work and bemoaning his fate the while, when a friend pointed out, by way of sympathetic consolation, that Brahms and Schönberg had had to do at one period of their lives, exactly similar work. "Ah yes," was the reply, "but they were able to preserve their anonymity and never put their names to this kind of work. The publishers of these potpourris insist on using my name, which, being known, will help sell their wares."

Publishers, business acquaintances and undiscriminating friends alike are always ready with some such advice as: "My dear fellow, we all know you have talent, but good heavens, why don't you, just for a year or two, turn your attention to *what the public wants?* Why don't you write a popular ballad or two, a few good jazz tunes, a comic pantomime-chorus song that the street-boy can whistle? It would be quite easy for you with your gifts. They would sell in thousands, your royalties would be immense, you would make a fortune in just a few short years. THEN, my boy, you could turn out the stuff you want

Music To-day

to do, everyone would then accept it, and you would have made the best of both worlds!" ... Two observations fall to be made upon this oft-tendered and so well-meant advice. First: no amount of taking thought will enable a composer to reach the millions if he be not of them. If he be of them he will, in writing to please himself, please them. Your Gershwins, Frimls, Linkes, and Heykens, are born, not made. They write as they do write by sheer glad gregarious instinct. Second: no man having once struck his flag and capitulated to Mammon, can ever buy back his lost integrity.[1]

The remedy for all these difficulties lies in just that more widespread and penetrating public judgment in music upon which we are focussing our attention in these pages. If, and when, such judgment reaches a point of any real discernment, any even approximately just evaluation, some sort of subsidization of our finest composers who happen to need it must surely follow.[2]

§ 3. A PRESENT-DAY ABERRATION

In even a superficial review of conditions in the musical world at the present time some consideration must be given to 'jazz' music just as, I suppose, a similar review up to 1900 would mention, if only in passing, the waltz and the polka. The waltz attained the dignity of being handled by such fine composers as Weber, Berlioz, Brahms, Schumann, Chopin, Tchaikovsky, Ravel, R. Strauss, etc. In our day this dance music of negroid origin is also sponsored by some

---

[1] "Whoever *mistakes his way* in the direction of triviality has to do penance towards his better self, but whoever *consciously seeks* triviality is lost" (Wagner).

[2] "My success in music I owe to just three things. Good health; *a small but secure income*; ... and, I suppose, my fighting spirit" (Dr Ethel Smyth).

A Present-day Aberration

of our serious musicians,[1] and one cannot go far without having to pass an opinion upon it—an opinion, be it noted, as to its real value considered *qua* music.

Excellent to dance to: evocative on a gramophone record, by way of recalling the delights of the (ahem) 'Terpsichorean art'; even capable of fitting into a music-hall programme without incongruity: further than this it can hardly go without doing violence both to itself and to us. And the spectacle of jazz music paraded in the serious-concert room, asking our suffrages, nay, demanding careful attention on equal terms with the works of serious artists, is one positively to stagger the imagination. It is a claim so preposterous that one cannot realize it all at once.

Jazz bears the same sort of relation to Music as does doggerel to Literature. It may be amusing, occasionally even witty; beyond this it cannot rise. No one in his senses would dream of feeding doggerel to children in order to stimulate their interest in real literature. But something like this is in danger of happening to our musical children when jazz is alluded to with portentous gravity as 'epoch making,' 'epitomizing the age,' and all the rest of the shibboleths of the professional publicist.

I am biassed? I know it! Brought up with a supreme contempt for the bounders, the larrikins, and the 'Smart Alecs' of the musical world, I cannot bring myself to countenance this attitudinizing as 'artists,' 'serious innovators,' 'emancipators from the fetters of rhythm' and the like, on the part of many of the protagonists of jazz music.

[1] Including Stravinsky, Křenek, *et hoc genus omne.* Why these gentlemen should have given their blessing to the thing I cannot imagine. But that is the fault of my imagination. I have immense confidence in their business acumen and powers of self-assertion and -protection.

Music To-day

"Oh but the world is a big place and surely there is room for all." Certainly there is room for all. Moreover there is a proper place for everything. Your 'good brown earth' proper to the upland furrows, is an offence in one's eye; that 'healthy smell' proper to the farmyard is an offence in one's *salon*, and jazz is an offence in the concert-room.

Further. Although there are strict limits to its powers of exaltation, there would appear to be none whatever to the depths of degradation to which it may sink. As may be noticed by the discerning in dozens of night-clubs and the like, it may descend deeper and deeper in its pimp-like office until eventually it reach a nadir of utter filth. If a man prefer this to Beauty, that may be no concern of ours, as artists. What is very much our concern is that jazz be not allowed to stalk abroad in the musical world in a robe of glory which rightly belongs only to the grandest of our fraternity; to assume the attitude of leader and dictator in a theatre in which its true position is that of coloured comedian; to steal the thunder of the gods and regurgitate it in piddling little muted hiccoughs, or bleats from the blastophone; and by dint of shouting its wares in season and out, in the gutter, the market-place, the dance hall, and even in the temple of art, to debauch the taste of those who have not yet reached the age of (musical) discrimination.[1] Its composers are they, and theirs is the work to which the term

---

[1] Only the other day they laid filthy hands on the *Götterdämmerung Trauermarsch*, and the big tune in Beethoven's *Ninth Symphony*. I heard it. True, it did me no particular harm, being tough and seasoned, an old campaigner; but think of youthful ears and virgin hearts being debauched in this manner, and robbed in advance, as it were, of untold riches and delights. For even the noblest musical ideas when besmirched and degraded in this manner have a way of sticking in the consciousness like viscous filth and defiling the recollection-thrill ever afterward.

A Present-day Aberration

'light' in its opprobrious signification may properly be applied.

A very brief examination of its constituents ought to help us to put jazz in its proper place . . . on the dance-floor; and keep it there.

Its protagonists are never tired of telling us how it has 'liberated rhythm.' Liberated fiddlestick! Any 'music' that is chained down to a persistent and undeviating basic pulse of such utter puerility as:

poum, poum; *poum*, poum; *poum*, poum; *poum*, poum; *poum*, poum;

(and so on *ad nauseam*) might indeed complain of being fettered, it can hardly boast of liberation.

The question may be asked: why, having so little sympathy with, or liking for jazz music, have we devoted so much attention to it here? The answer is that however much some persons may dislike jazz, even to the point of utter detestation, there is a modicum of truth at the back of it. And it is because of a desire to show this scrap of truth in its proper perspective, not as a discovery of jazz merchants but as a world-wide and age-old device, that we have turned aside from the main line of our study.

It would be useless to deny the profundity of the appeal to and effect upon us of long-continued repetition of recognizable rhythmic patterns. It is no new device, being indeed one of the most primitive, as every student should know. And it is freely used in modern music by such men as Strauss, Prokoviev, Holst, Falla, Hindemith, Ravel and almost all modern composers. Notice has been taken of the fact that this pounding out of a reiterated rhythm for long periods without cessation, has an almost hypnotic effect upon the hearer. The judgment, it has been remarked, is stunned, and

Music To-day

the question may well be asked, ' to what end ? ' The end is an escape from mere ratiocination (a temporary stopping down of the thinking apparatus), which escape is undoubtedly facilitated by such a device as we are discussing. One of the reasons for the widespread popularity of jazz is its undeniable efficacy in just this respect, *with the majority of persons.* By long-continued repetition of a rhythmic pattern which is sufficiently childish for them to recognize as such, these persons are ' helped to forget.'

§ 4. EMANCIPATED RHYTHM

The purveyors of jazz do not usually make any serious claims for its originality of melodic, harmonic, or structural content, but only for that of its basic rhythms. But the reason why jazz fails with more serious artists is precisely because of the inanity of the basic-rhythm it offers. " Two and two make four " may be a true statement; its continued iteration not only quickly palls, it positively annoys all but uncivilized persons or infants. So with jazz rhythm, which can only succeed with the (musically) uncivilized or the (in this respect) infantile.

Emancipated Rhythm

At (A) above, we have the naked banality that underlies jazz. Could anything that calls itself a basic rhythm be more inane and infantile? Can it be wondered at that some musicians, decently brought up to respect relative values in their art, grow pale with rage when the fanatical votaries of jazz calmly dub this unutterably abject apotheosis of intellectual deficiency — if you please — " emancipation of rhythm."

At (B) is something slightly less feeble, *i.e.* the basic rhythm upon which Ravel has constructed his notorious *Bolero*. It is probably of Moorish origin—begot upon Spain by the Moors, these, in turn, probably out of India.[1] Though no ethnologist, I can tell you that (even in a decadent specimen such as this) it is somewhat higher in the scale than the negroid infantilism exhibited in jazz.

At (C) we approach the rhythmic world of those who are (in this respect) really beginning to grow up. It is the rhythmic basis of a movement in a modern work for piano and orchestra, concerning which such an authority as Tovey says—addressing his audience in a programme-note:

[1] Cf. p. 259.

"Pronounce at a brisk uniform pace the words 'one two one two three one two three four' again and again without pause, and with an accent on each 'one,' and you will feel the powerful swing of this rhythm."

At (D) the interesting tri-rhythmic presentation of an idea in the second movement of Bartók's *Second Quartet*.

At (E) a *Tala* from India which, after several iterations, is accepted as an eleven-fold unit by the musical intelligence, much as example (C) is recognized as nine-fold after a few repetitions.

Rhythms of five or seven beats, quite familiar in modern music, are far in advance of the supposedly emancipated jazz rhythm. Albeit this five-beat rhythm is almost always made up of a three and a two, or a two and a three, as in Tchaikovsky's *Pathétique*:

or a seven-beat rhythm will consist of either a three and a four, or a four and a three, as in Holst's *Perfect Fool* ballet:

I can recall at the moment only one extended movement in five-four *tempo* which is, and remains, a real five-fold,

Emancipated Rhythm

and not a two-and-three, or a three-and-two rhythm. It includes various formulæ such as the following:

each bar of which is a pure five-fold rhythm.

The foregoing are just a few of the reasons for the keen dislike of jazz which so many artists betray—a dislike which is often thought by its protagonists to be due to fear or envy of its popularity; an arbitrary and entirely insupportable 'highbrow' attitude; or mere inability to understand its profundities.

Is there then nothing in it that is of real interest to the artist—of potential value to the art? I would reply, decidedly, there *are* three elements in jazz which are worthy of the attention of real music-lovers. First: the device of long-continued reiterations of basic rhythmic formulæ, with its potentially hypnotic results.[1] Second: the introduction of new tone-colours.[2] Third: the recognition of the possibilities and values of collective improvisation.[3] The last being by far the most important.

[1] Cf. p. 136.   [2] Cf. p. 331.   [3] Cf. p. 345.

Music To-day

§ 5. MECHANIZED MUSIC

A term which is frequently met with nowaday is: "mechanical music," and it is one that is often misused and perhaps still more often misunderstood. There is no such thing as mechanical music in the sense in which the words are frequently used. What is nearly always meant is mechanically *reproduced* music; just as you have famous pictures mechanically reproduced, duplicated, stereotyped, etc. What is important to remember is that none of these reproductions is as good in every way as the original. One will distort the colour-values; another alter the total dimension; another will omit colour altogether (perhaps an engraving), or will give you at best a sort of "facsimile" by means of the three-colour process; another will copy all the lines faithfully enough, but will content itself by merely suggesting light and shade; still another will be an approximation in monotint.

It does not seem to have occurred to many music-lovers that our processes of gramophone and radio are somewhat analogous to these picture reproductions. Up to the present time the world is still in the throes of excitement and delight in these discoveries, and enjoyment of the undeniable usefulness, edification, and educational value of gramophone and radio. None can have enjoyed them more than the writer—none be less inclined to undervalue their educative aspects. They may be very useful indeed: up to a certain point.

Anyone, however, who listens with a cultivated ear and attends carefully with an unbiassed mind is bound to detect certain glaring deficiencies which seem to escape the notice of many, but which ought to be mentioned here. Not, be it

Mechanized Music

noted, by way of cavilling at these delightful inventions, but in order to put in a warning against too early a sense of satisfaction, or too complete a faith in their ability accurately to convey to the listener a composer's message.

As a boy I was witness of the very striking difference of effect created by an orchestra as Hallé had trained it (or rather allowed it) to play the Beethoven symphonies, and that created by the same orchestra in the same works after a little coaching by Richter. Several other factors no doubt brought their quota to the general improvement, but the greatest single element, beyond all comparison, was that of dynamic, nuance, control of gradations of tone. This is indeed a most valuable and important factor in music and any diminution in its efficacy is bound to be a serious discount off the composer's message. In the hands of a fine composer it is one of the most potent elements in his equipment. By its means alone he can often move the listener deeply and, by its aid, transport him through the entire gamut of human emotions. One of his most potent factors, I repeat, lies in the use of dynamic, and it is for this reason that composers and conductors when preparing compositions for the press, or rehearsing for performances, are meticulous to a degree over the observance of 'expression' marks. Almost all depends upon this. Read the correspondence between Beethoven and his publishers relating to this subject and you realize what importance he attached to it. And rightly. Attend any orchestral rehearsal directed by a competent conductor, and the point will, I think, be conceded.

Now if we represent the distance between the *ppp* and the *fff* of a full symphony orchestra by the figure 100, I would hazard the opinion (without, it is true, scientific corroboration) that when translated *via* gramophone or radio, this figure is reduced to, at the highest, 25. In view of what has been said above of the importance of dynamic this would appear to be a severe indictment indeed.

In the early days of broadcasting I was directing the performance of an instrumental piece. Under the natural excitement of a novel occasion extra attention was paid, at rehearsal, to questions of *piano* and *forte*. In order to make sure of the balance I then went into an adjoining room, put on headphones, and listened to a page or so re-rehearsed. As a result of this experience I returned to the studio and directed the orchestra to play at a level *mezzo forte* throughout! The microphone could deal with no less and no more than that. No doubt improvements have been effected since those early days, but this serious defect has not yet been (cannot be?) completely remedied.[1]

Again: I suppose that no musician of any culture would deny that the orchestra is a vastly superior instrument to the brass band—superior in variety of tone-colour, in range of expression, and in beauty of tone. The following then, from an article intended to read *in favour* of gramophone recording by no less famous a company than H.M.V., would appear to be, on the contrary, an indictment: " Bugles have the advantage—an inestimable advantage in recording —of uniformity of tone. That is what makes records of brass bands more completely satisfactory than those of the

---

[1] In an ' official' article on this point which I have seen since writing the above, the B.B.C. admits that " the reception of broadcast music can be but a reproduction on a reduced scale of what is happening in the concert-room. For this reason the listener cannot expect to experience the physical and dynamic contrasts between the *fortissimo* and the whisper of an orchestra heard in the concert hall." Quite so. And yet, in the face of this admission, it is claimed that what is " launched on the ether " is a "*faithful reproduction* of what is being said, sung, or played." It is the gravamen of my charge that what is received, grateful though we may be for it, is nothing of the sort.

Mechanized Music

orchestra, the strength of which is just in variety of tone." That is clear enough in all conscience. The very lack of one of our most highly prized qualities, variety of tone-colour, is a *desideratum* for recording. But surely, if any method of recording gives superior results from an admittedly greatly inferior source it stands condemned, *ipso facto*, as an unsatisfactory method. It may, of course, be capable of improvement. Music-lovers should not, in their natural delight in the joys of the gramophone, forget the fact that it is an inadequate instrument in the ways I have mentioned, and should not cease to press for improvement.

Further: when Sir Richard Terry, speaking in favour of ' mechanical music ' says, " if you cannot see a real landscape, even a photograph is better than nothing," I agree. Corollarily: " if you cannot hear real music even a mechanical reproduction is better than nothing." Again I would agree. Especially with the ' if ' and the 'even.' But this is not a question of radio or gramophone being better than nothing. To me the case stands thus; if a man who has never seen the falls of Niagara is shown a photograph and objects that it gives him no thrill, at least *he knows* that he is missing the roar and the stunning crash, the colour and the swirl, and the magical quality of sunlight through blown spume, and he does not deny that the real thing might thrill him deeply. But a very great many persons of our day, hearing for the first time, and hearing *via* the radio say, one of the colossal Wagnerian ' purple patches,' do *not know* that they are missing the gorgeous orchestral surge, that they are hearing the balance grievously distorted, that they are hearing practically no weight of tone at all below the F which lies just under the bass-clef stave, that the percussion instruments are hideously misrepresented, and that the range of dynamic is perhaps, at best, a mere one-quarter of the reality.

The great necessity then would seem to be to recognize more frankly these inadequacies, and to let the great new music-loving public which is undoubtedly being built up by the agency of mechanized music know them also. In that way they can be led toward a closer acquaintance with the great masterpieces of the tone-art, and not, as I have sometimes noticed, urged away from them by reason of the lack of many of those qualities that should most profoundly affect the listener.

Another most important practical point that arises upon even a slight acquaintance with broadcasting is this: that whilst the dynamic, the nuances, the 'light and shade' produced by every instrumentalist is under the control of the conductor, the total dynamic of the orchestra is controlled by . . . a music-engineer! If he so choose, this official may vulgarize a subtle and enchanting *pianissimo* as a work-a-day *mezzo forte* to millions of hearers, or reduce a carefully built up and impressive climax to a grey and emasculate penumbra of what it should be: and not only what it should be but what it really is.

An instance came to my notice only the other day which is perhaps worth recording. The work was Haydn's 'Farewell' Symphony, in the finale of which the instrumentalists leave the orchestra one by one, thus gradually reducing the volume of tone from the *forte* of the full *tutti* to the *pianissimo* of one single violin. This *forte* was reduced by the engineer to a chaste *mezzo forte* " for fear of blowing out the cheaper sets," whilst the final whisper was increased greatly " in case the listeners thought it was fading out." Thus there was very little difference in volume of

Mechanized Music

tone between a *tutti fortissimo* and a *solo pianissimo*. Without suggesting that this is usually or even frequently done, one may draw attention to a curious state of affairs which surely ought not to be accepted as inevitable or even desirable. The engineer virtually becomes by this method a veritable Conductor-in-Chief, and unless he be a first-rate artist as well as mechanic, dire are the results he may bring about. If he can control the total dynamic by merely manipulating a couple of knobs, why should the conductor and the members of an orchestra labour strenuously at what is by far the most difficult part of their task, the attainment of perfect gradations of tone-strength? A plain level *mezza voce* in which the *timbres* of the various instruments will stand off from each other, the total dynamic being left to the man with the knobs, would seem to be the next logical step forward whilst using our present methods in this matter. Wise in his generation, Stokowski insists upon having this engineer under his personal control (sitting by the first violins of the orchestra) instead of being installed in some distant sanctum, working one of the most dynamic and therefore one of the most important elements of the performance entirely " at his own hook " as my master used to say.

Admittedly the volume must be controlled in some way before being cast abroad, and I have heard it suggested that the best thing would surely be, difficult though it may sound, to have a separate microphone for each instrument of the orchestra. There may be technical objections. Indeed I have heard some of them. I will not attempt to deal with them for the simple reason that I cannot; but they do not in any way nullify the above argument that separate microphones would seem to be *desiderata* at our present stage of

Music To-day

development. Yet, do what we may toward improving the balance of the component parts of the orchestra, the grave defects of dynamic and *timbre* remain, and seem likely to.

A curious phenomenon may sometimes be observed when listening to the classics. Schubert, Brahms, Beethoven (some moderns, too) have made magical use of the silent bar or bars in their works. This device can be extraordinarily arresting and impressive, and the concert *habitué* will recall many unforgettable instances of it. So far as my observation has gone it is entirely without effect by radio. Not only does its failure to 'come off' negative one of the composer's most powerful effects, it positively injures the performance. For everybody believes that something has gone wrong with the machine, or that interference of some sort has occurred.

Many years ago Berlioz noted the fact that mere duplication of harp-players in an orchestra, if they play the same part, does not increase the effect one iota.[1] In the case of violinists, on the contrary, duplication of players of the same part increases the effect greatly. *Via* the microphone, it may be noticed that duplication of players of *any* of the parts fails to increase the effect—indeed it often has the opposite result. For example, a large-scale choral work which I had performed several times in a huge auditorium with a choir of upwards of a thousand voices was broadcast some years ago from a studio. I listened at a distance of some hundreds of miles and drew certain conclusions. And it was quite surprising to be told afterwards by the conductor that his choir had numbered but twenty-one voices. Yet the effect had been

---

[1] Well knowing which, Wagner writes at the end of *Rheingold*, for instance, six *different* harp parts for his six players.

Mechanized Music

rich and full, and quite satisfactory, *up to the limits of the microphone*.

Again: loss of the most valuable characteristics of *timbre* is one of the heaviest indictments that could be brought against any reproducing apparatus. And I have actually heard the splendour of a full brass chord—three trumpets, four horns, three trombones and tuba—so ' stepped down ' by the microphone that a quite equal effect was obtained at another performance by a concertina played *ff* close to the microphone. The ' business-man ' might aver that if one player can produce as good an effect as eleven, that is a desirable thing: the artist will say that if your apparatus cannot transmit a finer thrill from a so much grander source it stands, by that fact, self-condemned: condemned that is to say, not as utterly undesirable, but as not yet so satisfactory to persons of discernment as less educated listeners are ready to take for granted.

Speed the day when improvements reach a point where characteristic *timbres* are more faithfully reproduced; dynamic (individual and collective) more accurately rendered; and total range of tone-power increased to something nearer reality. And let us hope that if and when the inventors have done their part of the work, no sordid ' business interests ' so-called will be allowed to step in and nullify the results. I saw a case of this kind years ago in Berlin. A Brahms symphony was being played on the gramophone. In the middle of a most subtle passage (alas, it always happens then!) the thing sagged like a deflated toy pig. You are familiar with the procedure. Someone rushes to the rescue. The plaque is turned over, a new needle inserted, the handle re-ground and we proceed. But all the physical, emotional, mental, and even spiritual effect the composer has been building up is dissipated in a moment. I complained bitterly of this mechanical ineptitude and was sharply pulled up by a friend who, the following day, introduced to me a machine which played the whole of the third act of an opera (*Rosenkavalier* if I remember rightly) without stopping. I was astounded and enthusiastically hailed it as an epoch-making improvement in gramophones. This is surely what should have happened, but the invention, so far as I am aware, has never been allowed to reach the market. We can easily imagine what miserable subterfuges may have been employed to preserve conditions as they are, and easily see that these forces are never on the side of the angels, but ever work together for the maintenance of the *status in quo*, depreciating progress, automatically tending to foster philistinism and stultify the growth of thousands of young music-lovers.

To sum up: I cannot bring myself to view with equanimity the distortion of dynamics and *timbres* which radio even at its best would seem inevitably to entail. The tendency which I have already regretted in a section upon the orchestra [1]—a tendency, namely, to lose the characteristics of the separate group-tones, is greatly exaggerated by radio and gramophone alike. To an ear naturally sensitive in the first place, and then educated to discriminate searchingly between various qualities of tone, these reproducing instruments impose upon each and every type of instrumental *timbre* a nodicum—sometimes more, sometimes less—of that 'hooty' quality which is so frequent and so undesirable in the 'stopped diapason' of church organs.

Flutes, Clarinets, Horns, suffer least: Violins, Violas,

---

[1] P. 75 *et seq.*

Mechanized Music

more: 'Cellos upon their C string, and Doublebasses, terribly. Oboes and Bassoons always emerge with the tubby quality I deplored in Chapter VI Section 5; whilst instruments of percussion (with the fairly frequent exception of the Timpani) are almost always unrecognizable. And inasmuch as this distortion invariably takes the form of reducing all instruments toward a dead level and overlaying their most characteristic divergencies with a pall of a particularly coarse brown texture, it amounts to a denigration of some importance.

Speaking generally it would seem that classical instrumental music is more faithfully transmitted by radio than is modern music. Complicated modern scoring, greatly more interesting *qua* instrumentation than that of former times, comes over far less well than simple linear work of the Bach type. Large-scale choral works are never satisfactory. An even approximately fair judgment of a first performance of a modern work *via* radio is generally agreed to be impossible, and one reaches the conclusion that its most effective use at present is in giving us the delight of the recognition-thrill by performances of works which we already know.

The arrival and the popularity of radio has considerably altered the orientation of the musical life of the nations. The whole civilized life of the world has been affected, and deeply. So far as the question is related to music, it focusses upon the following aspect: whether the people's love of music has been falsified and cheapened, or increased and broadened. I believe the latter. And it is one of the most promising of signs that the controllers of radio in several countries are alive to the importance of not killing the desire of the amateur to make his own music. This desire has admittedly been affected and has not yet been completely restored to its natural mobility; but the importance of the act of making his own music by the amateur, a function which every known age of musical culture has shown to be essential for its very existence, let alone its development, has been clearly recognized by the authorities, and efforts are being made further to foster it.

From much of the foregoing it may have been deduced that I am an opponent of radio. Not at all. Far from it. The good far outweighs the harm in any really broad view. Nevertheless, the defects noticed above have already, in a few short years, tended to hebetate the perceptions of thousands of music-lovers in just those particulars where their increased refinement and penetration is so eminently desirable. And it is because one recognizes the enormous power of radio in the musical world that one hopes so ardently for improvement in those directions to which I have ventured to call attention.

§ 6. CONCLUSIONS OF PART TWO

We have now glanced over the musical world of to-day upon the technical side—(1) noticed with what distrust much modern music is approached by the majority: (2) observed that an unparalleled revolution has occurred in the musical world since about the beginning of the century; that it is chiefly in its technical aspects that modern music is misunderstood and misvalued; and have therefore first paid attention to some of the more baffling of modern technical devices: (3) traced the derivations of our two (major and minor) modes, and indicated a greatly extended system of 90 modes, an understanding of which would help consider-

Conclusion of Part Two

ably towards a comprehension of Diatonal aspects of modern music: (4) surveyed the trends which have resulted in Polytonality, Atonality, and 'free' Chromaticism, without some comprehension of which an understanding of typical modern music is impossible: (5) reviewed the Quarter-tone, Tertia-tone and Microtone as used by certain modernists, and the aural possibilities, susceptibilities and vagaries of listeners: (6) paid some attention to the instruments at our disposal—voice, and orchestra: (7) considered the fascinating and hitherto little-explored correspondences between Sound, Form, Colour, Elements, etc.: (8) examined certain psycho-physiological reactions to music; and have (9) faced some of the severely practical problems and conditions as they are met with in the musical world of to-day.

It is time to turn our attention to those forces and operations which lie behind—which are the *raison d'être* of—all technical devices whatsoever. These are questions of inspiration, æsthetic, and the like, some acquaintance with which is essential to the music-lover in his efforts correctly to evaluate—indeed even properly to enjoy—the music he hears.

PART THREE
TOWARD A MUSICAL ÆSTHETIC

CHAPTER TEN: SOURCES OF INSPIRATION

Musical Æsthetic in a State of Chaos—Musical Appreciation —A Septenary Classification—Genius Defined— Relatively restricted Range of Music hitherto—A Five-planal Conception—Music and Sex—The Ensouling of Music.

SOME attention having been paid to the chief characteristics of modern music in their technical aspects, let us now turn to the qualities discernible in all fine work—qualities without some or all of which, no music in the world, be it never so accomplished technically, is worth writing or performing.

§ 1. MUSICAL ÆSTHETIC IN A STATE OF CHAOS

It has been observed as a depressing fact that whilst musical literature is daily enriching knowledge on technical, historical, and critical questions, the study of musical æsthetics remains in a state of chaos. It is extremely difficult to define the self-subsistent and specifically musical beauty, as it expresses no definite cerebral conceptions. Thus writers have been compelled to speak of it either in dry technical terms or in the language of poetic fiction. Yet it may be possible, whilst avoiding both of these extremes, to suggest a theory which is pregnant with far-reaching possibilities.

Questions of æsthetic are always difficult to discuss. Subtlety of thought in these and allied realms is not exactly a speciality of our race, and when we approach even the fringe of such a subject as metaphysic, for example, the paucity of suitable expressions in our language, nay, the downright lack of words in our vocabulary, copious though it be, is quite striking. If we desire, however, to be able to form any real judgment of the music we hear, apart from its merely sensuous effect or its technical adroitness, we must formulate some sort of scheme to which we may refer our impressions; some comparatively definite tabulation of qualities, states of consciousness or realms of nature, to which the various types belong and from which they have emanated. The very clarity of thought which is fostered by such a method, whether it leads to right or wrong conclusions, seems to me eminently desirable amid such a welter of diffuse speculations as that which faces the musician upon all sides.

§ 2. MUSICAL APPRECIATION

Of recent years a laudable attempt has been made to assist the growing number of music-lovers who desire to grapple more closely with the problems of music to-day. A cult of 'musical appreciation' has grown up, books have been written, classes held, and courses of instruction devised, and quite a busy-ness has resulted from this and allied endeavours. Opponents—of course there are opponents to every human activity, usually more vocal in proportion to the inherent force of the original effort—declare that the 'musical appreciation' teachers concentrate too much on analysis, parsing, and suchlike rudimentary technical aspects, which is certainly not what our searchers are after. The plain man does not look for such detailed orthodox musical training. If he did he would turn to colleges, academies, text-books

Musical Appreciation

and professors for guidance and teaching. Thank God he goes instead to the concert-room and endeavours 'all by himself' (alas, often in vain), to glimpse, through the complexities and newnesses of modern composers what it is they are telling him, and to 'place' them and their works in some sort of relation to each other and to his own innate ideals.

The 'musical appreciationists' hold that by their methods they "remove obstacles to sensitivity" from the path of their pupils. The objectors hold that if this were so, then the 'appreciators' themselves, being presumably post-graduate in their own teaching, would agree as to the relative values of composers, which, of course, they do not. The plain man needs some more definite method which shall be at the same time more comprehensive and more easily adjustable to his personal predilections.

We professional musicians have no excuse for trying to make him love what we love—other than the very natural desire to share a delicious thrill with one's fellow-men. Circumstances of birth, blood, nationality, environment and many other factors have succeeded in fostering a remarkable diversity of tastes in the human race. Each must be left to choose from the viewpoint of his own individual uniqueness what he loves, what he prefers, what dislikes. Subject only to these reservations: that he understand the 'language' any composer is using sufficiently to be able, more or less accurately, to understand his message; and that he familiarize himself with that music of the past which has been admitted by general consensus of opinion to possess real power and beauty. For it is to be observed that the feeling for music, like the feeling for art in general, is not only susceptible of cultivation, but very quickly responds to appeals which are

Music To-day

made to it by noble or beautiful thoughts or objects. It is made both more sensitive and more dependable by constant contact with those works which call it out. No rules for its development can be laid down; but the oft-proved-true observation may be made that if we listen to and become intimate with (only and always) that music which has real power and beauty, such intimacy will make the sense of delight more keen, will preserve it against influences which tend to deaden it, and make the taste more sure and trustworthy. A man who has long held in the forefront of his consciousness the best works of art of any type comes to have, almost unconsciously to himself, an instinctive power of discerning good work from bad, of recognizing on the instant the sound and true method and style, and of feeling a fresh and constant delight in such work. For the ability to distinguish a quality is conditional upon intimate acquaintance with that quality. To some such conclusions as these the person of culture would surely subscribe. But they are too vague, too ill-defined to be erected into any kind of codification to which judgment can be referred and from which clarity of thought and systematization of impressions may take their rise.

Æstheticians love to separate the arts into two classes which they speak of as the arts of presentation and representation. The former include (they say) architecture, music and various crafts; the latter, poetry, sculpture and painting. We need not proceed to particularization and discussion for we soon discover that this division into presentative and representative has little value besides convenience of classification. They are in fact all presentative as well as representative, the distinction everywhere breaking down.

A Septenary Classification

§ 3. A SEPTENARY CLASSIFICATION

We cannot go very far in this matter without being forced to consider the make-up of Man; of what diverse, though interpenetrating spheres his 'world' consists; and which of these regions his consciousness is exploring when he contacts those vibrations which he bodies forth for us in his music.

The only classification I have found to be at all satisfactory—certainly the most helpful—and the only one which seems to cover the facts as we see them to be, is an ancient system which has survived to us (in Sanskrit) from near the inception of our Aryan race. Taking then an atom from one tiny crumb of this ancient wisdom, and putting it for the sake of clearness into a diagram:

SANSKRIT	ENGLISH
UNMANIFESTED { 7. ĀDI	DIVINE
6. ANUPĀDAKA }	MONADIC
MANIFESTED { 5. ATMA	IMMORTAL INDIVIDUALITY { SPIRITUAL
4. BUDDHI	INTUITIONAL
3. MANAS	HIGHER / LOWER MENTAL
2. KAMA	MORTAL PERSONALITY { EMOTIONAL
1. STHULA	ETHERIC / DENSE PHYSICAL

we see that seven realms of Nature are postulated. At our present stage of evolution man cannot consciously contact the

Music To-day

two loftiest realms; Divine and Monadic. He can, however, through the medium of his own consciousness, range the five lower spheres. Now we are more or less familiar with the first (I say 'more or less' for it is only recently that we have begun to exploit part of the physical realm, *i.e.*, its etheric aspect [1]); also with the second (the realm of desires and emotions); and the 'lower' part of the third (the realm of the critical, ratiocinative, thinking principle).[2] Together, these constitute the 'mortal personality'; and nothing—no music, certainly—that emanates from these levels, *i.e.*, originates in them, holds permanent value.

The great dividing-line lies here, between the 'lower' and 'higher' mind.[3] And if it be true that it is the ratiocinative faculty, the 'lower' mind, which 'raises mankind above the brute'; it is equally true that through the 'higher' mind he may 'commune with the gods.' The brain is his instrument for the former: the properly-so-called psychic faculties for the latter.

It is the crucial dividing-line between ephemeral and permanent. Could we but learn to distinguish between the music which emanates from the first, second, and lower third of these planes of Nature, and that which reaches us from beyond that level, we should possess at once a most valuable touchstone to aid us in our judgments. It is possible. It is

---

[1] By means of 'wireless' *via* the ether: or more properly, one of the ethers.

[2] The dictionary derivation from the Sanskrit is given thus: *man*, to think, *manas*, mind.

[3] Aware that 'higher' and 'lower' are unphilosophical terms to use in this connection, as these 'worlds' interpenetrate and interact in a subtle way; the distinction does, however, I think, make for clarity of thought in these early stages of our study. Psychologists, in using the familiar terms *sub*-conscious and *sub*-liminal, would seem to lay themselves open to the same criticism. Why 'below'-conscious, or 'below'-threshold? we may ask, when it is admitted by them that many results derived from such regions of consciousness, transcend those from the 'normal.'

Genius Defined

more than possible: it is even not very difficult, though subtle and unfamiliar to most of us, and we shall endeavour to realize the various steps as we proceed. It is, of course, no part of our business to advise anyone which to prefer. To force people to choose the higher and eschew the lower is—in the arts no less than in life—an impossibility. Time, and Evolution may bring that about. Meanwhile, for those who do prefer the nobler, purer and more sublime, here is definite information which may help them to distinguish these qualities—at first maybe only sporadically, but with increasing sureness and celerity.

§ 4. GENIUS DEFINED

We have said that man at the present general level of evolution, can contact through the medium of his own consciousness the five lower spheres shown in our diagram. Few of us, however, can bring through into the brain tangible recollections of contact with the loftier of these spheres. Fewer still—very few indeed—possess a technique in any of the arts which is anything like capable of inducing in the listener, reader, or onlooker, a similar vibration. The test of any composer's relative value lies in his ability, first, to bring through the effect of his contact with the higher of these realms into his physical brain; second, to give this adequate expression in physical-plane terms.

He who can perform both these functions is a man of genius.

Let no nonsense about ' infinite capacity for taking pains,' [1] no misuse of the word, nor any sneer due to a fashion of the moment, disturb our conclusion. I have known a great many

---

[1] By parity of reasoning my housekeeper would be a genius were this parrot-cry true.

people in all walks of life who have been able to carry over into the brain more or less definite impressions from comparatively lofty realms: many persons also who possessed a good technique in one or other of the arts (and it is intriguing to notice how often the technically well-equipped artist is ignorant of such sources of inspiration; ignorant even to the point of denying them altogether.[1] The contrary is also the case; one frequently meets persons who can bring through into the brain some reflection, more or less vivid, of their contacts, but who lack a technique anything like adequate to pass on to us their inspiration): but the man who can bring the results of his contacts with 'higher' worlds without undue distortion across the frangible bridge which leads from the super-conscious realms to the mundane world in which his brain functions,[2] and can body them forth for the delectation of his fellow mortals in terms which are anything like commensurate with the beauty and power of these ideations—he is the man of genius. Such are rare; always have been rare; and perhaps always will be.

For the sake of utter clearness of thought on this matter let us state that just as definitely as in the physical world the range of musical sounds lies within certain vibration-numbers and the range of colours within others, and so on; just so in the emotion-world the range of passion and desire

---

[1] A worthy professor of music, well known and successful, who has composed an opera, quartets and symphonies, told his pupils that he " knew nothing of this so-called inspiration ! " His works contain ample evidence that the professor at least spoke the truth.

[2] This activity " is not like reasoning, a power to be exerted according to the determination of the will. A man cannot say: 'I will compose poetry.' The greatest poet cannot say it; for the mind in creation is as a fading coal, which some invisible influence, like an inconstant wind, awakens to transitory brightness; . . . could this influence be durable in its original purity and force, it is impossible to predict the greatness of the result."—(Shelley, in his *Defence of Poetry*.)

lies within another and greatly more rapid series of vibration-numbers; the mental-world within others, again immeasurably more rarified, and so on up to the 'highest' and most rarefied that we can reach.

Now the musically uncultured masses, the as yet undeveloped even though potential music-lovers, respond to vibrations of the two lower levels. From these all jazz music for example, music-hall ditties, shop-ballads and very much else emanates—all music in short which has for *raison-d'être* the titillation of the physical senses and the rousing of the emotions.

§ 5. RELATIVELY RESTRICTED RANGE OF MUSIC HITHERTO

Just 'below' this great dividing-line—*i.e.*, between the ephemeral and the permanent, the 'lower' and the 'higher' mind—is the realm of the Intellect, the brain being its physical instrument. Here, at this level, originates by far the greatest bulk of musical busy-ness at the present time. Vast numbers of compositions deal with material contacted at this level; are discussed and considered from this level; and are addressed to those of us whose musical consciousness functions normally at this level. It is, of course, somewhat more valuable than much that is found acceptable and, did it represent the limit of man's capabilities, no criticism could be directed against the tremendous amount of purely cerebral work in which the musical world is whelmed. It is not so. As intellectual beauty represents something far superior to the purely physical; just so spiritual beauty far transcends that of the purely intellectual.

'Above' our dividing line are the 'higher' mental (Manasic), the intuitional (Buddhic), and the spiritual

(Atmic) levels, and could we but learn to recognize those marvellous works, or those portions of works which draw their inspiration from such sources, we should indeed have made a tangible step toward a logical musical æsthetic—a step perhaps never before so sorely needed.

It should be said before we proceed further in this branch of our study, that each of the five planes we are considering is divisible in a subtle but nevertheless quite distinct way into seven sub-planes, a detailed examination of which would lead us far from our subject. Also, it would appear that they react and interact in the most delicate manner, giving rise to complexities and gradations of almost infinite subtlety. Further, in addition to these complexities and subtleties, all ideations contacted at however 'high' a level induce repercussions at 'lower' levels on the way through, so to say, to a physical-plane expression. And when this is realized any suspicion of naïveté, which a certain type of mind might believe to be inherent in this classification, disappears completely, and it is seen to be in reality one capable of the most stimulating and penetrating inflexions; of searching and illuminative deduction; and moreover, it is seen to be a system so comprehensive as easily to include not only all music yet written, but a great deal that has origin in realms as yet uncontacted by our composers, or at least, unrecorded by them in their music. For the sake of clarity I deal here with only the boldest outline and the baldest statement of this theory, leaving details to be fitted in as they arise; chiefly in the practical section devoted to an attempted evaluation of composers and their works[1]—an evaluation having our theory of æsthetic as background.

Let me add that in using such words as 'higher,' 'lower,'

---

[1] Part Four, p. 219 *et seq.*

A Five-planal Conception

'spiritual' and the like, I mean nothing whatever to do with morality, religiosity or ethics. We are here concerned with art and artists, and nothing else. But these words, which I agree might be misleading, seem to be the best we can do in translation from the Sanskrit.

Our codification then, furnishes us with standards as well as standpoints. And a further examination of our clear, though admittedly somewhat crude classification, forces several conclusions upon us—conclusions which, if and when they are accepted, throw light into the darkest chambers of our present ignorance of musical æsthetic.

§ 6. A FIVE-PLANAL CONCEPTION

All music to-day[1] *is a physical-plane expression of vibrations contacted upon one or other of our postulated five planes.*

1st. It may be a mere echo of physical-plane sounds (*e.g.*, certain of Vivaldi's pieces, Beethoven's cuckoo, or Strauss' sheep-bleat imitations. There exists very little of such, Nature being well able to supply it herself without man's aid. Honegger's imitation of a locomotive at speed, Mussolov's of a factory machine-room are similarly physical-plane in origin, though I do not say that they do not cause repercussions in other parts of our nature. More of this presently); or it may have its origin in those less dense sub-divisions of the physical realm which we call etheric: a great deal of the music of the so-called 'impressionists' and 'symbolists' is of this kind; (Debussy, Rimsky-Korsakov, Respighi, Falla, and, of course, Wagner and many moderns furnish examples).

2nd. It may be a record of impressions contacted in the

[1] Why 'to-day?' Cf. § 5, p. 163.

Music To-day

emotional plane, upon one or other of its seven sub-divisions. Almost the whole of our musical output since Bach has had its origin here, as well as all of our 'popular' music. Indeed, the whole huge gamut of emotions, passions, desires, has its root basic-vibration in this range. That emotional music which is not ephemeral takes inception upon Causal,[1] Intuitional or Spiritual levels, and is emotional only in a strictly secondary sense. But this is the restricted sense in which music is universally regarded. And it is accepted as axiomatic by almost everybody that only music having its birth and being on this level, and making effect on the emotional part of our make-up, is worthy of attention. In every condemnatory criticism, you may expect to hear some such phrases as "it left us cold," or "it failed to *move* us"; *i.e.*, our emotions. Every laudatory epithet from 'pretty' to 'sublime' will be expended on music addressed to and from this part of our nature. That music we do possess whose origin and appeal lies outside the emotional-plane (which emotional-plane is a mere one-fifth, be it remembered, of our potential scope) is either laughed to scorn, or at best may be dubbed 'amusing.' And the vast majority of us are so obsessed by the emotions that a recent pronouncement that no new possibilities in music remain to be exploited has gone almost unchallenged. No new possibilities! Think of that. Consider for one moment that most of the music you are likely to know has been contacted upon one or other of the seven sub-levels of the Emotional-plane or upon the 'lower' Mental levels, and then remember that the upper levels of the Mental-plane (the Causal world), the glories of the whole of the Intuitional world (the Buddhic) and the wonders of the Spiritual (Atmic) realm remain practically

[1] *I.e.*, higher Mental. See also footnote, p. 168.

A Five-planal Conception

unexplored by composers, or, more precisely, not conveyed to us in their music. Having realized this, what will be our reaction to such statements as these; that we have reached a terminal point; that to progress further is a manifest impossibility?

It will surely be abundantly clear to readers who have persevered thus far, that no additions to our technical equipment—no quarter-tonal, no modal systems, no additions of new *timbres* to our orchestral resources, in short, no technical means whatever—will in themselves aid us in our efforts to widen the field of musical appeal. What is needed is the spirit of the intrepid explorer; his contacting instrument the human consciousness; his driving power the Will, and his recording instrument the brain. Once able consciously to contact and freely roam the hitherto neglected higher-mental, intuitional and spiritual realms, once able to realize these extremely rarefied vibrations in his brain, assuredly all the technical devices we have so far evolved *and many new ones* will be needed by the composer adequately to transcribe for us the records of his pilgrimage.

3rd. Of recent years certain composers have shown a tendency to turn away from the emotional in their works; have tired of the appeal from emotion to emotion and have sought to make contact with, and translate into music, vibrations of the third (the Mental) plane. All too few, alas, are able to raise their consciousness to a degree at which they can contact the 'higher' sub-levels of this realm. They reach only the 'lower' levels whence emanates that plethora of merely cerebral works the super-abundance of which has already been deplored in these pages.

Nor is this the first time in the history of music that such a concentration upon 'lower' manasic activities has taken place. The whole of the Netherland School of the fifteenth century was marred by merely cerebral compositions and rule-of-thumb essays which, amusing enough as some of them may be, add nothing of real value to our musical treasury. This dividing-line between lower and higher Manas is the Rubicon which all must cross who would explore regions of permanent worth, records of experience of which form the rarest treasures of our art and the only ones of lasting value.

So much for the relative smallness of the field covered by the bulk of our music hitherto. It would have been a saddening philosophy indeed to have dwelt upon this [1] had we not also glimpsed the more remote regions whence yet unimagined splendours may be conveyed for the ravishment of future ages. For . . .

4th. Music may have its source too in the ' higher ' mental world—the Causal world of the philosopher [2]—the realm of Divine Intelligence of Dante, in which inhere those mighty archetypes to which Plato refers in his Dialogues.

The Causal world then (*i.e.*, the three sub-planes which constitute the ' higher ' mental world), is one wherein the consciousness functions as he " whose nature is knowledge." [3] In this realm the " Arabesque of Time and Space " is transcended. Ideations are here contacted as Unity whose translation in physical-plane terms appears as Diversity. Time and Space being non-existent in this realm, an ideation

---

[1] A saddening philosophy subscribed to by Busoni when he says, about the paths pursued by the " standard-bearers " of music in his day (composers whom he has " joyfully acclaimed ") : " and still it seems to me that of all these paths . . . none leads *upward*."

[2] So called because all the causes, the effects of which are seen in the ' lower ' worlds, reside in it.

[3] . . . In the region above the heavens [the causal plane] is the place of true knowledge.—*Phædrus*.

A Five-planal Conception

contacted here as a single illuminating flash may, when unrolled to our physical senses take an hour to perform. Anyone who has made such an experience, and they are more numerous than might be supposed, will readily understand what may seem somewhat obscure in this statement.

By contact with such an ideation upon this plane, Mozart was aware of a single chord which appeared to him when brought into his brain-consciousness, as a whole symphony. Another time he writes: that when his 'soul is fired' he hears 'in his imagination' the whole composition as it were *gleich alles zusammen* (all at once).

Further, such an ideation, undifferentiated upon the Causal level, when contacted by artists of different types, is translated in our world in terms of their own art. Thus the same ideation contacted by a musician, a poet, a painter, is given to the world as music, poem, or picture. Blake attempted a three-fold presentation of some of his inspirations. We have the poem and the drawing. His wife has told us how he *sang* many of his poems, and it was probably only because he lacked a commensurate mastery of the extremely complicated technique of musical notation that he left us no record of this side of his inspiration.[1] Wagner records many of his ideations contacted at this level as poem-picture-music. Scriabin aimed at a still more diversified presentation of the unity he glimpsed on this plane: Boito also.

Again: many are the instances, too well known to need reiteration here, of creative thinkers working quite independently on the physical plane, contacting an ideation

---

[1] I am not suggesting that the music sung by Blake was fine (which is extremely unlikely), but that he was impelled to translate the unified ideation in a diversity of expressions.

simultaneously and translating it in almost identical terms in physical-plane expression. 'Coincidence,' 'thought-transference'; these are accepted as satisfactory explanations unless the incident happens in the world of music. Here it will almost invariably be asserted that one composer has wittingly copied another. Sometimes, of course, it is so. Wagner, for example, borrowed copiously, but what generous interest he paid! Frequently, however, it is not so, and the foregoing is a hint which the student of these matters would do well to bear in mind. Truly, there exist much more exact correspondences in this branch of musical study than most æstheticians have yet realized.

Whilst the Mind has the mental body as its instrument, ranges the 'lower' mental sphere, and has concrete thinking as its activity; the Intelligence has as its vehicle the causal body, ranges the 'higher' mental sphere, and has abstract thinking as its activity. The Mind acquires knowledge by utilizing the senses for observation (its percepts) and by working on these and building them into concepts; its powers are attention, imagination, memory, reasoning by induction and deduction, and the like. The Divine Intelligence *knows*,[1] by the assonance of the outside world with its own nature, and its power is Creation, its products Ideas.[2] When it sends a flash into the lower mental body, illuminating its concepts and inspiring its imagination, we call the flash genius; and when this is in turn brought over into the physical-plane instrument, the brain, and is recorded at all adequately (in one or other of the arts, for example), we call the result a work of genius.

[1] Cf. footnote on p. 168.
[2] I am indebted for help in this concise summary to a learned Sanskrit student who desires to remain unnamed. Naturally I respect his desire, but he shall not go unthanked.

A Five-planal Conception

But the moment any composer glimpses this possibility, the moment he attempts to body forth in his music any appeal from and to a 'higher' part of our make-up than the merely emotional, be sure he will be attacked from many sides, pilloried, and scorned. Stravinsky, for one, has essayed to do this and you should hear the writer quoted on page 295 animadvert on Stravinsky's "comic attempt to avoid the temptations of expression and emotion in his music" and conclude that in doing so he is "denying the very god in music." If this god resides upon the emotional plane, functions there and only there, and is content with the appeal from that comparatively humble sphere to only such as are conscious within that very restricted part of their natures, then it would be true that Stravinsky and others who in this matter are thinking with him are 'denying the god.' It is not so. The 'god of music' ranges a vastly greater field than this. By reference to the thesis we have been developing, it will be seen that a five-fold world is postulated, from any and every realm of which music may draw its inspiration, and in the corresponding parts of our nature, according to our development, make its effect.

Music as we know it is the youngest of the arts, being barely three hundred years old, and its youthfulness is shown in no way more strikingly than in the degree of ineptitude displayed on all sides about musical evaluation. The man of average general culture would never expect to discover in a Sax Rohmer 'thriller' the soul-revealing penetration of a Marcel Proust. And if he did, and failed to find it there he would never dream of blaming Rohmer. 'A wrong choice on my part' would be his explanation. So narrow, however, are persons' reactions to music that a man of similar general culture expecting to meet in Schönberg passages of mellifluity equal with Mendelssohn, and not doing so, incontinently blames (not himself for lack of penetration, but) Schönberg for not supplying the ' medicine as before.' All music, you see, must contain the melodic, harmonic and rhythmic ingredients he knows, must be served up in the same scheme of orchestral *timbres*, and must emanate from the same restricted portions of the emotional sphere, utterly regardless of the fact that we are, or ought to be, free of all the ' five worlds'; *from any sub-level of any of which*—played upon, reacted upon, reinforced, fructified; either brought through ' simple of itself' or shot through with any admixture of vibration between its source and the composer's brain—a veritable inspiration may be transported for the delight and edification of mankind.

By parity of reasoning then, we see that the charge brought against music of the Causal levels, of coldness, lack of feeling and inability to rouse the emotions, is simply a *non sequitur*. Except by reflection it ought not to rouse emotion in the listener. It is not intended primarily to do so.[1] As sensibly say of Hinton's fascinating accounts of the Fourth Dimension that they do not directly evoke emotions such as love, heroism, self-sacrifice, generosity and so on. They are not intended to.

It will not have escaped the discerning reader that my sympathy lies with this trend of the ' new music.' But it is not at all a preference for the one type over the other; simply a welcoming of the broader range of experience which several composers of our day are endeavouring, perhaps subconsciously, to convey through their works. For it were as absurd to deny the value and beauty of the emotional, the romantic, as to deny that of the other, the non-emotional

---

[1] Cf. p. 238 *in re* Stravinsky.

A Five-planal Conception

type. Yet the musical world includes large numbers of persons who repudiate one or the other.

The Philistine will tell you that the art of composition has been attacked by a microbe whose activities have succeeded in infecting the whole inspirational stream; that no composer since the Romantics has been able to resist the influence of this naughty germ, and that, *ergo*, no typically modern music is worth listening to.

The Iconoclast, *per contra*, breaks away from the emotional, desires to free himself from the ideals which formerly did duty, and repudiates a ' sentimental expressionism ' in music.

We have indicated a point of view which reconciles these apparent opposites: have glimpsed a vista so wide as easily to include both; one, moreover, so extensive as to cover many regions hitherto unexplored by the consciousness (or, which is the essence of our argument, as yet unrecorded by composers), whose exploitation lies in the future.

Composers who are impelled in a direction apparently contrary to ' expressionism ' in their music are strongly championed by Paul Bekker, who emphasizes their attitude and supports it logically in his book *Organische und mechanische Musik*. He finds expression to be one thing; music another. Unfortunately, in his reaction against the overconcentration upon emotional aspects of music he can find nothing other than a purely mathematical conception to offer in its stead. And I mention his work here by way of drawing attention to a danger which undoubtedly besets the composer —namely, that non-emotional music, if it connote nothing more than a deliberate inhibition of vibrations from the second plane of our scheme (the Emotional), and a concentration upon the ' lower ' sub-levels of our third plane (the

Music To-day

'lower' Mental), will inevitably stultify his productions, and he will discover eventually that he has been pursuing a retrograde course. Thus the above writer, so far from increasing our scope, would decrease it to an anæmic and dessicated mathematical problem. In terms of the classification with which we are now familiar, he would confine all music to the 'lower' mental world (*i.e.*, would derive musical ideas from that realm only), and by so doing would degrade musical composition to the level of a chess game. Other writers also, as well as several modern composers are restricting the art in this myopic way. And although their thesis, as an argument against our long thralldom to the purely emotional in music, is both logical and convincing, as even a superficial acquaintance with our main schematization would seem to show, danger lies in that having freed themselves from the limitations of a solely emotional appeal they voluntarily accept those of an equally restricted (or even more restricted) sphere, *i.e.*, the lower levels of the mental plane.

5th. Pursuing our argument still further, we recognize the possibility that music may have as its birthplace, so to say, the fourth realm shown in our classification—the Intuitional (Buddhic) sphere. Rare indeed are those who can bring into their waking consciousness definite impressions of contact with a rate of vibration so rapid, so rarefied, as that which obtains at such a super-normal level. Of these rare ones very few, in the nature of things, happen to be musical composers. And of these rare, rare ones, who will be likely to have developed a technique at all capable of giving us the faintest echo of a world of such transcendent glory?

I can tell you of one. And at the mention of his name every composer, every musician, every music-lover should

A Five-planal Conception

summon his inner being to attention! For it is the loftiest name known to music in the Western world: Palestrina.

Do not think I use the word lofty in connection with Palestrina's music because his name is so closely associated with the Church that assumed responsibility for him, and because many of his works are settings of various portions of the Roman liturgy. Sacred words do not render holy the music that is composed to them.[1] Besides, a great deal of Palestrina's work is avowedly sæcular in the usual sense of the word.

No. I regard him as the loftiest, grandest, and purest composer the Western world has ever known, because he, more than any other, and with less admixture of 'lower' vibrations has habitually brought through for us records of the ineffable bliss and glory of the Buddhic sphere.

Every musician should study him. Every music-lover insist upon performances of his works. Not necessarily the Masses. The *Madrigali Spirituali* will suffice to open up new worlds to them. If denied the marvels of the Seraphic Mass *Assumpta est Maria*, the *Improperia*, the immortal *Salve Regina* (for five voices) and the *Illuminare Jerusalem*, at least sing and listen to the *Amor quando floria*, the words of which are taken from Petrarch's *ballata* in his *Death of Laura*. In these you shall find pure, passionless music of a true spirituality such as he of all musicians has best

[1] Shades of Sankey and Moody, of Torrey and Alexander!

This confusion between the so-called sacred and sæcular in the realm of music—a peculiarly English, or at any rate Teutonic affection—is rapidly dying out. And it is being realized that there is no such distinction in fact. The very superficial designation 'sacred,' applied to music written to various liturgical rituals and the like, however convenient as a cataloguing device, is fundamentally a misnomer. Nature takes no account of the ethical idea in the social economy of man : neither does music which, taking rise in some corner of her vast domains, brings to us a glimpse of her Beauty and her Life. With these things only does Nature concern herself and music sedulously copies her.

understood, and this expressed in an ideal and natural human vein without circumlocution or any 'art'-fulness.

And if you are willing, as so many of you rightly are, to take the *Wohltemperirte Klavier* for your daily bread, take the *Madrigali Spirituali* as your consecrated wine. Intoxication will assuredly follow; but intoxication from which there will be no sordid reaction—for this is the nectar of the gods.

6th. Remains only for consideration the remotest of the planes of our classification, the Spiritual (Atmic), direct contact with which connotes a very rare exaltation of consciousness indeed. Here an important observation falls to be made. It has already been remarked that music carries to us some record—more or less easily discernible according to the adequacy of its transcription in physical-plane terms, and according to our degree of penetration—of its plane of inception. Also that it causes reactions in other parts of our nature between the realm of its inception and the physical world. But further, and quite apart from these reactions, a series of reflections as between the planes themselves must be noted—reflections which, as it were, operate automatically. Thus:

> The 5th plane; Atmic, is reflected in the 1st plane; Physical.
> The 4th plane; Buddhic, is reflected in the 2nd plane; Emotional.
> The 3rd plane; 'higher' Mental, is reflected in the 'lower' Mental.

It will now be clear that any charge of *naïveté* regarding the application of our system to an evaluation of the æsthetic content of music falls to the ground. It appears, on the contrary, to be one capable alike of the clearest and simplest broad application, or of an almost impenetrable subtlety.

Having thus glanced at the characteristics of the various sub-divisions of the universal consciousness which it is within man's power to contact, from the 'lowest' to the 'highest,' let us be careful to disabuse our minds of any notion that we should permit ourselves to praise only music of the 'higher' planes. (For there still lingers a good deal of *snobbisme* in the musical world). To a starving man a cup of milk is more welcome than the holiest sermon, and there is room for good music of all types in the world of to-day.

Our classification may none the less be useful in the nebulous state of musical æsthetic at the present time, and if we avoid upon the one hand a pedantic didacticism, and upon the other help to dispel the vague mists that have hitherto enveloped this part of our subject, naught but good can ensue.

By way of illustrating how definite may be the results of such study as the foregoing, I permit myself to mention what is perhaps the first conscious essay along these lines: an opera, *Avatara*, each of the three 'Acts' of which is preceded by a *mantra*[1] apposite to it, which aims to set in motion the basic vibration-type of the whole act. The First—Mantra of Activity—appertains to the 'higher' third plane (Manas): the Second—Mantra of Bliss—to the fourth plane (Buddhi): the Third—Mantra of Will—to the fifth plane (Atma).

§ 7. MUSIC AND SEX

We are now able to face a subject which, *inter alia*, becomes greatly illumined by our study of these differ-

[1] *Mantra*, see footnote, p 117.

entiated realms and their cognate states of consciousness, viz., Music and Sex.

It has frequently been urged against music as a damning reproach that it has been observed to accentuate and heighten sex. If I may say so without giving offence, so has religion! Any operation which brings rarefied, exalted—and therefore unusually rapid—'spiritual' vibrations to play upon the physical body may cause these results—may heighten sex, as well as produce other collateral reactions. I will not discuss here whether this is or is not a desirable result. One remembers Arnold Bennett's indignation when an antagonistic reviewer spoke of the close of Wells' *Tono-Bungay* as "an orgy of lust." "Orgy of fiddlestick," says he. "The most correct honeymoon is an orgy of lust; and if it isn't, it ought to be."

Apart from the fact, frequently observed, that dance-music of a low type stimulates the erotic impulses, it is noticeable that much of our finest and noblest music acts upon some persons as a sexual stimulant.

I have observed, at a performance of Wagner's mighty love-drama *Tristan und Isolde*, members of the audience so wrought upon by its fervour as to be physically affected: at the same performance others could be observed who sensed the Buddhic (the transcendent) aspect of the work—an aspect which Wagner undoubtedly contacted when he was composing it—and responded to that and its reflection in the Emotion-world, without permitting the creative urge to invade their physical make-up at all.[1]

How are we to account for this?

---

[1] Ordinary physiological reactions, as heightened blood-pressure, increased pulse-rate, and other *quasi*-automatic responses in the sympathetic-nervous system are beside the point of the argument.

The Ensouling of Music

We have seen that a vibration (or a series of vibrations) of creative type and potency, may be contacted at any level up to and including the Atmic (Spiritual).

It may be 'tapped,' so to say, at any point between the region of contact and the physical realm.

Also, it may be expressed at its place of inception, or brought down through intervening levels of consciousness into the physical world.

It may be expressed either in the Intuition-world as universal love; in the Mental-world as creative thought; in the Emotion-world as desire or passion; in the Physical-world as the creative sex-act.

Up to a certain point and strictly according to one's type and place in evolution, we can choose the level at which we will permit the original creative impulse to manifest.

§ 8. THE ENSOULING OF MUSIC

The voluminous labours of æstheticians in the world of music are usually expressed in one or other of two ways; either in dry technical terms or in the language of poetic fiction. That their conclusions are as a rule distressingly nebulous may be not altogether unexpected from the nature of the subject; that they should in almost every case fail to mention one of the facts of outstanding importance to musicians and music-public alike is, however, surprising. For the fact itself is one that has been observed countless times by vast numbers of musicians, however much their reports, or the terms in which they refer to the phenomenon, may vary.

This fact, which is quite frequently to be noticed in concert-room and theatre, in salon and in study, is what I call the 'ensouling' of music.

Music To-day

In using this term the reader who has not given much thought to the matter may imagine that I, in my turn, am making use of the language of poetic fiction. It is really not so. In approaching this question from the present angle unfamiliar thoughts may be expressed in unusual terms; but the phenomenon itself is a common musical experience, and a consideration of it should be of great practical value alike to performer and composer, as well as being of interest to the auditor.

Let us take as example an acknowledged masterwork, say the Brahms *Violin Concerto*, thus avoiding any complication of the issue, any side-tracking of the main question into a discussion of the value of the work itself *qua* composition. (For we are concerned here with a certain aspect of the *effect of a work in performance*, not its intrinsic merits). I must have heard this concerto quite fifty times. At one period I participated in a tour, every programme of which included it with Kreisler as soloist. The artist was in splendid form, at the height of his powers; the orchestra and conductor were the same for each performance.

Now it was plain for a sensitive observer to notice that, although there was a very high level below which this superb artist never descended, neither the excellent orchestra nor conductor, at times the effect suddenly became prodigious; soloist, orchestra, audience alike transported, the collective aura of thousands completely unified under a veritable spell of magic.

For the absence of this incandescent radiance what could be the explanation? Kreisler out of form: the audience unsympathetic: the conditions inconducive? None of these reasons would meet the facts, for the magic often happened

The Ensouling of Music

in face of such drawbacks, or, alas, on the other hand, sometimes failed to operate in conditions apparently most favourable.

Such instances could be multiplied from the experience of every music-lover of sensitivity. I can myself recall many such magical moments: Piatti playing the *Ständchen* of Schubert: the *Equali* of Beethoven blown from a turret of the Castel Sant' Angelo: Zelie de Lussan in *Carmen*: Joachim in the *Cavatina* from the op. 130 quartet: a specially memorable *Tristan* performance: Busoni playing some Bach chorales: a military band playing the *Bande Mataram*: Caruso in a Neapolitan street song: part of Scriabin's *Prometheus* in Paris years ago, and the middle section of Berlioz' *Queen Mab* scherzo in the old Conservatoire: the beginning of the last act of *Tosca*: Vougeot singing *La Marseillaise*, and others. A heterogeneous collection indeed; but remember, we are not discussing at the moment the intrinsic value of compositions, but the ensouling of them.

All artists of extended experience can recall instances of this miraculous lighting-up of the total vibration, and when it happens the best that is usually offered in explanation is 'he was in splendid form to-night,' or some such vapidity. Thus, the practising artist's conclusions are as unsatisfactory, as inconclusive and unhelpful in this matter, as those of the theoretical æsthetician.

A large body of teaching would be required properly to elucidate this fascinating but unfamiliar subject, and to link it with the numerous allied phenomena which musicians so frequently meet in their working life.[1] What I quote here are a few scraps of occult wisdom which seem to offer, in

---

[1] Such a body of teaching came my way some years ago which I intend one day to make available in *Consilium Angelicum*.

Music To-day

addition to positive information, food also for speculation and practical application:

> **Every musical sound projected through the air creates, as it were, a funnel between originator and recipient, and only when this is strong enough to resist any ordinary cross-current, is the performer really *en rapport* with his audience.**

This question of a strong and quickly-established *rapport* between the performer and his audience is one of the most important that could engage the attention of the interpretative musician to-day. And it is a question upon which there is an almost complete dearth of information. Note that it is not invariably the greatest music which makes the magical effect spoken of above, but that it is invariably music which is, so to say, 'ensouled' as it is performed, that does so. In many of his pieces Grieg is much more quickly *en rapport* than certain more gifted composers. He has to some small extent mastered the trick of writing music which becomes readily ensouled. Puccini also; Schubert, of course. Wagner still more so, but [cf. p. 290] other agencies are at work in his case whose results might easily be confused with these. In our own day several composers have written works or portions of works which readily become ensouled but inasmuch as it is, so to say, accidental in all these men's work, it is nothing like so constant or so powerful as it might be. Obviously then it is a matter of the greatest importance in the evolution of music for composers to understand the qualities which must be present in their works if they are to carry this enhanced power, and equally so for performers on their part to understand something of the rationale of the ensouling of music.

The Ensouling of Music

It is possible to ensoul musical sounds by several methods: 1. By projecting along the 'funnel' a thought, together with the note; 2. By creating a powerful 'thought-form,' into and through which the music plays; 3. By operating upon the *timbre* of the notes by means of the Will, thereby causing them to affect different parts of the consciousness of the listener. The first is the method most frequently used nowaday, but the least powerful or lasting.

The above short quotation contains one of the most potent suggestions regarding the practice of music in its dynamic aspect that has reached my notice in a long and intensive musical experience. How often has it happened that music given by a huge and splendid orchestra, say of a hundred instrumentalists, playing admittedly great music, playing it excellently, conducted by a musician of knowledge and authority, has failed to make the music 'come alive' for a single instant during a two-and-a-half-hour concert. (Note that I do not say this in disparagement.) At other times, and apparently fortuitously, a piece of quite inferior music has suddenly 'lighted up' and the magic has resulted. Experienced artists know very well that the current jargon about a performance 'coming off well' and the like, does not cover the facts at all, and they are in almost total ignorance of even a possible explanation of the facts as they are seen to be.

Hence I venture to attach a degree of importance to the above information which might well seem extravagant to the inexperienced or the unthinking. A further short quotation may shed more light on this subject:—

One reason why at your present stage of [musical] evolution it is mainly slow music which becomes ensouled, is because performers need time to get

'inside' the music themselves. For the ensouling of music can not be done accidentally. At your present stage, performers are only able to ensoul such quick pieces as follow well-trodden paths. You have seen [*e.g.*, Braga's *Serenata* performed with extraordinary effect at a soldiers' concert in 1916] how quite inferior music may be ensouled and delivered with more effect than great music. That is one reason why at present not more artists are taught how to ensoul their music. Even a poor piece of music (like that mentioned), having a pure intent, may be ensouled and no harm done; the great danger would lie in undiscriminating persons having the power to ensoul music of evil intent, inferior or otherwise. The conscience needs to develop along artistic as well as ethical lines, and when people have learned to discriminate between the Bad and the Good (music) and have learned to prefer the Good, then they will be taught how to ensoul their music.

Not to lose my way in metaphysical speculations upon questions which, I am well aware, the above quotation opens up, I content myself with the remark that there is a reality behind the phenomenon itself. By drawing attention to it as a dynamic aspect of the art and one which, although widely recognized, has never to my knowledge been seriously examined, not to mention studied and practised scientifically, I have at least indicated its importance to both creative and interpretative musicians. Several more-than-hints are contained in the foregoing as to the lines along which, and the methods by which, its further study may be pursued; and those who may be impelled to 'seek truth' in this direction are likely to be more than amply repaid.

Chapter Eleven: Qualities of Inspiration

Of the Vital Principle in Music—Of the Beautiful in Music—Of Idealism—Of Purity in Music—Of Spirituality in Music—Of Individuality and Originality—Of Mysticism and Mystical Inspiration—Conclusions of Part Three.

ONCE we have accepted the schematization sketched out in the planal tabulation in Section 3 of the preceding chapter, it becomes a joyous and fascinating task to trace out in the works we meet the composer's contacts with the various realms shown forth as *qualities* in these works. Between a Beethoven struggling unsuccessfully (for he was pouring new wine into old bottles) to express in the *Grosse Fuge* an ideation contacted in the Causal world, and, say, a Johann Strauss expressing superbly adequately a contact with some not very lofty Astral (emotional) vibration in the *Wein, Weib, und Gesang* waltzes, what a range is covered. And these by no means indicate the limits in either direction. For the scheme already put before the reader is so comprehensive as easily to include the superbities of Palestrina's Buddhic records as well as the obscenities of some of the jazz purveyors. And it becomes increasingly easy to ' place,' to our satisfaction at least, any and every work upon which we focus our attention. It will not, needless to say, bestow upon us ready-made a sound taste and a fine culture. Of the acquisition of these I have spoken elsewhere. But it does help us to concentrate our attention upon clearly defined qualities and states of consciousness, an invaluable and entirely necessary preliminary.

How then do these qualities show themselves in the music we meet, and how shall we render ourselves able to detect the finest and the highest? Or, again, how do the composer's contacts with the various sources of his inspiration show themselves in his works as qualities?

It is only by a process of elimination that we can hope to arrive at even an approximate definition of the finest and highest in music, and when, in this endeavour, we survey the whole field of music of the present day we are forced to make first of all a most trenchant distinction, namely between that which is infused with a vital spark—what one might call for want of a more philosophical term ' live ' music—and those moribund, dry-as-dust, merely scholastic compilations, or those trumpery catch-penny pot-boilers which constitute at least eighty per cent of our publications.

From this ' live ' music we may further portion off that which is definitely beautiful. This will be by no means all of it, though still a fair modicum.

When, however, we attempt to discern in the beautiful, that which is noble, sublime, or spiritually inspired, we discover what a startlingly small proportion of music exists or is being composed which can truly be described in such terms.

§ 1. OF THE VITAL PRINCIPLE IN MUSIC

Certainly not more than twenty per cent, I estimate, of the enormous masses of music put forth by the music-presses of the world, is informed by the vital principle. Yet only ' live ' music is of any real interest—using this

Of the Vital Principle in Music

term to indicate that which possesses the primary charm of freshness of feeling and statement. Any music which discloses fatigue, weariness, deadness of psyche *in the composer*, has parted with its magical spell; for vitality of emotional, mental, or spiritual content, and vitality of statement of that content, are the prime characteristics of music in those moments when its power is most dynamic.

Music to deserve our attention must have this freshness of feeling, this ' live '-ness, first of all. And it is the beautiful quality of the true art-instinct that it contacts everything, even the commonplace-familiar, with a kind of childlike directness and delight.

This term, in the sense used here, covers a fairly wide field, and if it were the only test to which our music were put it would include a very great deal that the musician of any degree of real culture would find intolerable. Still, if we insist on our music possessing even and only this one quality of ' live '-ness we are helping separate the gold from the dross. For remember, you cannot get it by paying for it. " Money will not buy life."

It is this quality, distinguishable in a moment by a fellow artist, that marks off at once the true from the false: pains and patience will not give it: it comes into the world with the creative artist as a natural gift, and we should demand first of all that our music possess this quality of life: (not live*liness*, for this may be either true or simulated), and train ourselves faithfully to distinguish it—a not very difficult matter for the average intelligence. Having done which, a further step would be to turn our attention to that ' live ' music which can be truly termed beautiful.

§ 2. OF THE BEAUTIFUL IN MUSIC

Throughout the eighteenth century, and indeed in various other epochs of our history, scorn has been poured on the art of music on the grounds that it is immoral in tendency.[1] The priggish or the puritanically inclined—and there are still some of these ' left over ' from an unhappy age—persist in regarding music as nothing more than sensuous tittilation. And this maugre the clearly expressed views of Plato, Pythagoras, Aristotle, Napoleon and many more, as to its educative value. Others—and I am afraid we have to include Wagner, Beethoven, Scriabin in this group—claim for music, somewhat pretentiously, a direct moral value. It has nothing of the sort.

Nature takes no account of the moral or the ethical idea in the social economy of man. She is indifferent to everything except the struggle for Life and Beauty. Life (vitality) we have already considered as it demonstrates through music. What of Beauty?

A sensual force (as differentiated from a moral force), it is, according to Amiel, " sans pudeur et sans probité." Ethical values (the good and the non-good) differ from day to day; differ as between one country and another; as between society and individual (*e.g.*, what is good for society may be bad for the individual); and the same thing may be at the same time both good and bad for a person (he may know it is bad for him but still like it). Moreover, " there are no such things as Good and Bad," says a great philosopher, " only degrees of Ignorance."

A thing cannot however be both beautiful and non-

---

[1] *E.g.*, St Augustine's well-known diatribe, betraying his apprehension lest music should lay hold of the imagination to the detriment of church dogmas.

Of the Beautiful

beautiful at the same time to the same person. When a thing is judged to be bad the judgment is no longer an æsthetic but an ethical one. The Good is always a relative, a derived value. The Beautiful is an intrinsic value. Moreover the ethical value, as having its home in the mortal world, that of diversity, is presented to the mind surrounded with subjective impositions and interpretations; the æsthetic, as pervading all realms, is indivisible. The mind is merged in the object. Beauty is self-sufficient. And the 'higher' the source of any particular manifestation of beauty the more complete is its effect.[1] For the Causal presentation is, of course, complete.[2] Lest however, in pointing out how Nature in her efforts toward Beauty dissociates herself from the ethical idea developed by man, this should be read as meaning that there is anything inimical to his best interests in following her in those efforts, we may remind ourselves of Goethe's dictum: The Beautiful is higher than the Good; the Beautiful includes in it the Good.

The Beautiful, then, is beautiful because it is of the essence of Beauty. With the true artist—creator, interpreter, or participator—intimacy with Beauty is the only kind of familiarity which does not lead to contempt.

We must however be careful to avoid the common notion that Beauty implies only charm, suavity, and such like sunny characteristics, for it must be realized that Beauty in every degree and in all its many appeals, has always two sides. It can rise to the sublimest altitudes of bright and joyous vibration which we can conceive: but it can also penetrate the "depths of a dark inversion." The concord retains

[1] Cf. 174 et seq.
[2] Music taking inception in the Causal realm is sometimes regarded as lacking in 'warmth,' but this is a mistake, for the Causal conception and presentation is complete. It is a question of familiarity.

much of its dynamic power by contrast with the discord: together they constitute one of the pairs of opposites—as Night and Day, Heat and Cold, Happiness and Despair—to which in this world of diversity we are bound to submit, willy-nilly. But hands have at all times been raised in holy horror of discords, related or unrelated, resolved or not, prepared or piquant. The component notes of discord however are just as certainly present as resultants from any given root-bass, as are those of concord. They are therefore just as 'natural.' And this is a point which modern musicians constantly find it necessary to make, however childish it may seem in itself.

Beauty, however, is a quality not necessarily present in all live and true music, neither does its application as a criterion narrow down our field of inquiry in any very drastic way. For there is a vast mass of music, especially of songs, dance-music, so-called ' comic '-opera, etc., which, whilst it might, broadly speaking, be designated beautiful, holds little or nothing of the ennobling or elevating.

It is necessary to bring into play another factor, namely, Idealism.

§ 3. OF IDEALISM

When, however, we attempt further to narrow the field of inquiry and separate off from the ' live ' music and that which is beautiful (broadly so-called) that which is rooted in the ideal, we begin to touch the realm of spiritual principles and lay ourselves open to misunderstanding.

Idealism has so often been associated in recent years with vagueness of thought, slovenly construction and a weak

Of Idealism

sentimentalism, that it has been discredited even among those who recognize the reality behind it and the great place it must hold in all rich and noble living. The relation which the ideal bears to the real is penetratingly defined by Goethe when he says that the Ideal is the completion of the Real.

A rigid and unfecund Realism sees in the sonata, symphony, overture or quartet, nothing but its key-structure, its ' form,' its clever (or otherwise) disposition for the chosen instruments, its fugal imitations, modulations, related subjects, *codettas* and what-not-all; a true and rational Idealism sees all these things, and values them too, but it sees and values at least as highly the Life behind the Form, the spirit informing the matter; sees (again to quote Goethe) the ' object whole.'

Now, in a demand for this quality of Ideality lies the first hint of a true eclecticism, for, as we have seen, the insistence upon Life and Beauty in our music, without which it is unworthy of the name, still leaves us with a very wide field, and includes much that a cultivated artist would consider beneath him. But so soon as we apply the test of Idealism to our music we lift it at once into the realm of the enduring; and lacking any other quality than these three and maugre any adverse circumstance whatsoever it will surely find at some time or other a response in the human heart.

No quality is more essential than the inspiration which results from such an Idealism—none is more easily lost or dissipated. Immersion in mundane affairs, a blighting routine, a drab and colourless daily round of duties, the decline of moral energy, all these conspire to chill the faith and paralyse the aspiration. Against which nemesis the

Music To-day

familiar companionship of the great Idealists is one of our grandest resources.

§ 4. OF PURITY IN MUSIC

Of the vast amount of music to which the term beautiful may be allowed to apply only a small proportion, that which has been composed by men having a living and dynamic Idealism deep rooted in their natures, can be said to possess the quality of Purity as I use the word here.

I have already spoken of the great exemplar of Purity in music when, in discussing the world of Intuition (the Buddhic realm), the name of Palestrina was mentioned. We know that the transcendent purity of this truly inspired master's work has never since been surpassed, and there have been at all times and in many European countries since his day, groups of Palestrina devotees who have found in the study and performance of his works a more elevating, purifying and inspiring effect than in the works of any other composer.

For some reason which I am unable clearly to formulate, this quality is the rarest in music to-day, and it would probably baffle most of us to point to a single passage of any length in any fine modern music to which this word could be applied without straining it beyond all ordinary meaning.

§ 5. OF SPIRITUALITY IN MUSIC

When we endeavour to recollect the impressions made upon us by the works we have listened to, especially after a lapse of time sufficiently long to blot out the memories of all but the most striking, we often find that certain characteristics which escaped our judgment at the hearing are never-

Of Individuality and Originality

theless present in the consciousness, and this apparently unaccountably. And two broad distinctions may be made into either of which our more permanent musical memories will naturally fall: the one characterized by a delicacy and charm, a nearness and tenderness which has its place among our most intimate experiences (music possessing any or all of the qualities named hitherto); and the other by a sublime majesty, a mysterious grandeur which loses none of its effect by the passing of time, but inspires us with an undiminished awe ' like that felt at the presence and operation of some great Spiritual power.' These are the two great divisions into one or other of which all that is enduring in music may be classified. The Persians, we are told, say: "*Jemâl*, the grace, the sweetness, the beauty of God is greater than *Jehâl*, the glory, the majesty, the power of God." Certainly in so far as they are reflected in our music the qualities of grace, beauty, sweetness and charm, are much more common than those of majesty, power and sublimity. Indeed the last-named, as emanating only from the Causal (Manasic), Intuitional (Buddhic) and Spiritual (Atmic) realms, is extremely rare, and only to be found sporadically even in the finest works of the greatest composers. Nor is this at all surprising when we consider how miserably inadequate are our means, even in the hands of a master of technique, to parallel the mighty vibrations of these supernal worlds.

§ 6. OF INDIVIDUALITY AND ORIGINALITY

I suppose that every truly great artist has been accused, at any rate during his lifetime, and by those who do not read beneath the surface of things, of overweening egoism, not

Music To-day

to say conceit and vanity. And this surely arises from the fact that the " infinite capacity for taking pains " commonly thought to be synonymous with genius, would mean nothing at all without that consciousness of superiority which they have one and all possessed.

With what reverence did Schumann and Mendelssohn study the immortal Bach; Beethoven sit for awhile at the feet of Haydn and Mozart; Wagner in early years play the ' sedulous ape' to Weber; Brahms to Beethoven and Schumann, Berlioz to Gluck, Tchaikovsky to Mozart, Strauss to Brahms and Wagner, Scriabin to Chopin: and yet they all possessed, and necessarily so even if hidden beneath a modest exterior, an inner impulse—a conviction of the superiority of their work in some one way or another —that should on no account be confused with conceit or vanity. When a man of genius takes up a special line of work there is always the conviction that the task to be accomplished will be better done by him than by anyone else. (*Exegi monumentum aere perennius!*)

In his individual manner of conveying to us either his view of life in general or his more rare and elevated contacts, a great artist marks himself off from the average men and women of his time, and it is against the personal expression of this aloofness that all that is petty and mean in the character of the mass cries out. If it be true that democracy and socialism tend to strip society of any false aristocracy, socialism in its turn will be conquered and governed by the aristocracy of the intellect and the intuition, the only unconquerable things in the world.

Of course a distinction may be made, even in the ranks of the greatest men, between those who belong to the militant and those who naturally express themselves in a more

Of Individuality and Originality

meditative manner. A militant genius may, in the overstating of his case inseparable from pioneer work, incur the danger of counteracting the effect of his very virility and originality. The more meditative type, he who has no new systems to erect or theories to uphold, is usually positive as a personality but passive as an artist, and does not run a similar risk.[1] But every man of true originality may be said to be an alien in his own country until, by one and one, friends gather round him with sympathy for his message and some understanding of its purport. It takes years to attain sufficient understanding of a new message rightly to value its creator: indeed we cannot get the true measure of a man of genius without to some extent approaching his plane of culture; and it needs a genius perfectly to understand a genius.

We are not therefore to be surprised that true originality may seem at first to push us away, whereas novelty tickles and invites. We know that devotion to the higher induces true culture and will reap for us a very real reward. Everyone then, who wishes to get the most out of music, or indeed any art, should have a right attitude towards originality, avoiding on the one hand the mistaken notion that novelty is synonymous with originality; and on the other, recognizing that strict conformity to routine is one of the surest signs of intellectual inferiority.[2] Only broad and independent minds can afford the luxury of originality, and to this fact the Philistine is ever blind. He is infallible and he is sufficient unto himself. What he accepts, believes, or has, is not only the best of its kind, but nothing better can ever supersede it.

---

[1] " I really do not study or aim at any originality " (Mozart).

[2] There is no rule that one may not break for the advancement of beauty (Beethoven).

Music To-day

The keen-minded Schumann and the more profound Wagner exposed and exploded many of the fallacies of Philistines and mortally wounded more than one " Goliath of ignorance and conceit," but the work must be done anew in every generation and the way kept open both for records of new ideations and restatements of old ones. Thus you have two fundamentally different types of 'originality.' The new-contacted ideation (for I am not of those who believe that every archetype has already been contacted and expressed in music); and the well-known ideation newly expressed. This last is a perfectly legitimate form of originality, for " the same thought uttered a thousand times is his at last who utters it best." And this is the originality which is affiliated with the Personality (*i.e.*, with the first, second, and lower third divisions of the table shown upon page 159).

When a new composer ' swims into our ken ' there immediately arises in certain circles a buzz of admiration, calculation, appreciation, attempted evaluation; and underlying all these as a sort of persistent *basso ostinato* the query, " is he original? " By which is usually meant, or I am the more mistaken, does he perform any musical antics with which we are not already over-familiar—any gymnastical contortions which we can immediately recognize as his, and display our cleverness by some such remark as: " Ah! A thing of so-and-so's. I would know his touch anywhere." This is the kind of originality associated with Personality, and is a much less valuable matter than that fundamental originality which results from a far deeper penetration and a far ' higher ' contact—the originality which is associated with Individuality (*i.e.*, with those realms in which the Ego, the ' pure Activity,' operates). It is when, and *only* when,

Of Individuality and Originality

the great composers of any age are expressing the freely generalized vibrations of these 'higher' realms and states of consciousness that their Individuality is making its real contribution to the art. And it is at these moments, transcending the limitations of Personality, enlarging the horizons, and referring only *en passant* as it were, to the emotional states and lower-mental concepts of the Personality, that the great composer succeeds in 'universalizing a personal state.'

We are not concerned, when moved by the *Symphonie Fantastique*, with Berlioz' infatuation for Harriet Smithson, which undoubtedly helped to call it forth; nor in his *Nocturnes* with Chopin's regard for George Sand; nor in Tchaikovsky's fourth symphony with his attitude toward Nadeshda von Meck; nor in *Tristan* with Wagner's personal relations with Mathilde Wesendonk.

It is important to realize clearly this distinction and difference, for there is a great confusion noticeable in the minds of most persons on the question. And a very familiar note in the jargon of the artistic world of to-day is the exaltation of 'great personality' to a status out of all proportion to its importance relatively to that of great *individuality*.

This exaggeration of the importance of the lesser at the expense of the greater has not been without consequences in the ranks of artists themselves, and of late years we have had the spectacle of more than one composer concentrating upon his own idiomatic characteristics, tricks of speech, idiosyncrasies of diction as it were; stating and restating *ad nauseam* his small personal predilections, and purposely refraining from any attempt to stretch upwards to Individuality and outwards to Humanity. That way lies sterility.

And an impartial examination of the works of Debussy, Stravinsky, Ravel, Schönberg and some others betrays the presence of this canker.

All the qualities spoken of above become coloured by the individuality and the personality of the composer on their way through, so to say, to a physical-plane expression. But it is not this personal aspect—this quasi-accidental colouring as we might almost call it—for which the world hungers. Re-translations, reflections of the glories of the eternal archetypes, these it is for which the world waits, for which it is always craving, and of which it will never tire. For man can never penetrate to the holiest adytum, or expose the innermost altar. And this is at the same time his greatest incentive to labour on, and the surest safeguard of his humility.

§ 7. OF MYSTICISM[1] AND MYSTICAL INSPIRATION

Mystical inspiration is the essential element that assures immortality to any work, whether in poetry, art, music, science or philosophy. It is the crux of our studies in their non-technical aspect. And the products of the highest creative activity of man in his mystically inspired moments —the finest moments of his life—are memorials of a happi-

---

[1] It should not be necessary to explain that Mysticism really does not mean mysteriousness; mystery in the conjurer's sense or that in which the writers of 'thrillers' use it; or vague, dreamy, nebulosities of pious tendency. The word is used here as meaning: a seeking to commune with inner realms by means of internal illumination. As the dictionary has it: 'a communication between man and his Maker through inward and spiritual perception.' Why 'Maker?' unless we substitute 'God,' and regard Him as Everything. In which case we may define Mysticism as 'a seeking to commune with higher realms of Nature by means of exaltation of human consciousness.' Some may boggle at 'Nature' for 'God,' but surely the greater includes the lesser; and in any case, thank heaven, it is no part of a musician's business to attempt to split theological hairs.

Of Mysticism and Mystical Inspiration

ness which may have been brief indeed, but which had in it a touch of the divine. Beethoven may have been deaf, but in the composition of the great works that bear his name he surely knew moments of purer happiness than other mortals. Wagner in exile wanted many of the lesser comforts of life, but there were hours of transcendent joy in his stormy career —joy that had nought to do with the applauding audiences or adoring sycophants. Tortured by the many ills that the flesh is heir to, Mozart, Schubert, Weber, Berlioz, aye and many among the moderns no less than the classicists have known the rapture of mystical inspiration and the joy at the moment of completion of inspired work, before the period of reaction and depression—which is the heavy penalty demanded of the creative artist—has set in.

This is not mere sentimental vapouring. Those persons who deny the possibility of man's power to raise his consciousness to the 'higher' third, fourth, or fifth plane, (which is to be 'inspired') are just as wide of the truth as those who chatter eloquently of inspirational hyperæsthesia. But whereas the former *may* know what the business of being an artist is, the latter certainly do not, for this way lies a negative type of spiritualism and all the ills that may arise when Intelligence vacates his place at the helm and leaves the barque of Reason either rudderless or else at the mercy of something or someone unknown. No creative artist of understanding and experience will pursue such a course. He is the captain, and he alone is ultimately responsible. And to yield up his intelligence in this way would be as common-sensible as to traverse some doubtful back-alley at midnight with bank-notes bulging from his pockets and his eyes closed. Seriously, the following of such unhealthy practices is to risk eventually reaching a point of saturation and induration, the nemesis of which is a complete and unprofitable anæsthesia.

Happily enough from this point of view, creative artists are usually strong individualists, at least to the extent of preferring to be able to say of their work, even if " 'tis a small thing," yet " 'tis mine own." Such is the useful obverse of their type, the reverse of which is a rather objectionable egoism.

The conclusion at which we arrived at an early stage in our studies that " the occult power of sound is at the same time the most important and the most neglected of the many and varied aspects of music to-day," supplemented by the suggestion that " what is needed is the spirit of the intrepid explorer; his contacting instrument the consciousness; his driving power the will, and his recording instrument the brain," may profitably be examined here in some of its various implications.

In the first place, why, in the face of reams and tomes of expatiation upon modern technical newnesses, fascinating as they are, is it asserted that the inspirational is the more important aspect? Simply because, if the ideation contacted by the composer be sufficiently powerful and sufficiently clearly brought over into the brain-consciousness, commensurate means of expression will follow ultimately; and this is the proper order. Instead of this we frequently see nowaday the spectacle of composers who clearly have not reached a worthy source of inspiration at all, forcing themselves upon the attention of the musical world by the employment of quaint new-seeming oddities which are mere technical tricks. This is not the proper order. Inspiration will not result from this procedure.

It would perhaps be kinder to say of most of them that

Of Mysticism and Mystical Inspiration

they are too much occupied with style to be aware of the necessity for any matter. But the time comes when a man should "cease prelusory gymnastic, stand up, put a violence upon his will, and, for better or worse, begin the business of creation" (Stevenson). And where shall he look for guidance, for examples, for precedents in this elusive but pre-eminently important part of his studies?

Now there are many and various ways of achieving the exaltation of consciousness referred to above; probably as many and as various as the temperaments of those who achieve it; and to dogmatize on the point would be merely stupid. The conscientious, systematic, daily application to work of a Haydn, a Turner, an Anthony Trollope, a Bach or a Da Vinci, no more puts it out of court than the 'waiting for an inspiration' of your half-baked dilettante induces it. It is, if you permit the word, a sort of trick, and probably every artist who has made the experience will court it by a different method. Beethoven evidently found that it was favourable to the attainment of his condition of 'raptus' to walk abroad in thunderstorms; Haydn to sit in his court costume wearing a favourite ring; Gluck to place himself in the middle of a beautiful meadow with his piano before him. Schubert, it appears (amazing creature!), could manage it in a common pot-house; Coleridge, Poe, de Quincey and, I suppose many more, needed the assistance of drugs. Some sort of fussy physical activity such as smoking, or circumambulating their den like a caged animal (which is exactly what their physical body is) is part of the *modus operandi* of many literary men, and I well understand the need they feel of pandering to the nervous system in their attempts to quieten it and thus temporarily

Music To-day

free themselves from the gnawing insistence of the physical body that the consciousness shall be focussed upon or in itself.

Consider how Einstein copes with this difficulty. We are told [1] that, unlike most mathematicians, he feels through the emotions results which are 'justified' intellectually later on. More specifically a student of occultism would say that he keeps the physical-body and the emotion-body occupied (in some way analogous to the string-twiddling or eyebrow-teasing habits of some thinkers—mere tricks to keep the sympathetic-nervous system quiet) what time his consciousness is focussed at the appropriate level whereon his problem can be dealt with. . . . "He seats himself at a small table blue pencil in hand, with a blank piece of paper before him, and strives mutely with chaos.[2] Suddenly he will leap to his feet and fly to a piano and improvise, perhaps for hours, returning then to his table with the problem at least on the way to solution." Which I take to mean that music whilst occupying the physical-body (including brain) and the emotion-body, has at the same time helped him to 'tune in' his psychic faculties to the vibration of those realms—a vibration incredibly more rapid than any physical-plane one—in which all knowledge, all beauty, all truth inheres.[3] It has also assisted him in the delicately subtle task of bringing the results into his brain, by far the most difficult part of the operation. We know that he is able adequately to state his conclusions (this is analogous to the music-composer's technique); therefore by parity of reasoning upon our

---

[1] In a newspaper interview which I noted at the time but regret I cannot trace.

[2] That is to say, he endeavours to focus his consciousness in one of the super-physical realms, *i.e.*, 'higher' third, fourth, or fifth of our table.

[3] In the case of Einstein I would hazard the opinion that his inspiration is contacted, in the main, at a certain sub-level of the higher third plane—Causal.

Of Mysticism and Mystical Inspiration

thesis we would expect him to be a man of genius: and as such the world has agreed to regard him.

Scriabin (so I have been told by one who knew him well), pursued a definite line of meditation in, or rather concentration upon, the various plexuses in the body. In these (or their counterparts, the *chakras*), he focussed his consciousness in a certain order, until, upon reaching that situated over the top of the head, he became aware of those premonitory symptoms of inspirational activity well known to the *illuminati*.

The novelist Galsworthy gives us a hint of his procedure when he tells us: "I sink into my morning chair, blotter on my knees, the last words or deeds of some character in ink before my eyes, a pen in hand, a pipe in my mouth, and nothing in my head. I sit. I don't intend: I don't expect; I don't even hope.[1] I read over the last pages. Gradually my mind seems to leave the chair and be where my character is, acting or speaking, leg raised, waiting to come down, lips open ready to say something. When the result is read through, it surprises one by seeming to come out of what went before, and by ministering to some sort of possible future.[2] These pages, adding tissue to character, have been supplied from the store-cupboard of the subconscious."

The old philosophical distinction between the self and

---

[1] Note particularly that he has soothed the physical-body (pipe in my mouth); inhibited the emotion-body (no hopes, or expectations); and informed his brain that he does not seek its aid *as yet* (no intentions: nothing in my head). His consciousness is focussed away from these bodies and the planes upon which they respectively function.

[2] Exactly the same sort of 'surprise' was experienced by Stevenson when receiving *Jekyll and Hyde*, the surprise only arising from the fact that we are so unfamiliar with the working of the consciousness apart from the brain: so little familiar in fact, that many would even to-day deny the possibility—though instances can be met with almost daily among quite ordinary folk, and still more frequently among creative thinkers.

the not-self, as well as that between the self and the Self, is never more clearly to be noticed than at those times when the consciousness is functioning upon levels higher than the physical. It is at once realized that the physical body with which we are so closely acquainted and in which we so constantly focus the consciousness, is merely the self and not the Self.

So familiar are we however with the physical, and so unaccustomed to working with the consciousness apart from the brain, that our natural tendency is to regard the physical plus the consciousness working in it, as our*self*, and to imagine that the consciousness functioning apart from the brain—superiorly to it—is a separate entity. It would seem that Socrates thought of his dæmon in this way. Certainly a great many cases of this sort could be cited which were misunderstandings. Later in this work[1] we shall have to glance at well-authenticated instances of a real co-operation between non-human entities and creative artists, and it will be seen that there is some danger of confusion between these two quite diverse types of inspiration. Quite probably it was Stevenson's own consciousness functioning out of the body which gave him the ready-made plot and solution for *Jekyll and Hyde*; equally probably he contacted at other times entities apart from his own consciousness, for he was a man of unusual sensitivity, and when he did so he attributed the striking results to his ' Brownies.' *Olalla* amongst other of his ' Fables ' was probably given to him thus, from outside as it were. He somewhere remarks significantly that they have not " a rudiment of what we call a conscience." Naturally not, since ' what we call ' conscience is compounded of ethic and morality—the values of

[1] Cf. p. 279.

Of Mysticism and Mystical Inspiration

which are constantly changing in an ever-changing world; are moreover different upon various parts of the earth at the same time; in any case, apply only to humanity; and even so, only to our activities in the two lower worlds and part of the third of our table. They are ruled by conditions which do not at all obtain in the world of 'elementals,' nature-spirits, 'Brownies,' or any beings of the grand Deva evolution.[1]

The possession of the inspirational faculty, necessary, indeed obligatory as it is in all fine work, must not be thought of as an unmixed blessing. Man being an incompletely evolved, imperfect adumbration of divinity, his Dyonisiac flair, even at its best is a sporadic, fugitive business. One of the grandest artists who ever lived, William Blake, was out of touch with the fount of his inspiration for twenty years, and just hear him upon its return: " I am . . . enlightened with the light I enjoyed in my youth, and which has for exactly twenty years been closed from me . . . Oh! the distress I have undergone . . . I thank God with entire confidence that it shall be so no longer . . . I am really drunk with intellectual vision whenever I take pencil into my hand . . . In short, I am now satisfied and proud of my work, which I have not been for the above long period."

So many interesting points emerge from a reperusal of Mozart's well-known letter on his inspiration, when regarded from the present viewpoint, that it is worth while to quote it here: " When I am, as it were, completely myself, entirely alone, and of good cheer—say, travelling in a carriage, or walking after a good meal,[2] or during the night when I

[1] But cf. p. 279 *et seq.*

[2] *I.e.*, occupying the physical body and keeping the sympathetic-nervous system at bay. (See *ante in re* Einstein's piano-playing and Galsworthy's pipe-smoking with like results.)

cannot sleep; it is on such occasions that my ideas flow best and most abundantly. *Whence* and *how* they come, I know not; nor can I force them. Those ideas that please me I retain in memory, and am accustomed, as I have been told, to hum them to myself. . . . All this fires my soul,[1] and, provided I am not disturbed, my subject enlarges itself, becomes co-ordinated and defined, and the whole, though it be long, stands almost complete and finished in my mind. . . . When I proceed to write down my ideas, I take out of the bag of my memory, if I may use that phrase, what has been previously collected into it. . . . But why my productions take from my hand that particular form and style that makes them Mozartish and different from the works of other composers, is probably owing to the same cause which renders my nose so large or so aquiline, or, in short, makes it Mozart's, and different from those of other people." [2]

The poet A. E. Housman made, quite recently, a most interesting personal confession of the inspirational process as it operates in his own case.[3] It is prefaced by two remarks which confirm observations already placed before the reader. First: "I think that the production of poetry, in its first stage,[4] is less an active than a passive and involuntary process."[5] Second: "I have seldom written poetry unless I was rather out of health." A well-known cause-and-effect: the explanation being that in rude health the physical body is clamantly egoistic, tending to imprison rather than free the consciousness. He continues: "Having drunk a

---

[1] In the terminology we are using here—raises his consciousness.

[2] Exactly: the 'same cause' being racial and personal heredity, environment and so on. Cf. p. 222.

[3] In a lecture delivered at Cambridge.

[4] Cf. p. 211. "It is fatal *at this stage* for the brain to be allowed to intrude any critical or ratiocinative operations whatever."

[5] 'Involuntary.' Cf. p. 213, '*unsought* ideations.'

Of Mysticism and Mystical Inspiration

pint of beer at luncheon—the beer is a sedative to the brain, and my afternoons are the least intellectual portion of my life—I would go out for a walk of two or three hours." [In this way keeping the physical body, as it were, at bay. (Note that he has already, to some extent, stilled the brain). Mozart's " travelling in a carriage, or walking after a good meal ": Galsworthy's " pipe in my mouth ": Einstein's ambulations between piano and writing table: the peripatetic behaviour of numbers of creative artists—all these are tricks to soothe the nervous system and help liberate the consciousness.] " As I went along, thinking of nothing in particular,[1] only looking at things around me and following the progress of the seasons, there would flow into my mind, with sudden and unaccountable emotion,[2] sometimes a line or two of verse, sometimes a whole stanza at once." . . . Sometimes his inspiration fails him and the poem has to be " taken in hand and completed by the brain,[3] . . . a matter of trouble and anxiety, involving trial and disappointment, and sometimes ending in failure . . . a laborious business ": (and one of which Beethoven knew something, as the Sketch-books bear eloquent witness). Other symptoms besides the above-mentioned, are clearly physical results due to activity in the various *chakras* which are situate just outside the surface of the physical body as already described, opposite (1) the base of the spine, (2) the solar plexus, (3) the spleen, (4) the heart, (5) the throat, (6) the point between the eyebrows, (7) the top of the head. The poet is aware of the activity of the fifth which causes in him a ' constriction

---

[1] Almost Galsworthy's very words (p. 203) ' nothing in my head.'

[2] He surely means unaccountable by any physical-plane cause. The ideation from a ' higher ' source impinging upon his emotion-body on its way through to the brain, of course stirs the emotions ; and powerfully.

[3] ' On one's technique,' as we musicians say.

of the throat': also of the sixth which causes a 'precipitation of water to the eyes.' But, for some reason upon which I am unable to throw any light, he appears to be quite uncomfortably aware of activity at the solar plexus. (This is a symptom not unknown to nervous soloists before making their bow). When he is inspired it appears to him, ' so far as he can make out,' that " the source of the suggestions thus proffered to the brain, is an abyss which I have already had occasion to mention, the pit of the stomach." His consciousness can free itself from brain and intellect and contact more remote states, but apparently has difficulty in completely inhibiting the intrusion of vibrations from the physical body. Briefly, he is aware, when in his poetic ' raptus,' of the activity of the solar plexus *chakra*. He permits this to lead him to the conclusion that " Poetry indeed seems to me more physical than intellectual." Which may be true in the light of the above explanation. What may also be true, is, that it is more spiritual than either intellectual or physical.

The following self-analysis is given by Berlioz with reference to the effect of music upon his own highly organized and uncommonly sensitive nature: " My whole being seems to vibrate; at first it is a delightful pleasure, in which reason does not appear to participate at all," *i.e.*, the first effects are sensuous; physical. " The emotions increase in direct ratio with the power and grandeur of the composer's ideations, and, by degrees produce a strange agitation in the circulatory system; the pulse beats violently; tears, usually giving evidence of the crisis of a paroxysm, indicate only a progressive stage and greater agitation to follow. When the crisis is really reached there occur spasmodic contractions of the muscles, a trembling in all the limbs, a total

Of Mysticism and Mystical Inspiration

numbness of the feet and hands," (*i.e.*, the 'prâna'[1] is leaving the physical body) "and there is a partial paralysis of the nerves of vision and hearing" (*i.e.*, the *consciousness* is being detached from the physical senses and what is properly described as a psychic condition is beginning to supervene).

Wagner speaks of "an internal sense which becomes clear and active when all the other senses, directed outward, sleep or dream. It is precisely when I no longer see or hear anything distinctly that this sense is the most active and appears before me as the producer of calm; I can give it no other term." This 'calm' for which Wagner can find 'no other term' is a condition well known to mystics of all ages and lands and was probably familiar to Wagner's mentor Schopenhauer through his studies in ancient Sanskrit literature. Here the several varieties of this 'calm' are explored and expounded under the terms Dhyana and Samadhi.[2]

Upon so little explored and yet so vitally important a branch of our study it may be well, even at some risk of arousing the ire of the sceptic and the irrision of the *blasé*, to particularize still more clearly. There is the case of a fairly well-known composer whose physical body had been brought to a rare state of sensitivity by a thirteen-year period of clean dieting and abstention from alcohol, and a long course of training in stilling the mind,[3] inhibiting the intrusion of outside thoughts[4] and many other technical

---

[1] 'Prâna' is usually translated 'life-energy.' See footnote, p. 112.

[2] Cf. also p. 313.

[3] How many of us can still the mind at will and hold it poised and yet keenly active? (like a top spinning so rapidly that it 'sleeps').

[4] How many of us can hold a single concept in the mind for one minute, thirty seconds, ten seconds even, without it straying about all over the place like a peripatetic monkey?

practices. These, whilst much less protracted than had been his technical musical studies (*i.e.*, of harmony, counterpoint, composition, orchestration and the like), resulted eventually in endowing him with a measure of clair-voyance and clair-audience. (Clair-sentience would be a more accurate description, because contact is not achieved by use of differentiated senses as upon this plane of diversity; rather the whole being is 'aware of' the contacts.) His studies also put him in possession of a fact which is of great interest in the world of music; namely, that as the whole of the manifested world is constituted of matter of varying degrees of density, vibrating at varying speeds, the whole of this matter—demonstrably that which is physical—is amenable to the range of vibrations which we call sound. Shortly; that every physical object has a basic sound—a keynote as it were—to which it responds automatically. Further and corollarily, that every human body possesses a 'keynote': not only this, but that each of the *chakras* corresponding to the nerve plexuses or centres of the physical body, also responds to a musical vibration-rate. 'By accident,' as we say, he discovered the *order* in which his own *chakra* 'notes' were arranged (the order varying in each individual case), and was in the happy position therefore of being able to harmonize his body by the projection and application of the appropriate sounds, by singing them, to the corresponding centres in his body. He possesses the faculty known as 'fixed pitch,' and it is perhaps worth noting that, when in the clair-audient state, he always hears all 'inner' music at an invariable pitch which he is constrained to describe as 'Nature'-Pitch.[1]

[1] At this pitch, by the way, music seems to be immensely more potent than at our normal pitch. Cf. also p. 347.

Of Mysticism and Mystical Inspiration

The physical body in tune, he follows the sounds as it were into the inner realms *without losing consciousness*. He is now aware of multitudes of collateral phenomena, some of them of the most arresting and fascinating nature, but as he is first and foremost a composer of music, he concentrates one-pointedly upon that and cognate matters. So far removed is this from the invertebrate mediumistic trance-condition so often described, that the brain, far from abdicating its throne, is functioning at a high degree of activity. A condition of ice-cold efficiency as of the brain standing to attention with its mass of data, recollections, and experiences, immediately available for reference and illustration—this is the prevailing condition *so far as the brain is concerned*.

It is fatal at this stage for the brain to be allowed to initiate or intrude any critical or ratiocinative operations whatever. The time for work of this type, extremely important, indeed invaluable as it is, comes later.

Many a potentially valuable ideation has been lost to this composer in the past through lack of knowledge on this important point. It is but one illustration of our ignorance of the rationale of inspiration.

The artist is now in a state of positive-negativity, that is, he is positive to impacts from 'below' (inhibiting all but the most insistent physical sense-impacts, for example), but negative to impressions from 'above.'

According to many conditions will depend the 'height' to which he can raise his consciousness, the length of contact he can maintain, and the accuracy with which he can bring across undistorted into his brain the vibrations he is contacting. Anything which throws out of alignment the 'bodies' between (and including) that in which he is making contact and the physical in which he is recording such contact (*i.e.*, his brain), will almost immediately sever the connection and cut off communication.

As may readily be imagined, questions of health, circumstance, immediate environment and a thousand others affect this operation, which, whether you like the word or no, is one of elementary magic.

At this stage, his whole being is keyed up to the nth degree; his brain is on the *qui vive*; and his consciousness is free to penetrate, so far as it have power, into the wonders of the Spiritual plane, the ineffable glories of the Buddhic (intuitional), the marvels of the Causal world in which inheres all knowledge—in which time and space are not, but all of past, present and future, as well as far and near, are available in a great Here and Now—and the unspeakably moving vibrations of the Emotion (astral) world whence has emanated almost the whole of our modern music.

It is now, in his attempt to record some of his contacts in music, that your artist, be he never so self-sufficient in his everyday attitude, will pray for the polyphonic mastery of a Bach, the dramatic-logic of a Beethoven, the unifying force of a Wagner, the ethereal purity of a Palestrina, the inner refulgence of a Scriabin—yea, and the wide-embracing tunefulness of a Verdi and a Puccini, the poignant harmonic *nuances* of a Debussy, perhaps even the deva-touch of a Grieg, a Delius, a Sibelius—all these, all their technical mastery and more, will he need faintly to shadow forth even a distant echo of the wonders that have been revealed to him.

For in the state to which he has now attained, emotion, resulting in and from an alchemical change powerfully impinging upon the sympathetic-nervous system, is (though the normal) by no means an adequate vehicle by which to

Of Mysticism and Mystical Inspiration

express the contacts he is making. He is now aware of the white-hot therefore ice-cold crystallization of ideas through the *Brahmarandra*.[1] Cold airs circulate through his aura. An indescribable sensation results from the vivid activities of pituitary body and pineal gland (those supposedly atrophied or moribund ducts; ducts of what we know not, nor whence they lead). For in this region of his aura unsought ideations as it were, distil like beads of dew upon his mind.

In bringing over into the brain and setting down even in the veriest sketch some record of such experiences, an extraordinary degree of concentration is required. The operation of converting a single synthetic vibration—an ideation, that is to say, that seems upon contact to be one and indivisible—into a physical-plane expression, involving as it does the factors of time and space, is one requiring the utmost delicacy, positivity, steadiness and skill. The idea has to be, as it were, spread out in physical terms, and an ideation contacted and cognized in an instant, complete and perfect, may well occupy an hour or more, when unrolled upon the physical plane even as concisely and tersely as possible. The experience is one not unknown to the writer, and this and collateral experiences, experiments and studies relating to the rationale of inspiration appear to him of such importance that he cannot tacitly agree to their utter neglect.

Examining myself—which is perhaps the honestest method of trying to add to the available data—I can say that a good deal of my stuff has come into existence in the way described above; and although we cannot assume that

---

[1] *Brahmarandra.* The *chakra,* or centre in the aura, situated over the top of the head. The 'thousand-petalled lotus' of Sanskrit mystical literature.

any other music has been brought through in exactly the same way, yet, upon studying the subject closely we may well find reason to believe that a good deal of it has, whether consciously or subconsciously.

This book is no pandect of occultism, no treatise of the rationale of inspiration—not even of the small branch of it which affects so profoundly the art of music, and we cannot go more deeply into the subject here. It must suffice if our ' modern instances ' have, in however small a degree, caught the attention of the reader. For there be those who deny that behind the panoply of the sound-art is anywhat at all of inner import, of soul-substance, who assert that the be-all and end-all of music is a mere sound and rhythm pattern, an unsubstantial mirage, a local and ephemeral vortex of no provable causation and of briefest effect; an imponderable ripple that appears out of Nothingness, for a moment troubles the air, and . . . is gone.

It cannot be so.

Listen to the *Amor quando floria* of Palestrina; listen to the *Mass* of Bach; to the *Coriolanus* of Beethoven, the *Sanctus* of Berlioz, the *Schicksalslied* of Brahms, the *Charfreitagzauber* of Wagner; Scriabin's *Prometheus*, Delius' *Song of the High Hills*; listen to any great musician whose heart is uplifted, and then ask: " Is it possible that that inexhaustible evolution and disposition of notes, so rich and yet so simple, so intricate yet so regulated, so varied yet so majestic, should be a mere sound which is gone and perishes? Can it be that those mysterious stirrings of the heart, and keen emotions, and strange yearnings after we know not what, and awful impressions from we know not whence, should be wrought in us by what is unsubstantial, and comes and goes, and begins and ends in it-

Conclusions of Part Three

self? It is not so: it cannot be. No: they have escaped from some higher sphere: they are the outpourings of eternal harmony in the medium of expressed sound: they are echoes from our Home: they are the voice of the Angels, or the Magnificat of Saints, or the living laws of Divine Governance, or the Divine Attributes: something are they besides themselves, which we cannot compass, which we cannot utter—though mortal man . . . has the gift of eliciting them " (J. H. Newman).

§ 8. CONCLUSIONS OF PART THREE

To sum up this Third Part of our studies: we have adopted, for the sake of reducing to some degree of order a branch of musical study which is in a state of pitiable nebulosity, an extremely ancient table which presents the idea of seven interpenetrating spheres related to and including the physical, and of the states of consciousness by which Man may contact and investigate the five 'lower' of these realms. In the light of this we have been able to indicate to a certain extent the main types of vibration which emanate from these differing realms: to assert that a vibration or series of vibrations of creative potency may (according to certain circumstances) be 'tapped,' so to say, at any level between 'highest' and 'lowest': to define Genius: to bring forward a theory of the ensouling of music whose practical importance to both creative and interpretative musicians appears to be real.

By a sort of eliminatory process—examining the qualities of Vitality, Beauty, Idealism, Purity, Individuality and Originality, and Spirituality—we gradually arrived at a definition of what is noblest and most sublime in music.

Music To-day

We further linked these qualities with the spheres in which they take inception.

In order to *real*-ize still further in our minds these inner realms and the states of consciousness in which they are contacted, we quoted first-hand reports by a number of writers, and clearly laid bare some of the processes by which such contacts are brought over into the brain and externalized.

We may now proceed to study from this angle as well as from a purely technical one, some of the foremost composers of our time.

PART FOUR
MODERN MASTERS AT WORK

Chapter Twelve: Generalities

Obiter Dicta—Nationality in Music—Impressionistic, Post-Romantic, Neo-Classicist, Verist, Expressionist, etc.

§ 1. OBITER DICTA

Having in some sort reviewed the field of music in our day, and having attempted to arrange our ideas of a musical æsthetic in a system of such clarity that it may (without pretending to be exhaustive), be applied to all or any music; we may now devote ourselves to a consideration of the work of some outstanding composers of this epoch—a series of swift vignettes; no more.

It would be interesting to attempt an evaluation of the works of the accepted masters of the past in the light of our suggested æsthetic. We are concerned here, however, with music and musicians of to-day.

This section comprising as it does only some forty or so names, makes no sort of claim to completeness. As the vast majority of books on music concern themselves entirely with the lives and works of various composers, however, no reader need suffer any lack of special personal information, if that is what he desires. No great believer myself in the possibility of teaching anybody *what* to think (though a study of Logic—which surely ought to be an early and compulsory study in our schools—might help us *how* to), I assume no magistral attitude and attempt no final placement of any composer under consideration. Rather, I offer a few sketches, mere *obiter dicta*, along lines which bear some relation to the scheme outlined in our Third Part. In doing so we not only reduce to some degree of order our estimates of the few contemporaries mentioned herein, but we enable any reader who can accept our outline of a musical æsthetic as a working hypothesis, to arrange his own ideas regarding other composers and marshal his reactions to all the music he hears in some sort of broad categorical order, a 'consummation devoutly to be wished.'

§ 2. NATIONALITY IN MUSIC

The various composers considered here are not grouped under national headings. For the characteristics of nationality affect only those ideas of a composer which emanate from certain not very lofty levels,[1] and the source of all our music of lasting value lies beyond this. No listener of perception can hear much of the music written by our modernists without realizing too that the musical world, since the advent of gramophone and radio, has rapidly become supernational to a greater extent than ever before: that though in their technique one may notice nationalistic differences between Italian and German composers; Hungarian and Belgian; Russian and English, and so on; yet there is an increasing similarity in the thought-stuff itself of composers of all nationalities. If one thinks of the differences in actual basic musical thought (apart from its manner of presentation), of the contemporaries Wagner and Verdi, of Humperdinck and Puccini, of Beethoven and Piccini, Sullivan and

---

[1] Glance at the diagram on p. 159 and consider that national characteristics properly so called, are connected only with the lower triad; any idea which emanates from a higher source being necessarily, *qua* idea, devoid of mere nationality.

Nationality in Music

Planquette, Grieg and Leoncavallo, Berlioz and Schumann; and then compares the salient basic musical matter (not its handling) of four-fifths of present-day composers, the question answers itself. We have already noticed in considering Atonality, how strikingly similar are works employing this idiom by French, German, English, Russian, Italian, Belgian, Greek, American, Spanish, Indian, and other composers, and we can plainly see that the narrow nationalistic barriers are quickly disappearing. Opinions vary as to whether this is a sign of progress or decadence. It will be gathered from our previous studies that I cannot think it other than the former.

Controversy on this question of Nationality in music has raged backward and forward for years. And not alone in this country. The protagonists of Nationalism preach salvation as attainable only along this road, and they would base an exclusive school of musical composition upon their country's folk-song. To this type belong Cecil Sharp, Vaughan Williams and several other important musicians, to speak only of this country. The opponents of such a restricted and localized point of view declare[1] that " only out of a new realization of world-wide solidarity—even sodality—can the real music of the future be born."

But the reconciliation of these divergent views and the extraction of something of real value from them is an impossibility so long as we remain in ignorance of what 'nationalism' in this connection really means. This is clearly the state in which both parties to the discussion remain, and unless and until some light be thrown upon such ignorance, all discussion must remain largely a waste of breath and paper. Yet the vitality of the controversy

[1] Cf. p. 18.

and the persistence with which it is revived from time to time would seem to indicate the existence of an underlying truth, for which we might do well to probe.

Ethnological studies—considerations of Nordic, Alpine and Mediterranean derivations—questions of language, environment, heredity and similar lines of research, while interesting and indeed engrossing from a certain point of view, throw no light whatever upon the broader issue. And the discussion might go on indefinitely, emphatic statement on the one side, contemptuous denial upon the other, with nothing but a somewhat naïve personal preference at the bottom of both; and even this expressed in terms of loose generalizations.

This very vexed question resolves itself with consummate ease if we regard it from the viewpoint indicated in a previous section.[1] And once this viewpoint is accepted the two main aspects of nationality in music (that of folk-music and the folk-idiom upon the one side, and the more subtle and involved one of personal style—due to birth, antecedents, racial heredity, environment and so on—upon the other), fall into their respective places and assume their proper proportions in a perfectly intelligible and natural way.

Folk-music bears a relation to the art of music analogous to that which local dialect bears to a language; and just as local dialects are dying out under modern conditions of life, so is localized folk-music. As music is not a national, but a universal language it follows that its ' dialects ' (to continue our analogy) will be less narrowly confined than those of a national language. Thus you find similarities between Keltic and Teutonic folk-music; Scandinavian and, say,

[1] Cf. p. 159 *et seq.*

Nationality in Music

African; Irish and Indian; North American Indian (Appalachian) and, for example, Hebridean, which many have found impossible of reconciliation by the usual methods of research.

Ethnological considerations have always failed and always must fail to explain those phenomena whose place of inception is far removed from mundane realms, upon the ' higher ' mental, the intuitional, and the spiritual planes of Nature. These are realms of Unity; of Archetypes and universal Ideations which are the same for all, of whatever nationality, who can contact them.

In bringing through these ideas for statement in physical-plane terms as music, they become coloured by the personality of the composer—his ' lower ' manas, emotional nature, and physical characteristics (as nervous sensibility, power of concentration, brain control, and so on; these in their turn depending on racial and personal heredity, environment,[1] etc.), and it is here that a consideration of the second aspect applies. Many composers who have no fondness for folk-music, who may indeed admit an aversion from it, are nevertheless spoken of as typical of some one or other nationality by virtue of the fact that their personal idiom shows characteristic national traits.

When one speaks of the greatest music and composers as transcending narrow nationalistic boundaries one is sometimes met by such arguments as this: " Could anything be more French than Berlioz, more German than Beethoven, more Italian than Verdi? " Of course it could; particularly so as regards ideas. Hear Weismann on a sudden leap forward in Berlioz' art: " Berlioz needed just this experience [acquaintance with Beethoven's symphonies] to lift him

---

[1] Also, if you admit the idea, previous incarnations.

above his racial limitations." It is all very well for Vaughan Williams to scoff at those musicians who profess in their art what he calls a 'backboneless cosmopolitanism,' and to instance Wagner's *Meistersinger* as his greatest work because it was his most German one in its philosophy. If, for you, it is as great as *Tristan*, that is simply because the ideas are as great. If, as for many, *Tristan* is the greater work, the argument falls to the ground. For neither in its plot, setting nor music, is there a hint of anything German or even Teutonic, save those unavoidable personal traits of idiom and the like, the reason for the presence of which has already been explained above.

No 'backboneless cosmopolitanism' for me, but also, and equally emphatically, no 'little Englander' music either. English music in the main has been of little or no effect abroad because—as E. J. Dent says somewhere or other—" it has been the wrong kind of English music, because it was composed for purely English audiences;" and again, *à propos* certain 'Victorian' composers of this country, that they never get "entirely away from the atmosphere of pale cultured idealism, and the unconsciously hypocritical, self-righteous, complacent, Pharisaical gentlemanliness which is so characteristic of British art in the last century."

It is just because so many of our composers have responded to the English national vibration that they have done so little work which may be described as universal. No creative artist who cannot transcend the levels at which (up to which) *nationality* manifests, can be capable of work of *universal* appeal. It is nothing to the point that, " such as Byron, Shelley, Landor, Delius, have passed the greater part of their actively creative life abroad." Palestrina lived the greater part of his creative life in Rome, Beethoven in

Nationality in Music

Vienna, Shakespeare in England. It is, I repeat, the consciousness ranging worlds far beyond those of nationality, and the possession of a technique able to express the contacts made in such exalted states that alone constitute the great creative artist.

Once this point is apprehended we may readily admit that a 'change of air' in the sense in which a doctor would use the phrase, is a good thing; loosens the aura; aerates the faculties. But it no more gives the power to raise the consciousness to realms whence 'greatness' emanates than long-continued residence in Soho or Lambeth robs a Blake of the power to do so.

Upon the question of the musicality or otherwise of the English, it may be worth remarking that our viewpoint again helps toward a solution. They are often alluded to, particularly in the Latin countries, as unmusical. It is easy to see what is meant. As has often been pointed out in these pages, almost all the music composed since Palestrina has addressed itself from and to the emotional part of man's make-up. Those nations, therefore, which respond most swiftly to emotional stimulus are regarded as the most musical. It was always a superficial categorization, and, as music in the future enlarges its range of appeal to include other than emotional fields of inception and application, it will appear to be more and more superficial; therefore less and less really true. Already in 1929, Suzanne Demarquez wrote in the *Revue Musicale*: " Though we (French) do not believe it, we are immovable conservatives. . . . Having made up our minds once for all that an Anglo-Saxon cannot be a creative musician, we pay no attention to the very real renaissance that has taken place among our neighbours in the past twenty years."

Music To-day

§ 3. IMPRESSIONISTIC, POST-ROMANTIC, NEO-CLASSICIST, VERIST, EXPRESSIONIST, ETC.

Nor shall we group our composers in categories such as Impressionistic, Post-Romantic, Neo-Classicist, Verist and so forth.

In certain musical circles to-day a tremendous fuss and pother is made about labelling the various types of work. A word that looms large in such circles is 'Expressionism.' It is used not only of music and poetry but of the plastic arts also. Reams of near-metaphysical descriptions and discussions are written about it—especially in Germany the land of its birth. And what does it all amount to? Just this: that the artist is attempting to give you, in the terms of his art, not the physical-plane appearance, but the inner vibration he has contacted. This may be a noteworthy step in the arts of painting and sculpture, and also perhaps in a lesser degree, in poetry. Music, however, has always attempted to do this and therefore the word as applied to a modern tendency in music is a redundancy. Music has always been an Expressionist art.

It is true that occasionally musicians have paraphrased physical sounds. This has always been rare however, and when a Beethoven does it his apologists pray our indulgence for the master's 'little joke': when Mussolov and Honegger do it they emphasize, in the modern way, psychological reactions also. In a word they too, like all the rest of us, are 'expressionists.'

In this matter I am in agreement with Stravinsky who says: "Characteristic of musical art in our time are the numbers of catchwords used to denote different symptoms and axioms of style, such as the 'realistic school.' One can

Impressionistic, Post-romantic, Neo-Classicist

see, however, that these slogans, intellectual as they may sound, will hardly have any lasting recognition, as the right names for present-day styles belong to the musical historians and critics of the future." Moreover, in many cases a composer properly belongs in several categories,[1] and redundancy and repetition seem bound to occur. A better method which, though looser will be more consistent, is to note their characteristic technical traits and purely personal idioms, their response to nationality, heredity and environment, but more particularly in what degree they are able to penetrate to those regions, and retranslate to us in their works those states of consciousness discussed in the Third Part of our studies.

[1] Béla Bartók, for instance, could be regarded as 'Nationalist,' 'Neo-Classicist,' 'Neo-Romantic,' or Anti-Romantic.'

CHAPTER THIRTEEN: A SERIES OF SWIFT VIGNETTES

*Strauss—Elgar—Stravinsky—Reger—Busoni—Ravel—
Wolf—Schönberg—Bartók—Kodály—Falla—Hinde-
mith—Honegger—Milhaud—Poulenc—Szymanovski—
A German Group—An American Group—A French
Group—An English Group—An Italian Group.*

AMAZING fecundity of invention characterizes the work of RICHARD STRAUSS (German; born 1864). He is as proliferous as a Balzac. Generous of melody; prodigal of new-minted harmonies; dexterous and adroit—occasionally over-multilinear—in polyphony;[1] superbly master of his favourite instrument, the orchestra; often verbose, occasionally terse; richly opulent in sheer musicianship; Teuton in weight of brain and in thoroughness of workmanship; Latin in a certain fiery-witty-nimble quality of the mind; I count him to be, all in all, the biggest figure *in musical achievement* of the period which saw the end of the former dispensation, the revolution, and the dawn of the new era. His influence upon the musical world from about the year 1890 to the present day, has been prodigious.

During the period from about 1886 (*Aus Italien*) when

[1] For example, I well remember studying with Hans Richter the new work *Ein Heldenleben* and how the great conductor remarked (à *propos* the section apotheosizing the Hero's—that is, Strauss' own—works, in which the composer forces together no fewer than twenty-four musical quotations from his previous composition in a perfect welter of polyphony): "Anyone can write prodigious counterpoints if he doesn't care *how they will sound.*" The two-fold point of which is that the conductor did not comprehend polytonality, and that the composer has written, on occasion, a closer web of polyphony than any human ear at our present stage of evolution can possibly disentangle.

A Series of Swift Vignettes

his technique was, so to say, of Mendelssohn-Schumann type, to 1909 (*Salome*) when his equipment was far more complete than that of any other composer, his growth was formidable. He freed himself entirely from the old key-consciousness. When it suited his purpose he became polytonal or atonal with ease. He increased his command of orchestration in a superlative degree, and in a highly personal way. His resource and suppleness in the development of his ideas within self-imposed forms became admirably lucent. His productivity has been immense. And in the fields of Symphonic Poem (*Don Juan; Tod und Verklärung; Till Eulenspiegel; Also Sprach Zarathustra; Don Quixote; Ein Heldenleben*); and Music Drama (*Salome; Elektra; Rosenkavalier; Intermezzo; Die Frau ohne Schatten*): he has created veritable wonderworks and given enormous delight to millions.

The *crescendo* of his powers is quite clearly traceable up to and including *Elektra*; and sheaves of paper and gallons of ink have been consumed by various learned musicologists in their efforts to explain why and how it came about that from this time a rapid decline in his powers manifested itself. Even a cursory acquaintance with his works dating after this period undoubtedly confirms the fact of this rapid and almost total eclipse of his genius. It is as clearly to be noticed in his ideations as in his technique. More than once this has been somewhat naïvely summed up in the phrase " he had not sufficient genius," but it may be possible to suggest an explanation which is a little more illuminating than that.

There is abundant evidence in his work up to and including *Elektra* of astonishing virility; of sheer brainpower. And the story that has been going the rounds for

Music To-day

years quoting his assertion that music ought to be able to depict a spoon in perfectly clearly recognizable terms, is an infallible indication, especially when coupled with the many essays in a similar direction contained in his works, that he has his feet very firmly planted on the earth. In every work of that period you may find proof that he also ranges almost all sub-levels of the emotional realm with consummate mastery and, what is equally important, has a means ready at hand fully capable of interpreting his feelings to us. The sensuous beauty of his exotic moments such as the 'Anna' episode in *Don Juan*, the discourse upon the profession of knight-errantry in *Don Quixote*, and the love-song in *Heldenleben*, has perhaps never been surpassed and rarely so well expressed. The portentous, the awe-inspiring (as at the beginning of *Tod und Verklärung*); the sardonic, the witty or the merely vulgar, the robust, energetic,[1] the egocentric (as in *Heldenleben*); the joyous, merry, gay (*Till Eulenspiegel, Zarathustra, Rosenkavalier*); the strangely haunting, perhaps morbid, sensually erotic (as in *Salome* and *Elektra*); all these and many more subtleties of the realms of emotion are well within reach of his consciousness, and so well within his powers of expression that he can readily re-evoke similar vibrations in millions of listeners. It is perfectly true, and quite easy to understand how 'young' Germany—that of Hindemith, Krěnek, Schreker—finds his art with all its opulent lusciousness unsympathetic to it, even old-fashioned. But that is another matter, and one which is relevant rather to an historical survey than to an evaluation of the master's own work.

One may detect here and there glimpses of the 'higher' mental realm. One such he struggles hard to convey to us

[1] Cf. musical examples, pp. 82, 83.

A Series of Swift Vignettes

in the 'Von der Wissenschaft' section of *Zarathustra*—and fails. I believe he was able by a very great effort to project his consciousness just so far and for a brief space of time. In spite of his exceptionally well-furnished technique he fails to give us an even approximately adequate transcription of such an experience. Beyond that realm, it is my settled conviction, he has never penetrated. His efforts to do so, and to touch the Intuitional and Spiritual realms would almost certainly have borne better fruit had they been successful. For I believe his technique would have proved capable of growing commensurately with the higher demand made upon it.

To what cause then can we reasonably assign the rapid diminution of his powers? Remember that the Will is man's dynamic; that where the will is focussed, is concentrated one-pointedly and directed undeviatingly to an end, results more or less great and strictly in proportion to the power of will employed and the degree of concentration attained to, are bound to follow. Apply this observation to the case of Strauss. Recall to mind his own famous pronouncement regarding his aims and ideals, and it is neither an exaggeration nor an unwarranted intrusion into his private affairs to say that in the early 'fifties'—the 'dangerous age' for creative artists—he struck his flag; he, the prosperous, the popular and the world-widely celebrated. In doing so we shall be able to formulate an answer to our question. In the phrase of Talleyrand "a married man will do anything for money." Many persons would say that so he ought; and to have chosen as he did was Strauss' own affair, or at widest, one between him and his dæmon. We shall not pry into it. But we cannot fail to notice that almost from that fateful moment a rapid decline set in, his ideas deteriorated to the point of banality, his technique also. Even his most ardent followers can have no further hopes of anything of real value from his lifeless pen, and only the faintest trace can be descried in his latest opera *Arabella* of the once virile, often beautiful, occasionally aspiring and even inspiring figure they erst had loved.

But even so, surely none of the millions who have experienced delight and joy by contact with his work will think with less than real gratitude of Richard Strauss.

Occupying a somewhat similar position in English music as does Strauss in German, is EDWARD ELGAR (English; born 1857). Consider for a moment, however, the difference in worldly environment between them. The German recognized, encouraged, perhaps pampered but at least never starved of the pabulum which every creative artist needs in greater or lesser degree; and already at the age of twenty-four (*Don Juan*) or twenty-five (*Tod und Verklärung*) an arrived and —in a comparatively wide sense—an accepted master. The Englishman failing at thirty-two to make any real impression on the London musical world and retiring to the country temporarily checked.[1] The story of his first success at forty-two with his *Enigma* variations, and, at forty-three the production of *Gerontius* (which was not 'accepted' until two years later Strauss had made a public gesture of appreciation at a performance in Germany [2]), is one of

[1] There is perhaps a recollection of these difficulties in a letter he sent to the present writer in 1904. *A propos* of a large-scale choral work, *The Vision of Dante*, the score of which Elgar had asked to see, he wrote, after certain appreciative remarks: "It is a work of festival dimensions and scope. Don't you know anyone of power on any of the committees? It is very difficult to get in without influence."

[2] In the words: "I raise my glass to the welfare and success of the First English Progressivist, and the young school of progressive English composers."

which this country cannot be proud. Some will argue that the difference arises because the genius of Elgar developed later in life than that of Strauss. Of course it did. And it is not in the least due to our encouragement but to some godlike quality in the man's own make-up that it ever developed at all. We cannot sidestep our responsibility in these matters, leaving such things to chance or to the individual's *karma*[1] to put right. It is our common human duty to foster genius when we meet it and if our studies assist us in however small a degree to recognize true gifts when they are displayed to us, they will have been abundantly worth while.

Almost every theme and every bar of his orchestration bears the hall-mark of Elgar's personality. They are recognizable instantly as his. You may, or may not like them, but the man behind them is always clearly discernible. So far as characterization of melody and theme are concerned he is definitely more ' original ' in his utterances than Strauss. His orchestration, whilst deeply thoughtful and indeed masterly, is nothing like so bold or varied, nor does it cover anything like so wide a range as that of Strauss. His counterpoint is also masterly though often quaintly angular.[2] His harmonic sense is curiously restricted. Indeed it is far less evolved than, for example, that of Franck who was thirty-five years his senior; while comparison with Debussy who, but five years junior to him died in 1918, would be ludicrous. And I am convinced, after hearing many tenta-

[1] Colloquially—Fate; Kismet; reaping as we have sown.
[2] A French musician of eminence and wide culture to whom I was showing certain Elgar works in Paris, continued to play over some of the salient melodies for a while. Many of these, as everyone knows, contain melodic phrases having intervals of the seventh prominently displayed (for example, the slow variation in the *Enigma Variations*). " Eh bien ! " commented our friend, " il est vraiment un ' Angular Saxon,' n'est ce pas ? "

Music To-day

tive efforts to 'popularize' his music abroad, that this paucity of creative energy along harmonic lines is the chief technical reason for his lack of recognition among certain continental nations. For, be it remembered, it is principally along lines of harmonic freedom that the 'revolution' we have witnessed since the beginning of the present century has shown itself. Of course, harmonic originality is not extraordinarily valuable in itself, but as an indication of the depth and penetration of a composer's creative energy it is just as important as originality of melodic idiom or orchestral colouring, both of which Elgar possesses in abundance.

He has never grown to the point of accepting Polytonality—much less Atonality.

The charge of 'intrinsic vulgarity' recently brought against him rests upon two foundations. First, his admittedly 'light' pieces of the *Salut d'Amour* genre, about which, as also about the 'light' music of Bach, Beethoven, Brahms and others we have already had something to say.[1] To have written such pieces is no more an indication of essential vulgarity of character in the man, than are Bach's jigs and gavottes, Beethoven's German and Scottish dances, Schubert's waltzes or Smetana's polkas, and vulgarity—in the common use of the word—is hardly a charge we should bring against them. The second reason for the charge rests upon his imperialistic, flag-flapping, Kiplingesque efforts like the *Banner of Saint George*, and the *Pomp and Circumstance* marches containing the egregious 'Land of Hope and Glory.'[2] This again is

---

[1] Cf. PART Two, Chapter IX, Section 2, p. 127.
[2] One of the earliest performances of this march was given by Hans Richter, the members of whose orchestra were appalled by the principal tune and clearly showed it at rehearsal. "Gentlemen," he beseeched them, "let us play zis melody *werry slow*, it will not sound so wulgar."

A Series of Swift Vignettes

no more 'vulgar' than Bartók's *Kossuth* or Sibelius' *Finlandia*. Our minds—our English minds especially—are full of cant in this and allied matters. Those who dote sentimentally upon the 'English'-ness of Elgar's idiom must not at the same time blame him for using it in praise of England. They cannot have it and not have it. What will be clear to readers is that these partisans are really feeling that one aspect of nationality (cf. its dual aspects on page 222) as shown in his music, annoys them, whereas the other aspect, that of his much more subtle and characteristically personal type of expression delights them. The truth of the matter, from the viewpoint adopted in this book, will have been divined ere this, *i.e.*, that mere nationalism in art is essentially vulgar, and that only those artists who can transcend nationalism and reach universal levels can create work of real and permanent value.

Has Elgar been able to do this? If one is unable to say that he has created any single work of extended scope that fulfils this description throughout, there exist many episodes in his works which undoubtedly do so. If we yearn for complete and utter perfection, that is our natural right as 'sparks of the divine' ourselves, but none has ever as yet achieved it in this world of the ubiquitous 'pairs of opposites.' For us there exist spots even upon the Sun itself.

The Variations for orchestra (*Enigma*) and the two Symphonies, are his most valuable purely orchestral works. The Violin Concerto—with the passage-work of which Kreisler had more to do than is generally known—is superb, and no higher praise could be bestowed upon it than to say that it stands worthily beside those of Beethoven, Mendelssohn and Brahms.

His chamber works are in every way less striking.

Music To-day

Lacking the stimulus of the orchestral colours (his introduction to which he owed to Berlioz' immensely inspiring *Grand Traité d'instrumentation et d'orchestration modernes*), his ideas in themselves seem to be less valuable.

Closely associated with the first performances of *Gerontius*, the first Symphony, *The Apostles*, *The Kingdom*, *Falstaff* and other works, the writer can vouch that each production brought its own thrill to participants, audience, and critics alike. But this was not the thrill that arises when ' new worlds ' are ' brought into our ken.' It was largely that of pride in an Englishman who had been admired ' abroad,' admiration of his undoubted skill, and, more than anything else (so far at any rate as the oratorios are concerned), a wallowing in that type of religiosity which still abides in a large majority of those who congregate at places where they festival. Each occasion was what the French call a solemnity.

If *Gerontius* and the other oratorios, as must often have been remarked, owe a great deal to Wagner for their use of Leading Motifs, and particularly to *Parsifal* for their expression of the mystical, also to Franck for certain still more tangible traits, certainly *Falstaff* exists by reason of Strauss' Symphonic Poems, which in their turn, of course, derive from Liszt and Berlioz. *Falstaff* is counted a comparative failure however, and mention of Berlioz leads to a comparison between it and the *Symphonie Fantastique*. As a youth I heard an illuminating rendition of this masterpiece by Hallé who had studied it with the composer, and I experienced no difficulty at all in following the various sections with their few but cogent headings. *Falstaff* always seems to need too great concentration on the literary allusions to leave the hearers' consciousness sufficiently free for the music. I have watched them carefully with this

A Series of Swift Vignettes

question in mind. Perhaps the same criticism could be made of parts of Berlioz' *Romeo et Juliet* symphony, but, to the faithful, the gorgeous beauty of the Love Scene and the Queen Mab Scherzo more than compensates. Elgar admirers might well say the same of some of the delightful episodes in *Falstaff*.

And certainly there are in Elgar's works many things of great beauty; things that, if they die, will die hard.

Just as in the case of Debussy and *L'Après-midi d'un Faune*, we have in *Le Sacre du Printemps* of IGOR STRAVINSKY (Russian; born 1882) a single work of epoch-indicating character. This amazing piece of ballet-music created, or rather provoked, a *furore* unprecedented in modern times in every European and American capital where it was given as originally conceived—wedded to a Diaghilev ballet. This work was afterwards offered in the concert-room as a symphonic, *i.e.*, purely musical, item. I must confess to being one of those who cannot accept it in this form. A good deal less justification can be offered for importing it into the concert-room than for doing the like by opera-excerpts. Its origin seems to me to be in those mysterious and Pan-like kingdoms of nature which, in our present stage of evolution, lie beneath the normal consciousness of the human.[1]

In the incredibly far-off past the link between animal and human kingdoms was closer than is now the case. Memories of this bygone age still inhere in human consciousness however, and it is conceivable that just such scenes as are portrayed in this ballet might then have been enacted. When divorced from its representational half the

[1] Cf. musical example, p. 82, *Évocation des Ancêtres*.

Music To-day

music fails to evoke for most of us these race-memories which, in any case, are far below the surface of our normal waking consciousness.

On its technical side the music is astounding; harmony, orchestration, rhythm alike, being of a potency previously untouched and never reached by Stravinsky either before or since.

In many of his earlier works he makes free use of characteristically Russian folk-tunes or their derivatives and very well they have served him. For the novel *quasi*-oriental types of melody furnished him with a focus-point around which to construct his ingenious, engaging, witty and eloquent *pasticcios*. It is the best we can expect from folk-music borrowings and certainly Stravinsky justifies their use in *Petrouchke, Les Noces, Pribaoutky, Berceuses des Chat, Renard,* and the *Four Russian Songs.*

The composer has gradually modified his idiom since the production of the *Sacre*[1] until it has reached a point where it has (as he told us in Paris in 1929) discarded all appeal to emotions and now deals only " as is right and proper " with purely musical abstractions.

Quite recently he said " to my mind music should be a photograph of musical facts. It is not the expression of feelings, but movement and rhythm that seems to me to be the principal thing in a musical composition." Volumes have been writ on this ' extraordinary ' and ' unprecedented ' departure by those who have no such scheme as that we have outlined to which they may refer their judgments. Stravinsky, we clearly see from his works even if he had not told us so plainly, is tired of the restricted appeal of music

---

[1] In which may still be traced Russian folk-music influences. Cf. musical illustration, p. 80.

A Series of Swift Vignettes

from and to a very limited region of our postulated second level.

His appeal to the physical in physical-plane terms is undeniable; in earlier works he frankly retreads some of the emotional avenues once again (these, of course, as might have been expected, being his most popular works); and we have noticed his sub-human Pan-like excursions. Nowaday he addresses himself to the mental levels and to these only.

There is much to be said for thus widening the scope and appeal of music. I am all for it. Granted that music can very readily—perhaps more readily than any other art—move our emotions, should it voluntarily limit itself to that? By no means. A force in nature commensurable with those of Light, Heat, Electricity, it can and should be recognized as able to make direct effect upon all realms of nature[1]—certainly upon all those that our consciousness can reach—and not be directed merely from and to a tiny fraction of the second of our five levels (the Emotional) as has the enormously major portion of our post-Bach music.[2]

It seems doubtful whether Stravinsky has achieved such success in this quest as formerly he did with the *Sacre*. We are told he has gone back to Bach. That is not far enough. Pre-Palestrina is the nearest epoch from which a clear forward view can be taken.[3] Perhaps he has already seen this, and we do not know what new vein he may yet strike, for he has genius. So far his abstractions seem to emanate from the 'lower' mental levels and fail to bridge the hiatus

---

[1] Cf. p. 107 *et seq.*

[2] I repeat, for fear of misunderstanding, that music affects us upon all levels including and 'below' that wherein it is contacted. Upon the latter only by repercussion, however. I speak here of direct appeal.

[3] Cf. 52.

between these and the 'higher' mental or Causal realms whence only (as well as from still 'higher' realms) can enduring work take inception. To concentrate upon the geometry of music without a vitalizing influence from the Emotional, Causal, Buddhic or Atmic levels results in a barrenness that only depresses. Such dry-as-dust abstractions, conceived in the brain, expressing only brain-content, addressing themselves only to brain, cannot live.

It is not suggested that this is what Stravinsky aims at. I conceive him as having glimpsed, however unconsciously, some causal vibration which has seemed to him highly significant, and what he has to do is to convince us, *by his musical works*, of the high significance of his vision.

We have noted in the case of Stravinsky a definite attempt to concentrate upon the abstract, so-to-say geometric, possibilities of music. In his case I have always felt there is an attempt to paraphrase some sublevel of the causal world in many of his writings, particularly those of more recent date than the *Sacre*. With MAX REGER (German; born 1873) it is hard to trace anything having an origin outside the bounds of the 'lower triad' of our septenary classification.

He possessed a most active and fecund brain, but he was no adventurer; no explorer or discoverer. The old forms attracted him—sonata, fugue, variation—and he expressed himself easily in a complex polyphonic and not always too logical harmonic system, and remained an 'absolute' musician throughout his life.

His *Variations and Fugue upon a Merry Theme of Hiller* always gives great joy, and seems to me to embody all his best characteristics. The fugue is splendid; within its limits the orchestration is masterly (though in this respect he is no

A Series of Swift Vignettes

Strauss); and, with the reservation already made it may be considered a perfectly satisfactory appeal from the brain to the brain, with an unavoidable dash of emotion which (apart from that supplied by old Hiller) is naturally consequent upon the translation of any mental conception however 'low,' into physical-plane terms. Let this not be thought to be a cheap sneer. Whoever seeks to dismiss him as a nonentity is merely displaying his own lack of perception; for there certainly is a measure of intellectual nobility in Reger whatever else may be missing.

Reger was one of the first of modern composers definitely to turn his back on purely emotional work; and if, in the result, we find that he has often substituted ' lower ' mental cerebration for causal inspiration we are not entitled to withhold a measure of gratitude for what he did accomplish.

The greatest pianist I ever heard—the one who most profoundly affected me, physically, emotionally, mentally, even spiritually, was FERRUCCIO BUSONI (Italian; born 1866). The lambent flame of his intellect lighted up, or rather glowed through everything he played that was worthy of it. The loftier the work, the more easily he seemed to rise upon its inspiration till he scaled heights rarely reached by creative artists and seldom indeed by interpretative ones. Rachmaninof resembles him in this respect, if on a somewhat lower scale.

There is little room for doubt in the minds of many who have studied his works that, as composer, Busoni will bulk more largely in the estimate of future generations than he does in that of the present. In his major works he avoided just those qualities which make for popular success, and even when he was writing in lighter vein—in the Fantasy on

Carmen for example—exploiting a somewhat similar lode to that of Liszt in his compositions of this class; he worked in a *genre* which is quite out of fashion at the moment. But fashion in the arts is a damnable thing.

His work will take its proper place in due course, as also will that of Liszt, who still has a future! Indeed, in certain respects Busoni is a sort of second Liszt raised to a higher dimension. His pianistic prodigiosities take on a much higher degree of significance; his sheer intellectuality is far more highly developed than that of the earlier master. Still the analogy holds; and the closer one's acquaintance with their works, the truer it is seen to be. This is not to belittle either but to extol both. By all accounts personal contact with Liszt was a memorable event. I can vouch for it that Busoni radiated a quite unusually powerful personal vibration, one moreover, that was far removed from that grossly egotistical attitudinizing which so many misguided folk 'admire at' as 'wonderful personality.'

To a certain extent his possession of so magnetic a personality accounted for his great success as a performer. A similar success was denied him as creative artist and we may well ask ourselves whether the world's verdict in this matter is a true one and likely to be endorsed by posterity. In the first place we need not cavil at his universal success as a pianist, for his superb technical mastery was balanced by a powerful intellectual grasp of all the music he essayed, and added to these, the spiritual force he was able to concentrate and almost always to transmit to his listeners through the musical vehicle was as undeniable as it was unique. Over and over again in works like the 'Emperor' Concerto or the G major, the two Brahms works or even those of Liszt, not to mention such *genre* pieces as Saint-

A Series of Swift Vignettes

Saëns' *Africa*, I have seen him do veritable magical operations, changing the basic vibration of whole audiences in a quite unusual degree.

We might profitably consider alongside the specific case of Busoni, the general question of the relative importance of composer and performer. We have all seen many instances of the way in which audiences pay greater homage to the player, singer, or conductor, than to the creator of the works which they re-create. The composer is of course—even of necessity—performing the higher function, and many are the instances that could be adduced of outstandingly great performers yearning to evolve into great creative rather than remain as re-creative artists, whereas no outstanding example to the contrary can be adduced. Artists themselves, whatever critics or public may think, are usually agreed on this point. That the two functions—the creative and interpretative—are separate and distinct becomes clear when we remember how very few of the great interpreters who have made the effort to educe the genuine creative faculty have succeeded.

Think of Rubinstein, Paganini, Vieuxtemps, Wieniawski, Sarasate, Paderewski, Godowsky, Kreisler—many more will occur to the reader—whose performances revealed a magic power which seemed to approach that of the genuine creative artist. Their attempts to attain to equal stature in the rarer sphere signally failed.

To sum up this controversial digression in line with our scheme of musical æsthetic, we might say that the interpretative artist needs to be negative (receptive) to the composer upon the inner planes, and positive towards his audience upon the physical. Whereas the composer's physical-plane attitude matters not at all so far as his work

Music To-day

is concerned. The qualities he needs are the power to contact an ideation at a ' high ' level, the ability to maintain a positive-negative alignment of his ' bodies ' so as to conduct the ideation direct into the brain without distortion *en route*, and the technical skill to translate this white-hot intensity into intelligible musical terms which, in their turn, can inspire the interpreter and through him the listener. And they who can perform the latter functions (the fine composers), are rarer than they who command the former (the fine performers), and always have been.

That Busoni was one of the greatest interpretative artists of modern times is widely accepted. That he was a composer of equal power seems doubtful. What then were the inhibitions, what the inadequacies in his make-up, what the reason for his inability to succeed along his chosen path?

We may obtain a valuable lead by considering his attitude toward modern technical innovations. In his playing and choice of programmes he was unusually eclectic. From the most austere works of Bach to the most ephemeral of Liszt he ranged with equal ease. He included in his large and penetrating sympathy the intellectual severities of Brahms and the immediately appealing sensuosities of Bizet.

It was the more surprising therefore to hear him declare (if I understood him aright) that both Polytonality and Atonality were fundamentally wrong. ("Im Grundgenommen falsch.")

In these pages the view has constantly been iterated that side by side with the exploration of new worlds by our composers, new technical means will be needed by which their contacts may be expressed; and that therefore an increase and not a diminution in our equipment is desirable.

A Series of Swift Vignettes

That if we are ranging new worlds and opening new vistas, the present is not the time to belittle the tentative new vehicles by means of which records of them may be transmitted to the waiting world. As was said when considering them specifically, Atonal, Polytonal, Modal, Quarter-Tonal —all these and many more devices are needed by the adventurous spirit whose wings can bear him to the enchanted land of Hy Brāsil. And it is a shock indeed to find an artist of the eminence of Busoni accepting neither Polytonality nor Atonality but concentrating exclusively, so far as new technical methods are concerned, upon a resurrection of modal music in its practical form. Not an antagonist but emphatically a protagonist of practical modal composition,[1] I can not regard this as other than one of the *many* jewels which glow in the crown of modern music, and to reject any such well-proved means of enlarging the scope and expression of the art as Polytonality and Atonality, seems to me to be a retrograde step.

Certain composers have voluntarily narrowed and concentrated their personal style, their unique idiom, with the object, as it seemed, of strengthening their appeal and widening their personal influence. In every case it has vitiated their influence and sapped their virility.[2] Busoni was too fastidious a thinker and too finely balanced an intellect to err so grievously as this and his open-mindedness and sweep of imagination as expressed in *Entwurf einer neuen Ästhetik der Tonkunst*[3] almost amounted to genuine seership.

Seership, yes! But not perhaps practical musicianship.

[1] For see *ante* PART Two, Chap. III Modes, p. 41 *et seq.*
[2] See instances on p. 197. An outstanding exception among living composers is Van Dieren.
[3] Sketch of a New Æsthetic of Music.

For, curiously enough, after theorizing at some length on the possibilities of a tetra-tonal system—a purely intellectual system which, if adopted would speedily be erected into a dogma, as who can doubt—he pleads that we should " free it [music] from architectonic, acoustic and æsthetic dogmas." As a seer Busoni may have visualized the time when music shall have achieved this freedom, but the time is not yet. And the way seems to me to lie in directions which I shall indicate in a later section.

One eminent German critic, noting that Busoni is too deeply whelmed in intellectuality, offers us the not astonishingly recondite reflection that an artist's life must be of the senses as well as of the intellect. Naturally it must. And in this case Busoni's intellect was beautifully balanced by a rare sensitivity. What he lacked of greatness as a composer was nothing that the sensual or the intellectual worlds can supply. In the Causal, Intuitional, and Spiritual realms alone flows the inexhaustible fount of inspiration to which Busoni so nobly aspired. Whether or not he contacted it who may say? I believe he did. And if so, it was in an attempt to evolve a technique adequate to express these vibrations, that he made those purely mental and theoretical efforts which have caused the unpenetrating to dub him *merely* intellectual.

He has always inspired in me a feeling curiously allied to personal affection, and if it has been impossible to write of him as a gloriously successful composer it can be said of him, as of so many other single-hearted devotees, in Stevenson's moving words: " there, out of the glorious sun-coloured earth, out of the day and the dust and the ecstasy—there goes another Faithful Failure! "

A Series of Swift Vignettes

Anyone who has dwelt in Paris for as many weeks as the writer has years, will have had ample opportunity to notice a quality which pervades many walks of life in the capital: *Charme*. This quality with all its implications, (as well as wit, irony, and a characteristically Gallic savour of the *macabre*) runs like a silver thread through the work of MAURICE RAVEL (French; born 1875). As we are dealing in this chapter with none who are not admittedly masters of music, it should be unnecessary to remark that upon the technical side Ravel is of course a very accomplished artist indeed. It is nothing contrary to this to say that, viewed as a whole, his work gives an impression of being of the nature of the *petite*.

To the average English-speaking reader this may appear as a measure of disparagement. To the Latin, however, to refer to a thing, place, or person by use of this diminutive would be to denote a regard, even a love for it; and certainly Ravel is well loved in his own country at least.

By *quasi*-onomatopœic association you may discover the main trend of his mind. Child, Princess, pastorals, shepherdesses, flageolets and tambourines, mathematical elves and imps, hissing cats *Minchon* and *Môrnaunaon*; gardens, frogs, owls, birds, dragon-flies, nightingale, squirrel, a zoological madrigal to end all (as in the music to a play *L'Enfant et les Sortilèges*); *Ondine, Le Gibet, Scarbo* (three piano pieces called *Gaspard de la Nuit* inspired by Louis Bertrand); *Une Barque dans l'Océan* (an orchestral piece in which the frail barque of the composer's inspiration is whelmed beneath an ocean of confused rhetoric and pianistic orchestration); Beauty and the Beast, Queen of the Pagodas (*Mother Goose* suite); *Jeux d'Eau; Valses nobles et sentimentales; Histoires Naturelles* (a whole zoo faithfully reflected in music for voice and piano; peacock-pride, cricket-chirp, swan-shimmering, Pintade-peevishness): all these indicate what in fact we find reflected in Ravel's music, a subtle, kaleidoscopic mind, a mind, moreover, neatly arranged. Wit, irony, *bizarrerie*, *naïveté* (but simulated *naïveté*), are balanced by delicacy, artistic restraint, and a rare appreciation of the appropriate and the effective, the whole shot through with never-long-absent charm.

It would seem that Ravel is very rarely able to light up his inspirational flame of his own volition. The poets Burns and Tom Moore, we may remember, were inspired very largely through the tunes which had been written by musicians who had themselves made the necessary soul-effort; the poet, as it were, catching fire from the musician. Conversely, Ravel's is essentially a literary imagination. He does not make many of his contacts at first hand but, in a sense, obtains his experiences vicariously through literary allusions. It would be too sweeping a statement to say that he is, *au fond*, reproductive rather than creative. Yet a sympathetic review of his work from this point of view might well lead to a truer estimate of his gifts than reams of recondite discussion.

Ravel sometimes turns to Spanish types just as does Bloch to Hebrew, Bax to Keltic, Kodály to Hungarian, for the spark which shall fire his vision. In the *Rhapsodie Espagnole* they serve him fairly well. In *L'Heure Espagnole*, his best-known theatrical work, they are less inspiring to him, perhaps because he has had to concentrate his fastidious mind upon the coarse and not too amusing story of the worn-out old watchmaker, the lusty young wife and the brawny muleteer. There is wit, charm and, of course, adroitness in plenty in the work, but the fusion between form and content,

A Series of Swift Vignettes

without which no work of art can be great, does not occur till quite near to the end. The lustful young peasant woman, tearful from sheer physical desire, is a figure Ravel cannot paint. Strauss in his prime could have done it.

With reference to this composer, as well as, unfortunately, to many more, we must needs reverse the old axiom and render it: The Flesh is willing but the Spirit is weak.

He has made many notable additions to pianoforte music; indeed many of his orchestral pieces were first written for piano; *Ma Mère l'Oye* for example. Probably the ballet *Daphnis et Chloé*, written for Diaghilev, is his masterpiece. This is, of course, no very profound affair, neither is it possible to say that it reaches great heights. Indeed, I would say that his range of consciousness is one of the most strictly limited of all the composers of modern times. His adroit and penetrating brain is asked to body forth impressions from sub-human, Pan-like realms, to originate a good deal in itself, to render a limited range of contacts upon certain sub-levels of the second plane: beyond this, little or nothing.

Yet we can say of him, as we could not of the first of the masters treated in this section, that Ravel is emphatically one who has preserved his artistic integrity. He has never been false to his inner being. Even in face of the egregious *Bolero* one must admit this. And in an age which bristles with instances of the most bare-faced betrayals of artistic faith, and of cases of artistic prostitution galore, this is no mere empty phrase, but a claim of weighty implications and a title to honour.

One of the most striking examples of the sporadic behaviour of the inspirational faculty is HUGO WOLF

(Austrian; born 1860). He wrote an Opera, a String quartet, little orchestral work, but over two hundred songs. When the 'raptus' was upon him he was capable of prodigies. In a short four months he once wrote forty-three songs. Another time, between October and February he set some fifty or so Goethe poems. He seemed, like Ravel, often to need a poem to attune his consciousness and align his creative faculties; but once he had chosen his lyric he seemed able to adjust his musical make-up to it with the greatest ease and accuracy. One vein of his inspiration, that typified in such songs as the popular *Der Rattenfänger*, derives direct from Berlioz. Between this and the world of *Anakreon's Grab* he ranges widely and explores many byways of the emotion-plane.

I am unable to persuade myself that he does more than this, but this he does superbly, within the self-imposed limitations of the forms he chooses. And, with this proviso, we may regard Wolf as among the greatest of all song-composers.

The protean quality of the creative impulse, as it manifests itself in the work of musical composers, is strikingly illustrated by a comparison of Wolf with ARNOLD SCHÖNBERG (Austrian; born 1874).

First romanticist, then impressionist, afterwards atonalist, finally dodecaphonist; this pilgrim's progress has at any rate been logical. Without leading the reader into a detailed consideration of his evolution upon the technical side—an excursion which would probably interest none but the keenest 'professional' musician—we may observe that Schönberg has himself invoked the nemesis that appears to have overtaken him by elevating technique above inspira-

A Series of Swift Vignettes

tion, or, more accurately, giving it precedence in point of time.

From op. 1 to 10 he showed himself a timid romantic, reproducing ideas which had already been well rendered by the great romantic composers, and using a technique composed of all the *clichés* in common use by the lesser fry of the musical world at that time. He was, all the same, what would rightly be called a very good musician, as all would agree who can assimilate in any degree his grand-scale ballad-cycle called *Gurre-Lieder*.[1]

At this early period he showed his sympathy with the sister art of painting as have so many composers. Probably inspired by the new movement in painting he gave an exhibition of Portraits and Visions from his own brush.

In his op. 11, three piano pieces, he pushes out of his small environment and in this and succeeding works eagerly embraces a new type of 'expressionism,' hoping, against hope, as we now see, that inspiration would follow from the new method. We must not withhold from him a full measure of credit for the spirit of rebellion that prevented his decline into a spineless mediocrity such as contents so many. Particularly should we applaud his strength of purpose in face of a bitter struggle for existence—a struggle which necessitated the soul-deadening labours of scoring trumpery operettas and conducting at a variety theatre. The sickening misery of such work to any real creative artist cannot easily be imagined by anyone who has been spared a similar experience, and the qualities of character which enabled him to preserve his artistic integrity in the face of it is worthy of all praise, whether or no one sees eye to eye with him on purely artistic questions.

[1] Musical quotation, p. 337.

Music To-day

For the temerity of his early essays in atonalism earned him a fiercely-fought notoriety that had in it none of the easy comfort of popular success. Indeed, upon the production of his works of this period such storms arose—the opposition being, as is always the case, much the more noisy faction—that he fell naturally into the pose of pioneer and martyr, deriving new strength from this instead of from contact with inner realities.

Had he realized his paucity of experience in the world of ideations, or, realizing it, had he concentrated upon deepening and widening his contacts there, who can doubt that a brain of his power and a logic so convincing as his would speedily have found commensurate terms in which to convey his message to the listener. Instead, he formulated a theoretical outline of new musical principles, building as it were, a small but well-designed and beautiful vessel, only to find himself lacking a single drop of the elixir of life to pour into it when the appropriate time came.

The culminating work of this period is a cycle of twenty poems recited to music, *Pierrot Lunaire*, op. 21. The *sprech-stimme* style of recitation employed here is something between recitative and intoning, a medium that has several times been used since Schröder-Devrient electrified everyone at an opera performance many years ago by speaking instead of singing a dramatic phrase. This work bears a similar relation to the rest of Schönberg's compositions as does *Le Sacre du Printemps* to Stravinsky's other works. Thus, in spite of extraordinary vagaries of style and perversities of expression, and despite a lack of authentic inspiration, it has, like the Stravinsky work, a real historical value.

After this work which has had considerable success in

A Series of Swift Vignettes

the inner circles of the musical world, Schönberg threw himself wholeheartedly into the dodecaphonic system, in which, by the latest accounts, he still labours.

The value of Schönberg's contribution to the progress of music is that in the making it he has helped to hew out a new road. That he has become absorbed in his engineering to such an extent as to have forgotten whither his road leads; (so utterly obsessed indeed as to be indifferent to its leading anywhere at all), is all that need be said in depreciation of this sturdy iconoclast.

When dealing with the rationale of inspiration, I deplored the fact that all music academies, colleges, conservatoires, concentrate upon technique and largely ignore inspiration whose instrument only, technique should be:[1] when assaying the relative importance of interpretative and creative art it was seen that the latter is rarer than the former and, of course, prior to it in point of time.[2] Now in the case of Schönberg we have a specific instance of a composer elevating reason above imagination; allowing the machine to usurp instead of sub-serving the higher function. But, says Shelley, " reason is to the imagination as the instrument to the agent, as the body to the spirit, as the shadow to the substance." Despite all of which, he may be considered the most stimulating figure in the musical world to-day.

Among the young musicians of Austria are many who have become adherents to, and disciples of, the cause, and it is possible that one of his pupils or successors (Berg, Krěnek, Webern?) will attain to a truer balance in this matter than he; and from a happier synthesis will create works of greater worth and more enduring beauty than—admire him though we may, and do—has Arnold Schönberg.

[1] In p. 20.   [2] In p. 244.

Music To-day

About the year 1903 BÉLA BARTÓK (Hungarian; born 1881) brought to his compatriot and mentor Hans Richter, a work for orchestra which he had written under the impetus received from Richard Strauss. The latter's *Zarathustra* had made a profound impression upon Bartók whose musical education had previously been conducted on strictly classical lines. The exhilarating effect of this work, allied to his love of the Fatherland, resulted in a tone-poem having the national hero *Kossuth* as its central figure. It contained, I remember, a *fugato* upon Haydn's quartet-tune which had been adopted by Austria as a national anthem. As youths together we discussed the work, practically his first one for large orchestra (he was a modest, keen fellow, his English sparse, my German even more so), and his dissatisfaction with the *fugato* in question prompted the suggestion that a little research would probably have discovered a genuine Hungarian folk-tune which might more happily have rounded off the episode.

Whether or not he forgot this incident, the fact is that he concentrated thereafter upon the folk-music of his country and the results are to a great extent available to all. The effect of this study upon his style was naturally of great importance, and we can take the measure of the man to a certain extent by realizing that he did not remain content, as so many smaller composers have done, with adding a flavour of local folk-song and a mild modal tang (such as so many folk-songs possess) to his own idiom.

The study of Mode from such vestiges as remain in the peasant-music of European countries in a debased, decadent or perverted form is one thing; quite another is its study from fundamental roots, and this seems to be, beyond question, the more valuable *to the living art*. The preservation

A Series of Swift Vignettes

of such records as are to be met with in the folk-music of any country is eminently praiseworthy of course, and not without its own results, but a fanatical devotion to it is to be deprecated upon the grounds mentioned in Part IV, Chapter 12, Section 2.

Happily, as I think, Bartók's studies along these lines led him in 1913 out of the narrower localized aspect of even the more ancient Hungarian folk-music—he journeyed, for example, to Biskra and contacted there something of the farther East in Arab music—and it is highly significant that hereafter his own compositions are mainly non-nationalistic in character. He assimilated, that is to say, the larger aspects of modal music and, by the force of his own individuality, forged them into a personal idiom. He quickly added polytonality and atonality to his technique and, although his orchestration shows perhaps less certainty and mastery than the other branches of his musicianship, he is, in my view, one of the very finest of living composers. His phenomenal intensity of style is well shown in the following passage from his *String Quartet*, opus 17:—

Music To-day

Bartók seems, which is a rare thing in contemporary composers, to be more logical rhythmically than harmonically; owes a great deal of his terse masculinity of style to the late Beethoven quartets; often gives to persons of a certain type a quite false impression of coldness, lack of heart, almost repellent ugliness; scores beautifully though not easily; and has made, in his opera *Bluebeard*, one of the very few attempts in our day—Delius' *A Village Romeo and Juliet* and *Fennimore and Gerda* are the only others that occur to me—to solve the problem of 'representational' *versus* 'subjective' in the handling of this form of art.

His consciousness is able to explore a wider and loftier range of ideations than almost any other living composer, and if, as is only natural, his methods of expression occasionally fail to stir emotions or tickle ears, they never lack matter of extreme intellectual interest; and, which is more, once we have developed sufficient musical intelligence to recognize them, the very moments when he may seem to be most deeply immersed in merely cerebral regurgitations are those which contain genuine echoes from Intuitional realms with which we are only too unfamiliar.

The following moment in his *Second Pianoforte Concerto* is one of those the layout of which in its chordal, rhythmic,

and instrumental disposition, is so easily comprehensible that there is distinct danger of musicians of a certain type

A Series of Swift Vignettes

dismissing it as almost beneath notice on account of (as they phrase it) 'its cheap intellectuality.'

Take it to the piano, play it over several times, imagine the tone-colour of muted strings played *non vibrato*, and you will probably agree with me that at least there is a good deal more in it than 'meets the eye.'

It is to be hoped that he is one of those grand souls who face the 'slings and arrows of outrageous fortune' with lofty heart and unbowed head, an undiminished ardour in his soul and an unconquerable faith in his spirit; steadfast amid obloquy, a replica of many of his forerunners, an exemplar to many who shall follow.

Alas, one fears lest it be not so. Bitter scorn and bitterer neglect are beginning to do their blighting work (or so I hear) upon another rare and beautiful artist.

For such, and perhaps for every true artist, this is verily the Dark Age.

Musical nationalism in general and folk-music in particular have already been discussed in these pages and a definite—it is hoped not an unreasonable—attitude adopted as to the value of the former to the growth of the art, and the degree of importance of the latter as a basis for a national school of composition. Possibly the views put forward on these important questions will have seemed more rigid than in fact they are meant to be, for nothing is easier than to overstate a case upon which one feels deeply, and about which one has made up one's mind after years of experience and thought. It is all the more pleasant therefore to discuss an example, that of ZOLTAN KODÁLY (Hungarian; born 1882) whose work appears to traverse these views at certain points.

Music To-day

Just as with Debussy and Ravel, Elgar and Delius, Krěnek and Hindemith, Berg and Webern, the names of Bartók and Kodály are frequently coupled together. Alike in their almost fanatical devotion to folk-song (Hungarian, *videlicet*) and in their views upon music, many of our general observations regarding the one will apply to the other. But only up to a point. For whereas Bartók as we have seen, starting with local folk-song, widened his knowledge vastly by a study of further Eastern modes and types and ultimately freed his style completely in its melodic, harmonic, and rhythmic aspects; Kodály has not done so, but has evolved a style of composition whose idiom is founded in the peasant-music of his country, to which he has remained faithful. To larger works this localized idiom seems to me totally unsuited, and the popularity of his orchestral suite *Hari Janos* indicates a recognition of propriety of idea and expression beyond which Kodály, up to the present, shows no signs of soaring. And he may be taken as the most favourable example possible of what a composer may attain to who founds his whole style, both as to matter and manner, upon the folk-music of his native country.

With a real desire to do so I have been unable to find in his work any indication that Kodály is able to reach any lofty source of inspiration: if he were (and I do not say he is unable to), it is certain that the comparatively humble peasant-music idiom will be miserably inadequate to parallel it, beautiful, interesting, engaging and even fascinating as so many of us have found Hungarian folk-music in itself to be.

The influence of Russian folk-music in the work of Stravinsky, and of Hungarian in that of Bartók and Kodály, has already been noted. In each of these cases the composer

A Series of Swift Vignettes

has worked in both folk-idiom and in that of contemporary European musical thought, and in the case of Kodály the attempt has been made to evolve a style of composition whose idiom is founded in the peasant-music of his country.

Whereas Stravinsky made occasional use of folk-melodies in his earlier work but turned away from them toward the goal of a kind of musical classicism; and whereas Kodály declined into a mannered, restricted application of peasant-music in all his work; Bartók, as we have seen, widened his folk-music horizon enormously by a contact with farther Eastern modes, and ultimately freed his style completely.

Now, as the folk-music bases of both Russia and Hungary are Oriental in origin, just so are those of Spain. For, from about the beginning of the eighth century, the Moorish invasions brought Eastern influences into Spain, and the musico-ethnologist can easily trace these influences—as well as those of Russia and Hungary and other 'national' folk-styles—back to their origins in Persia and India.

Long ago the question of the advisability, nay, the possibility, of founding a country's music upon vestiges of its folk-art was thrashed out in Russia. More recently Hungary has busied itself with the same problem. England and Wales are to-day in the throes of it.

And the musicians of Spain too have covered the same ground. Oriental influences inherent in their folk-music; those of Western culture in their art-forms; these were the opposing forces to be reckoned with and, if possible, reconciled.

Felipe Pedrell and Joaquin Nin began what can be considered the renaissance of Spanish music in the middle of the nineteenth century. Followed Isaac Albéniz who, in something the manner of Stanford with Irish folk-tunes, Dvořák with Slav, Smetana with Bohemian, and in our own day, V. Williams with English, sought to present Spanish folk-music through the medium of a cultivated musical taste. In his *Iberia*, national Spanish tunes are presented *via* a rhapsodic method which is undeniably French. Granados and Turina serve up all the well-known *clichés* of Spanish popular music, the *tournures des phrases*, the castanets and all the other ear-tickling tricks dear to the café-concert musical intelligence.

Of another sort is MANUEL DE FALLA (Spanish; born 1876) who, whilst refusing to indulge in the cheap Spanish tricks spoken of above, does compose in a style which is recognizably Spanish. He avoids the common mistake that the use of Spanish 'words' will suffice, but offers thoughts which, original up to a point, can instantly be recognized as imbued with the characteristics of his country.

His technique, however, remains French (for he pursued his musical studies in Paris in his youth), and however lively and nimble his fancy, however adroit and charming his purely musical gift, it would need a greater measure of imagination than most of us are endowed with, to see in him the unique and powerful individuality for which the musicians of his country are longing.

The idea has often been iterated in these pages that folk-music of the past—*i.e.*, that of the 'people,' the 'peasants' of former times—however vital, beautiful, charming, sentimental, or rousing, is too restricted in its field of inception to satisfy the real creative musician once his inspiration has really found its wings.

As amenable as anyone to the charms of simplicity,

A Series of Swift Vignettes

naïveté, rustic joviality, forthright rugged commonsense and all that sort of thing, and as capable as the next man of enjoying tunes like 'Lord Bateman's Daughter,' I do not see these peasant qualities with their strictly localized application, translated into terms of music (equally localized), as capable of initiating, in any sense, a real forward step in the art. Similarly, the 'Peasant Arts' (wrongly so called for they are crafts in almost every case, not arts) are out of place in a cosmopolitan *salon* however admirable in themselves.

It is a significant commentary upon this point of view that so many composers who, early in their careers, have attempted to base their style upon folk-music have, upon reaching a stage of greater maturity, forsaken it and tried their wings in a grander flight, one more worthy of the endeavours of those who have reached adolescence if not yet complete maturity.

Stravinsky, Bartók, have grown out of their peasant stage; Falla also has realized that devotion to local colour is a definite weakness in his style, not a source of strength as certain pundits maintain, and in *El Retablo de Maese* has essayed a wider flight. It is but a miniature; a series of puppet-show *tableaux*, but it is full of vitality of musical thought, melodic and harmonic.

It would be fair to say that, admirable composer as Falla undoubtedly is, and much as one may, nay, must, admire his abstention from the easy popularity which he could so readily have achieved by use of the usual *clichés* of Spanish music and lavish local colour—which is fashionable at the moment—he has insufficient power to raise his consciousness to heights at all far removed from the mundane, and therefore must remain, in any critical view, a lesser figure in the musical galaxy. Notwithstanding which, we may love him for the qualities of vitality, light-heartedness, beauty and joyous verve with which his work is so liberally bestrewn, as well as for his bravely outspoken declarations about religion and patriotism as basic elements in his music.

A likeable fellow and a great musical chatterbox is PAUL HINDEMITH (German; born 1895). Upon hearing the first performance of his *Concerto for Organ and Orchestra* in Paris in 1930, I wrote the following:—" The soloist was that eminent and masterly performer Marcel Dupré, and the orchestra that so frequently alluded to as " the best in Paris at present," viz., the *Orchestre Straram*. The work had, I happen to know, been more carefully rehearsed than is usual with new works in that country, and in fact, the circumstances were favourable to the reaching of a fair conclusion on the merits of the new Concerto. Due in part at least to the judicious registration of M. Dupré we were spared the experience that is so common in works for organ and orchestra, of a sort of trial of strength between them. In this work the effect almost throughout is that of a conversation. As to the purely musical value of the Concerto I was more than ever impressed with the idea that in this prolific, versatile and consistently polyphonic writer we have a present-day Max Reger. As with that composer, his themes are in themselves largely insignificant. They never (as they do with Brahms for example) grow in importance, beauty and profundity. All that happens to them is that they are subjected to Hindemith's everlasting device, that of canonic imitation. They are served up atonally over and over again in this fashion, and I personally cannot escape the conclusion I arrived at some time ago regarding this

A Series of Swift Vignettes

composer—that he is mainly occupied in pouring new (atonal) wine into old (canonic) bottles; a raw wine without bouquet, and old bottles with which we are only too familiar."

Hindemith is the typical professional musician, just as was Bach, Purcell, Reger. Just as certainly Berlioz is an amateur, and Delius and Boito. Which is not intended as a reflection upon these fine composers. It is, however, a distinction worth making. And I would say that the outstanding characteristic of the professional is his certainty, humanly speaking, of never falling below a certain level. The good amateur violinist or singer, for example, sometimes achieves a really beautiful performance. This most frequently happens in private and is often something in the nature of a fluke, if he will forgive the expression. The good professional, however, must in the nature of things be able to 'deliver the goods' to order. Thus according to his ability there is a limit below which, as I say, his work rarely if ever falls.

Berlioz, Delius, Boito, Sibelius, are capable of lapses into a banality so utter as to appear childish by comparison with their more happily inspired periods. But you may search for a long time for really feeble passages in Bach or Reger.

This is so to a certain extent in the case of Hindemith. Even when his message is verging on the trumpery and its expressive value exiguous to the point of vapidity, he will state it with an air, intrigue your judgment with witty devices, side-track your perspicacity by use of a consummate craftsmanship, and invariably leave you with at least a sense of having been entertained. He is bold and self-sufficient. He remains within his own personal idiom as securely as a Scriabin or a Schönberg. He will make no concessions *on the purely musical side* whatever he may do by way of selecting an appealing libretto or sub-title. His is not the astounding calm assurance of mediocrity, but the strength of a balanced and 'arrived' artist who is well aware of the value of what he has to say. He has, too, a very ready tongue. Piquant *badinage* is his natural speech.

He is as verbose as a Reger, but a Reger entirely without reverence for the classical idiom. And his thoughts are no more valuable, however they may engage the modern ear as being couched in the latest musical slang. Where the ordinary man would say " wait for a moment " the slangster says " 'arf a mo' ": where the ordinary composer would say, as being *all that he means*:

Hindemith, *meaning no more*, will say:

Now the clumsiest of expressions will often manage to convey somehow or other, a suggestion of the mystical experience behind it, whilst a glib ready pen may fail

A Series of Swift Vignettes

ignominiously to carry conviction. Indeed, technical facility of itself is no criterion of artistic worth either in a performer or a composer. And it is at this point, when, accepting the fact of Hindemith's easy volubility we probe deeper for convincing evidence of the value and beauty of—nay, the depth of the first-hand experiences about which he is so engagingly holding forth, that doubts begin to assail us. Some such negation of the realities behind all great art as we noticed in our section upon Æsthetic[1] as being put forward by Paul Bekker—some such danger as we have seen many musicians succumb to, would appear to be threatening Hindemith. For in his didactic, almost peevish refusal to concern himself with any extra-musical associations in his work, he is courting the nemesis of an empty formalism.

Many modern composers are not artists at all. They are craftsmen. It is only by the addition of inspiration to his craftsmanship that the craftsman evolves into the artist. Contrarily, by a denial of inspiration—a common attitude in the post-war period—the artist may decline to the level of a mannered and mechanical artisan. Form becomes crystallized into formalism, rhythm into a formula, new idioms born of the urgent need to express become tricks, and the whole style becomes as barren of inner vitality as a cross-word puzzle. These novel technical formulæ are but so many ingredients, they are not the secret of the magic philtre.

It is because in the *Third Quartet* there is a satisfying balance between idea and expression; in certain of the ballads in *Die junge Magd* a *naïveté* and charm which unite subject and matter; in the short opera *Das Nusch-Nuschi*

[1] Cf. p. 173.

several episodes which undeniably come to life; and in the opera *Cardillac*, perhaps his most important work to date, a wealth of real invention and originality which is not overlaid by unintelligible rhetoric; that so many passages in his works, where the object seems to be to conceal rather than reveal thought,[1] may be taken as temporary aberrations, and faith in the importance of Hindemith's contribution to the art can remain unshaken.

Exactly as with Hindemith, ARTHUR HONEGGER (Swiss; born 1892) often seems to force his ideas, fresh, characteristic and striking as they often are, into old fugal forms which are by no means commensurate with them in value. His frequently atonal harmonic schemes and his bold voice-leading would be still more convincing were they not so often stated in the most banal of *fugato* terms. It is still another case of new wine in old bottles. As freshness of impression is of some value in assaying the works of various composers, let me quote from notes I made when resident in Paris and making close acquaintance with the *Groupe des Six*, which consisted of Germaine Taillefère, Poulenc, Milhaud, Durey, Auric and Honegger.

My notes upon the last-named were as follows:

"I have heard a good deal of Honegger's music now, some of it many times, most of it several times and almost all of it at least once, and have reached a considered conclusion upon what he has written down to date. His is a peasant's music. Understand I am diagnosing the music, not the antecedents or birth of the man. I know nothing whatever of his circumstances, birth or antecedents. But

[1] For example, *Neues vom Tage*, News of the Day, whose interest is as ephemeral as the title implies.

A Series of Swift Vignettes

this, I repeat, is music from the emotional-mental make-up of a peasant.

" This must not be misunderstood to mean that peasant emotional or mental reactions are necessarily vulgar, commonplace or banal. One might as reasonably say that all music by aristocrats would, *ipso facto*, be noble and elevated. The truth is, of course, that music by either a prince or a peasant may convey any of these characteristics, good or bad; desirable or not. Neither do I mean to infer that Honegger's choice of subjects is not lofty—though the crash and clatter of a moving locomotive,[1] the splash and splatter of a Rugby scrum,[2] or the jar and snarl of a submarine[3] are appeals to no very exalted parts of a man's nature. It is the manner of the man to which I refer, his thought-stuff, the presentation of his ideas—his style.

" Contrast his manner in long-continued *fortissimo* passages, which is brutal, physically robust, near to the soil, with the styles, for example, of Beethoven, Scriabin, Wagner, Strauss, etc., in their *fortissimo* passages of highly wrought emotion, which approach the pathological condition known as hysteria, and you will glimpse my reason for the use of the word 'peasant-like' regarding Honegger's music. You may say you prefer a healthy peasant to a super-sensitive artist. All right! *Ça c'est votre affaire!*"

And again: " There is no doubt that Honegger in his *Pacific, Rugby, Submarine*" [and I may add, in his latest *Mouvement Symphonique*], " cutting out all direct appeal to the sense of beauty, and concentrating upon arranging his sonorities in a telling and pictorial manner,[4] does educe

---

[1,2,3] Honegger's best-known works at present are his *Mouvements Symphoniques* entitled : *Pacific 231, Rugby, Submarine*.

[4] Cf. musical quotation, p. 84.

Music To-day

a physical response in the listener. Your colour heightens, breathing becomes more rapid, pulse beats more quickly. All of which was clear once again at his recent Festival in Paris. The origin of this music appears to be the brain, the whole conception to be a cerebral one, and the effect to be primarily physical. Just so, if not perhaps quite in the same degree, is one affected by the facts themselves.

"Honegger must (will?) do more than this. To have one's blood pressure raised is, of course, something for one's money, but music, said Beethoven 'should strike fire from the *souls* of men.'"

The association of this composer, in his incidental music to *The Tempest*, with our great figure, is one of the oddest that can be imagined. Equally so is the result. His *Le Roi David*, an oratorio, magnificent in certain moments, is a *pasticcio* of styles which must seem unsatisfactory to a fastidious musical mind. *Horace Victorieux* is also unequal in the same way, though of unquestionable inspiration in certain of its subsections.

His most recent work, *Les Cris du Monde*, a kind of cantata, demonstrates an even greater degree of assurance upon the technical side than the above-named. Clearly his art is maturing and he uses all his former devices with finer and riper skill. His powers of inspiration, it is saddening to notice, seem to be declining *pro rata*, and this is a disturbing thought in connection with a creative artist in his early forties.

A certain reticence (yes, reticence!) in the scoring proclaims his French training. He is a completely emancipated Atonalist. It is all the more surprising that his use of antiquated forms as means for the display of his inspiration is as constant as that of a Reger.

A Series of Swift Vignettes

This is a distinction we have had occasion to notice in the work of many modern composers, and, although we must beware of the idea that novel form-structure is necessarily more easily comprehensible than any other new device, and must therefore be careful not to condemn as formless those works whose form-structure may elude us at a first hearing, it would not be too much to say that lack of real originality in their architectonic outlook is the technical weakness most frequently to be noticed in the work of modern composers.

Of the remaining members of the *Groupe des Six*, two must receive further attention; DARIUS MILHAUD (French; born 1892), by virtue of his powers of mind and the rich promise of his works; FRANCIS POULENC (French; born 1899), because he has achieved a rapidly growing success without either, thus presenting a side-light of some interest in the world of music.

Milhaud resembles two other Jewish composers in a very curious way, showing the mathematical bias and the intellectualizing tendencies which Schönberg has so grossly exaggerated, as well as a devotion to nationalistic Hebrew subjects in the manner of Bloch. I have been deeply impressed by several of his works—the *Poèmes Juifs*, one or two of the quartets, and even the completely artificial ballet *Le Train Bleu* written for Diaghilev to an *Opérette dansée* of Jean Cocteau, with Nijinsky. Like Honegger, he is a completely emancipated Atonalist and Polytonalist, his command of technical resources being both wide and profound. Remains to be seen whether he has the soul-power to be able to range wider inspirational fields than those provided by the *zeitgeist* and the special characteristics of his

Music To-day

own ubiquitous and mentally tenacious race. For it is too early in his career to be able to form any definitive judgment upon his work as a whole. If the Fates are kind to Milhaud he may well create some of the outstanding works of this epoch.

So, emphatically, will not Poulenc whilst pursuing his present course. For his procedure, now become a personal idiom which his admirers have learned to look for, and recognizing, to applaud in all his recent compositions, is this: by way of tickling his hearers' aural palates and giving them something they can readily understand, he serves up jejune imitations of lyrical Mozartean scraps. Anon, bethinking himself of those of his audience who may have a flair for the modern, and equally anxious to prove to them that he is *dans le mouvement*, he offers, sandwich-wise, slabs of pinchbeck modernities, between the two-hundred-year-old regurgitations already spoken of. And in the whole there is not, for me, one sincere bar.

Either the Mozart idiom, in its ingenuousness and (now-seeming) simplicity, is Poulenc's normal attitude, and we cannot help reflecting that the master did it all rather better; or the modern melodic-harmonic methods are his normal ones, and there are plenty of living composers who are incomparably his superior in these ways. Frankly, I cannot believe in either. Certainly both cannot exist side by side in any even moderately evolved musical style.

When Grieg writes a suite *Aus Holberg's Zeit* or Schubert an overture *In Italian Style,* or when a modern composer is commissioned to write music for a production of Shakespeare's *Henry VIII—in the period*—you have legitimate examples of, as it were, copies of the old masters. But a

A Series of Swift Vignettes

hybrid between the two styles in the same work, offered moreover with no acknowledgment to the older master (no 'Lines in imitation of Spenser' as Keats modestly announces), results in a confusion, a bastardization, which is nothing less than abhorrent to the sincere artist. With few exceptions, and these must carry their own justification, a work of art should be, as Whistler said of pictures, 'all under one skin.' There must be uniformity of idiom throughout the work, however much this may differ as between work and work. *Tristan*, from first note to last; *Meistersinger*, from first note to last, although they differ from each other signally, obey this artistic necessity. Modern styles aspire to a purity of their own, says Tovey; introduced into older styles or *vice versa* they are mere impurities. Bach's own style would be a ghastly impurity if introduced into a Palestrina Mass.

The outstanding Polish composer of the present time is KAROL SZYMANOVSKI (born 1882). He is a completely free Atonalist, a superb master of counterpoint and orchestration, and a modernist in all his personal idioms save perhaps that he is too much addicted—and the same may be said of Honegger, Hindemith, Holst and others—to a pedantic fugal exposition of some of his ideas. Colouring his type of inspiration is a swift response to certain strata of Eastern thought as is the case with so many musicians of our day.[1] This is shown concretely in *Songs of Many Colours* to words by the Persian mystical poet Hafiz, and in *Songs of the Mad Muezzin* to words by Rabindranath Tagore. But many traces may be seen throughout his later works. One hears that he is immersed in studies of Eastern mysticism, which

[1] Cf. p. 343.

studies, it is hinted, are profoundly affecting his musical style. I mention this *en passant* for what it is worth.

GUSTAV MAHLER, when I met him in Frankfurt in 1910, was in the throes of the production of his colossal *Eighth Symphony*. My private notes on the performance said: " the first bars were almost completely overwhelming—physically. The gigantic orchestra, the colossal chorus, the full grand organ, plus that imposing line of drummers stretching entirely across the back of the orchestra, emitted the opening passage with such a titanic concatenation of prodigious ponderosities that the poor listener was very nearly put to sleep (in the boxer's sense of the phrase). . . . Thenceforward the work proved to be, in effect, one long *diminuendo* until the end." His compositions sometimes show oversubtlety in workmanship. But although they are not without idealism I believe they will not endure the test of time because of sheer lack of creative imagination.

Similarly, those of Hans Pfitzner, whilst including such a subject as the opera *Palestrina*, seem to be too derivative in actual musical material (Schumann, Brahms, Wagner, so it goes) to fire the imagination of any wide circle of modern music-lovers. Perhaps more interesting is the outlook of Ernst Křenek who, like so many typical composers of to-day, turns away from the sensuous side of the art. His *Symphonic Music* for nine solo instruments embodies the chief traits of his style; linear counterpoint, utter clarity of statement sometimes amounting to aridity, and a personal idiom full of character. Another of similar basic type is Anton von Webern, who resembles our own John Ireland in the extreme exiguity of his output.

One work, an operatic experiment, *Wozzeck*, has sufficed

A Series of Swift Vignettes

to spread the name of Alban Berg throughout the musical world, so daring, so original and so vital is its mode of presentation: *in all ways save one.* How many times have we not noticed in the foregoing pages, that new wine is poured into old bottles. We even reached the conclusion that the architectonic sense is less developed than any other part of the modern equipment. Berg's wine is certainly a new vintage, not to say a heady. What of the form in which he chooses to present it? In *Wozzeck*, Act I consists of a Suite (prelude, pavane, gigue, air), Rhapsody, March, Passacaglia and Rondo: Act II of a five-movement Symphony—Sonata, Fantasy and Fugue, Largo, Scherzo, Rondo: Act III of a set of six Inventions. Thus he expresses new ideations in arrestingly unfamiliar terms but in the old familiar shapes.

It is one of my theses that a new-contacted ideation, if completely seized, and if realized in the brain *in toto*, will impose, in addition to new melodic, harmonic and other media, original forms also in which these will be shown forth.

Medtner, though he was born in Russia and has lived there all his life, has been little affected by environment. He is a German, and heredity has been the strongest factor in his case; for his musical thought is German through and through. The operas of Erich Korngold are performed in Vienna but seem strangely unable to spread abroad. A sidelight on his point of view may be obtained from a remark he made to the present writer in 1925 to the effect that he considered the first act of *Tosca* the best work Puccini ever did and a 'great modern masterpiece.'

America has not yet 'found herself' in the world of creative music. Perhaps her great period of efflorescence

Music To-day

in this as in some other directions lies in the future. There can be no doubt whatever about her passionate interest, and of this is born, ultimately, the power to will and to do. As in all the other countries we have noticed, opinion is divided as to the advisability of founding an American national music upon the folk-types (in this case Negro) or upon the supernational classic-romantic schools. Men like Henry F. Gilbert, Paul Whiteman, and Gershwin, pursue the former course; such as Ernest Bloch,[1] Leo Ornstein, Edgar Varese, Charles Loeffler, E. Stillmann Kelley, J. Alden Carpenter, John Cadman, George W. Chadwick, C. T. Griffes, H. K. Hadley, and John Powell, the latter, and perhaps the true main road.

In French music of to-day the twin influences of Fauré and d'Indy may still be traced. The former has, both by precept and example—for he was a prolific composer—wielded a very great power. The latter, in his youth a pupil and devotee of Franck, founded in Paris the *Schola Cantorum* with the definite aim of cultivating the study of religious music, plain-song and the like. The living inspiration of Berlioz, Franck, and Debussy is still in evidence and Roussel, Dukas, Schmitt, have kept the torch alight. Of the youth of to-day—Taillefère, Durey, Auric and others —I like best Georges Migot, a true artist, who expresses, *via* the most admirable characteristics of his French birth, heredity, education and environment, a truly supernational type of ideation.

[1] Who, however, declares for his race, and often chooses Jewish themes (*e.g. Schelomo* and *Trois Poèmes Juifs*) for his works. In addition to a certain oriental elaboration of detail and incrustation of arabesque, he is capable of great surges of emotion and a wide sweeping expressiveness that can be very moving indeed. The dual influences of the National Devas (see p. 280) of his own race and of America, as they show in his work, are an interesting study.

A Series of Swift Vignettes

In England also many composers are working in the plenitude of their powers, whose ultimate achievements, and still less their effect upon the development of the art, cannot be prognosticated. Among those not dealt with elsewhere in these pages, perhaps the most commanding figure is Vaughan Williams. He is a pronounced and confessed Nationalist in music, and betrays in many works a deep and close affinity with the contrapuntal English Tudor school. His modal excursions appear to go no farther back than those vestiges which remained in the church- and folk-music of mediæval times. He is rarely chromatic—always freely contrapuntal. And his novel and occasionally arresting harmonies are far more often results (in a sense accidental) from his free part-leading than self-conscious essays in harmonic creativeness. Strength and solidity are the chief characteristics of his texture, but the accusation of heaviness in his orchestration so often brought against him is not justifiable. It results rather from his habit of moving blocks of harmony contrapuntally (as in Bach) than from any fault of instrumentation. The idyllic opening of his *Pastoral Symphony* shows one such threefold strand:

and if other counterpoints of block-harmony be juxtaposed we can easily see whence the accusation arises. This composer's expressed opinion that the greatness of *Meister-*

singer lies in its nationalistic characteristics I have already ventured to traverse;[1] and it is in no spirit of petty carping that one observes that obedience to his own dictum in the composition of his opera *Hugh the Drover* has by no means resulted in another *Meistersinger*.

His mystical tinge and natural religious instinct never succeeds in transporting him to any great height. At its least inspiring it results in an effete sacerdotalism which informs many of his works such as the *Mass* and the *Sancta Civitas*; at its best it lands him in the placid piosities of the 'Summerland' of the Spiritualists (the highest sub-plane of the second sphere of our classification) as in *The Shepherds of the Delectable Mountains*, and the suite *Flos Campi*. So much for one aspect, at least, of his inspiration. Upon the technical side he is a fine all-round musician, whose parallel can be found in any country which is musically civilized, and his influence upon his immediate circle (just as theirs in their own countries) can easily be traced. As, chiefly, upon Gustav Holst whose *Somerset Rhapsody* parallels his *Norfolk Rhapsody*. Holst's *The Planets* is a splendid work and well stands comparison with any contemporary composition in the whole world of music to-day. Granville Bantock's output has been copious and facile.[2] At the opposite pole in this respect is John Ireland whose extraordinary reticence and severe self-criticism leads to a constriction of output which his admirers often regret. Early under the Keltic influence that he has never attempted to shake off, Arnold Bax's 'mystic wistfulness' is often compared with that of the poet W. B. Yeats. His output is considerable and important, as is also that of Arthur Bliss,

[1] Cf. p. 224.
[2] And his large-hearted efforts long ago on behalf of Sibelius and Delius should not be forgotten.

A Series of Swift Vignettes

a somewhat less highly concentrated musical intelligence. Cyril Scott has, in the opinion of W. H. Hadow, " listened too readily to the twin sirens of atonality and metaphysics." But it is not in listening to siren or any other voices that danger lies for the musician, but in permitting them to glamour his senses, becloud his higher Intelligence, beguile him into the spiritualistic ' Summerland ' and call it the ultimate heaven, entrap him in a maze of bye-alleys with the suggestion that he is treading the grand high-road, and filch away his devotion and his fidelity to his real soul's Mistress. Scott well knows all this. Holbrooke is of quite different sort, but a very gifted artist. A ' close-up,' which is the only picture we can have of him, shows one who has been hardly dealt with by fate. The reverse can be said of William Walton, whose recognition as a very able composer indeed has been unusually swift.

Of contemporary Italian composers one of the most illustrious though hardly associated with the most advanced group, is Pizzetti, whose chamber music is perhaps his most valued contribution to the art. Respighi is a purposeful master of modern orchestration and his works for this instrument are popular wherever a symphony orchestra is available. Castelnuovo-Tedesco is one of the most interesting of the younger men. Casella is as many-sided in his art as a Saint-Saëns, and, in the trite phrase, he adorns everything he touches: adorns it, that is to say, with Italian generosity of colour, opulence of mass and vitality of line. An eclectic musician. More strictly in the current of super-nationalistic musical thought is Malipiero; in my view the most powerful and truly inspired of living Italian composers. His symphonic fragments for orchestra *Dalle tre Commedie Goldoniane* are really very excellent indeed, as also the *Variazioni senza Tema* for orchestra. By way of illustration of the non-nationalistic basis of fine music, compare the above quotation of the opening of Williams' *Pastoral Symphony* with the beginning of these *Variazioni*:

It is in no spirit of disparagement of them, but of acknowledgment to him, that one mentions the deep indebtedness of almost all modern Italian composers, to Puccini. His *cantilena* has imposed itself upon them strongly, and recognizably, in innumerable moments of emotion, passion, or desire, as distinct from the more typically modern mental-plane stuff which is as frequent in their works as in those of any other country. Think what one may of Puccini's gifts—and he modestly refers to himself as a mere mandolin-strummer by comparison with the Wagner of *Tristan*—one cannot call to mind any living composer who would be equal to the task of completing his opera *Turandot* as, we can imagine, the master would have done, had he lived. The excellent technician Franco Alfano was entrusted with this awesome task, and it is with no sneer, either overt or implied, that one is able only to record that he did his best. On the whole I regard the contribution of Italian composers to the progress of the art as equally important with that of any other country to-day.

CHAPTER FOURTEEN: A DIGRESSION WITH SOME CONSIDERATION OF THE DUAL WORLD OF MUSIC; HUMAN AND DEVA.[1]

THAT artists are a race apart is recognized upon all sides, sometimes with scarce a veneer of toleration by those who belong to the race apart from artists. These latter function more readily through the cerebro-spinal system, artists through the sympathetic-nervous system. This fact is at the root of a good deal of misunderstanding of the one type by the other. Cold, unresponsive, insensitive, often seem the non-artists to artists, whilst these are dismissed as ultra-emotional, butterfly-brained, irresponsible or worse by the others. Control of the sympathetic-nervous system seems to be more difficult than that of the cerebro-spinal, hence those frequent exhibitions of the 'temperamental' which have been wittily defined as ninety per cent 'temper' and ten per cent 'mental.' Nothing is to be gained by concentrating our studies in this direction.

But another fact, one of much greater import and fraught with far-reaching consequences, falls to be noticed here,

[1] Deva, *Sanskrit*; literally 'shining one'; plural (*anglicè*) Devas. So called because when perceived they appear to glow with an inner radiance. I use this word for two reasons, neither being due to a devotion to Orientalism. First: I prefer a Sanskrit word deriving from the inception of the Aryan race to a much more recent Greek or Latin one. (Zeus and Deus with our own words 'divine' and, by inversion, 'devil,' are derived from this Sanskrit root.) Second: the English word 'angel,' through association in the minds of millions with puerile piosities, or with females (why always females?) in shapeless white nightgowns, has lost the significance which the glorious splendour of the facts themselves warrants. The usual mistranslation of this word as 'god' is also misleading. Bunyan, rather surprisingly, refers to devas in these identical terms as 'shining ones.'

for it is one which operates in the ranks of artists themselves, is the cause of a great deal of misvaluation of their work, and is indeed one without some appreciation of which certain composers' works cannot fairly be judged at all. Hence this digression in the midst of a section devoted to modern masters' works.

A theory was long ago propounded as to the parallel evolution of devas and humans. Instances of excursions into the human kingdom of nature-spirits, undines, and so on, are quite frequently to be met with in the traditions of almost all races, and folk-stories of changelings abound. Instances also of the contrary—of invasion of the devic world by humans, may be studied by anyone interested. It is a fascinating mystery. What is now widely accepted as a fact is that side by side with the human evolution runs another—that of the deva—which from lowly, sub-human levels of 'elementals' (of Paracelsus), fairies, gnomes, nymphs and salamanders; stretches upward through nature-spirits and 'individualized' devas (of stature roughly parallel to human in their evolution); to national devas, and those of the four great regions of the Earth; to 'Thrones Dominations, Princedoms, Virtues, Powers, Cherubim and Seraphim;' and to those mighty Archangels who are viceregents of Almighty. Innumerable as the sands of the ocean, graded and ranked in a vast hierachy, their influence can be discerned from time to time in the history of our world. Pertinent to our present subject is a comparatively small group of devas, those whose being *is* music—the *Gandharvas*.

It matters nothing whether you regard them (as I do) as Entities who may be contacted objectively given the requisite faculty, or as Forces which may be perceived by

A Digression

the intuitive powers. Suffice it that they exist and that by contact with them and their world glories unimaginable in the terrestrial realms may be glimpsed. Pythagoras, speaking of the harmony of the spheres, did not say that the movements of the heavenly bodies made an audible music, but that *it was itself a music* (says Schelling); and again: Beauty [in music] is a Divine Being perceived in a form adapted to our human condition.

At certain levels there is a measure of interaction between devas of a particular type and the world of music. In the occult fragment about the ensouling of music quoted on page 183 it was stated that one of the methods by which music could be ensouled was " by creating a powerful ' thought-form ' into, and through which, the music plays." This is what appears to be done by music-devas at rare times and probably for specific purposes which lie outside our ken. What is more easily understandable and indeed clearly to be noticed, is that composers of a certain type respond to and are inspired by the deva life whilst others are not. It is no part of our thesis that one type is more beautiful, more valuable, or in any way preferable to the other, *chacun à son goût*. But it is surely desirable to be able to understand both types, and thus help to obviate the misunderstanding of one type by the other; a misunderstanding which results in misvaluation throughout the world of music. And I believe this fact of the co-operation of devas with composers, rare though it be, throws a flood of light not only upon the misvaluation of the artist type by the non-artist, but upon the congenital antagonism of the one type of musician toward the other.[1]

---

[1] As I write this my attention is drawn to a remark in Cyril Scott's recently published *Music: Its Secret Influence throughout the Ages,* to the effect that

Music To-day

Thus, there is a divergence between what might broadly be described as the human and the devic types of artist. In nothing is this divergence more clearly to be noticed than in the terms used in appreciation by the two types. To the one, such phrases as " his music affects us profoundly and stirs us to the depths " (of our emotions, understood); or " his large humanity," are the strongest they can use. And these seem to them to be the terms which carry realist approbation. To the other type such encomiums appear somewhat uninteresting or at best uninspiring. To them eulogy would better be expressed by such phrases as ' unearthly beauty,' ' other-worldly,' ' emanating from far-off realms,' and the like. A typical illustration of this divergence is the fact that many persons, disliking the gods, undines, dwarfs, etc., of Wagner's *Ring* (reflections of various nature-spirit, or devic realms), extol wholeheartedly the ' rich warm humanity ' of *Meistersinger*: and *vice versa*.

Once we have assimilated the idea of the possible co-operation of a certain class of deva with a certain type of composer, or even admitted the possibility that the latter are responsive to vibrations of the devic realms, we are at once in not merely a more favourable position, but the only one from which a fair estimate of the stature of certain composers can be made. It is true that a composer may be touched by the devic fire only rarely; that only certain of his works, or even portions of works may reflect the devic

---

" Foulds in his *World Requiem* attempted to simulate that music " [*i.e.* the music of the Devas] " with the employment of quarter-tones." A misconception all the more strange in that whenever attempts were made to " simulate Deva music " in that work, the procedure adopted, as I afterward realized, was invariably diatonic. ' False relation,' however, as the above writer truly remarks, as well as polytonality, atonality, and especially devices of contrasted *timbres*, were other means employed with this end in view.

A Digression

vibration. But in the main, a more profound, a more basic demarcation is noticeable.

Bach belongs to the one type; Palestrina to the other. Bach, so far as I can remember from a fairly extensive acquaintance with his colossal output, never touches devic realms at all: Palestrina rarely forsakes them. There are glimpses of devic vibrations, albeit of lesser ones (nature-spirits), in the music of Haydn. Handel undoubtedly attempts to paraphrase the music of the *Gandharvas* in some of his choruses and, although nothing is more obnoxious to me than vague speculation in these matters, I venture to accept as literal facts the composer's own descriptions of " hearing a choir of angels singing," of his desire to make music of like sort, and the records of friends who found the composer in tears from the ineffable glory and bliss of the angelic vibrations with which he was temporarily in touch. He is reported as saying, " I seemed to hear the music of angels." Now " seemed to hear " is particularly suggestive. For whereas in the mundane world we make our contacts by use of differentiated senses, such is not the case with rarer vibrations, of which we might more properly speak as ' becoming aware of.' For my part (ingenuous creature), I attach this sort of significance to his remark during the twenty-four days' ' raptus ' in which he created *Messiah*: " I did think I did see all Heaven before me, and the great God himself." If we may take this remark literally—and the time is long past when the possibility at least could not be conceded—there need be no surprise at the master's mistaking one of these indescribably resplendent music-angels for " the great God himself."

Gluck exhibits unmistakable signs in certain of his works, of having been touched by the devic fire; and a characteristic *naïveté* in the harmonic lay-out (not altogether due to his period) rather strengthens than nullifies this opinion. At least it may be said that his purity of style is of all time. Berlioz is right, " the beautiful pages of Gluck will remain always beautiful."

Mozart gives many a hint to those who can ' hear between the notes,' (his own account of the inspiration which we know as *Batti batti* in *Don Giovanni* is exceedingly suggestive to a practical student of these aspects of creative art); Schubert also.

Schumann too, touched the mighty deva-evolution. But alas, lacking any guidance so far as I am aware on the all-important question of the regulation of his life so as to avert danger which results from a lack of co-ordination between the extremely rapid (because rarefied) vibrations of devic life, and the physical instrument in which he tried to record them, he was thrown off his mental balance, with what result every student knows. Judging from the somewhat meagre accounts, it would seem that Schumann in some way opened himself to the vibrations of the *Gandharvas* (whose being, remember, is music). Once having done so, the poor composer became obsessed by this ever-present, never-ceasing flood of music, and, lacking the power to regulate, inhibit, or deal with it in any way, the result was inevitable. A somewhat similar fate befell Smetana, and also Jullien, and, of course, others whose obscurity leaves all but alienists without reliable data.[1] In these three cases contact was established with music *in esse*, before the trick of breaking contact at will had been learnt.

[1] It is, then, an adventure fraught with danger. But I am all for living dangerously anyway, and conscious contact with the deva-world is worth a good deal of risk.

A Digression

We are in fact surrounded by an ocean of unheard music: Nature being a Cosmic Symphony. The power to 'tune in' and thus to 'hear' it at various levels is one that is just beginning to be apprehended by mankind and practised by a few persons widely scattered over this tiny globe. The phrase 'Cosmic Symphony' is therefore not used here in the imaginative sense of the minor poet but in the severely practical sense of the professional musician.

Much of the misvaluation to which Berlioz has always been subjected is dissipated in the light of this information concerning devic influences. Many and extensive are the 'holes in his technique'; many his harmonic and melodic *gaucheries*.[1] And lacking some understanding of the deva impacts which he so frequently transcribes in his works (*i.e.*, either a subconscious, intuitive understanding, or an understanding due to knowledge), it is impossible fairly to evaluate Berlioz' work. The same is true of many composers around whom controversy has raged, is raging and will rage.

There is a wonderful passage in the introduction to the *Symphonie Fantastique* (p. 286) which is an awe-inspiring marvel.

Familiar as I have been with it these many years, it never fails to induce in me an answering vibration which I have learned to recognize as devic. Sensitive persons will readily perceive its unique quality, a quality which it is beyond my pen-power to describe in words.

Music-lovers will remember also his records of sylph-vibrations in the ballet of that name in *La Damnation de Faust*; the *Minuet des Follets*; the inhuman music of the Demon chorus toward the end; the magic of the opening of the *Scène d'Amour* in his *Romeo and Juliet* symphony;

[1] About which Ravel holds forth so smartly—so unnecessarily.

Music To-day

the *Queen Mab* scherzo; the *Ronde du Sabbat*. Much of this is music of the lesser devas, of elementals and nature-spirits who are at a point in deva-evolution which is below

a level corresponding to the human stage. But Berlioz is able to go further than this. From realms which are the venue of devas beyond a stage parallel to the human, have emanated many of his indescribable inspirations. The un-analysable *ambience* of the Angel chorus, Marguerite's apotheosis, in *Faust*:

A Digression

holds a devic vibration impossible to detect (as Saint-Saëns so acutely remarks about much else of Berlioz) in the written notes.[1] Many other deva-inspired passages occur in his works. The *Sanctus* of the *Messe des Morts* is certainly one, and much of the music of *Les Troyens* is of this nature, though by this time he had realized the hopelessness of expecting people to respond to the things which had most deeply moved himself.

Grieg, Sterndale Bennett, Mendelssohn less than might be expected, but MacDowell, Dvořák, Smetana, Debussy, Franck, Sibelius, Delius, Holst (*e.g.*, the end of the *Neptune* movement of his *Planets*), Bloch (national devas these), and a hint here and there in the work of Szymanovski; these and others show devic influences in their music. These are also very strikingly present in Rutland Boughton's opera *The Immortal Hour*; particularly in the *Fairy Song* and certain other passages. This work had an almost uncanny effect upon many people, quite a number becoming genuinely fascinated and attending performance after performance, not, be it noted, in order more clearly to grasp the plot or to understand any recondite passages in Fiona Macleod's poem

[1] How lacking in just this quality is the *Verklärung* of Strauss' *Tod und Verklärung*.

Music To-day

or obscurities in the score, but simply to bask, as it were, in the undeniably magical *ambience* of the work. Yet, the consensus of informed opinion would hardly be so favourable to its purely musical value. Indeed, when judged by ordinary standards I doubt if it would be considered as very distinguished, because of a certain characteristic absence of sheer intellectual weight—a trait to which I shall refer presently.

Beethoven shows traces of devic influence very rarely indeed, though there is a point in the slow movement of the *Pastoral* symphony (clarinets are holding an F with its major third, violins are hopping about busily with the chord) during which I can always dream off into a delicious *rapport* with a world of (to be sure, not very-highly-evolved) nature-spirit intelligences. Through lack of perception of this kind most people (Grove for example), find this to be Beethoven's poorest symphony. Certainly if music is to be judged by the power of its appeal from the brain to the brain, this would be a just evaluation. Surely it is not so. But there is a kind of childlike *naïveté* which goes with the ready response to devic life which even Beethoven's powerful and highly organized brain did not throw off. From this contact, by the way, results a certain childlike *naïveté* which is wrongly ascribed to *all* artists. And it is the lack of stark intellectual values in so much deva-work which blinds so many people to its other and magical qualities.[1] Not many years ago a slight piece was published bearing the title *Gandharva Music* which is of a *naïveté* almost incredible from a purely intellectual point of view. Yet I have seen veritable magic result from its performance.[2]

From this fact arises another, namely, that composers

---

[1] But cf. p. 290 also for another angle on this question.
[2] Described in *The Bright Messenger*: Algernon Blackwood.

A Digression

who work along these lines are naturally prone to greater inequalities than the non-devic type. Berlioz, Grieg, Delius and all the others lapse into puerilities at times such as never do Bach, Reger, *et hoc genus omne*. But apart altogether from this, it is a lack of the proper attitude on our own part that has mitigated against our enjoyment of devic types of music in the past, and has operated against a correct evaluation of composers of like type.

In attempting to convey through music these vibrations of the devic kingdom, two ways are open to the composer. First: he may endeavour so far as is possible by use of our incredibly clumsy, coarse, unsubtle instruments,[1] to paraphrase or to imitate what he 'hears.' Second: he may attempt, by use of such means as he thinks most suitable, to induce in his listeners such a degree of *rapport* with the deva kingdom that they, the listeners, will themselves be able to respond, in however slight a degree, to their vibrations. The latter was the procedure adopted in the little piece quoted above. In listening to music of this sort the mind has to be held in abeyance, for our object is other than mental enjoyment. (If I take a powder against headache I do not concentrate upon its flavour. My interest is other than gustatory.) In cases of this kind, which of course are comparatively rare, the interposition of the mind is inhibitory of, and not contributory to the desired effect. So accustomed are we in the West nowaday to referring every sensation to the brain for its judgment that it has become difficult for us to confine it to its proper duties. Worse still, we allow it to intrude its ratiocinative operations long before the appro-

---

[1] At one time, after a prolonged period of concentration upon Deva music, I found the tone of the violin, which is, after all, one of our most subtle instruments, almost unbearably coarse and jarring.

priate time, and thus build up a barrier as it were, across which the sensitive vibrations we are discussing are unable to make their way. And ours is the loss.

But, as an ancient Eastern writing has it: "The mind is the great slayer of the Real. Let the disciple slay the Slayer." And this is an adage the application of which, *at the right time and to the appropriate type of work*, would be of incalculable advantage to composers, performers and listeners alike.[1]

It is also instructive to examine the works of that most comprehensive genius Wagner from the point of view under immediate consideration. His method is dual. In addition to the second method mentioned above, he provides a type of music which readily becomes 'ensouled'[2] by entities of the deva world. This, be it understood, only when he chooses to do so. In the whole of *Meistersinger*, for example, you shall find but one hint of this range of vibration, but how magically it imposes its more rarefied vibrations upon the 'warm humanity' of the rest of the comedy (I refer to the passage early in Act III where Sachs sings "*Ein Kobold half wohl da: ein Glühwurm fand sein Weibchen nicht*"): nowhere at all in *Tristan*. The *Ring* of course, obediently to its subject, is full of the music of water-elementals, undines (Rhine-maidens), mineral- or lower-earth-elementals (Mime and Co.), fire-elementals, salamanders (under the fire-deva Loge), and many more. The Flower-maidens (sylphs), in *Parsifal* are a complete failure from this point of view—one of the master's few. All these are vibrations of devic life up to, and roughly parallel with, the human

---

[1] The remark on p. 25 about "music going in at one ear and out at the other, missing the brain *en route*" carrying, as it appears to, a measure of satire, is quite beside the present point.

[2] Cf. p. 179.

A Digression

kingdom. Those regions of deva evolution which transcend the human, those, namely, which stretch from thence up to the highest Cosmic Archangels, Wagner is less concerned to translate for us, though he makes a tremendous and awe-inspiring effort to reach those of a certain grade in *Parsifal*, where, such is the evocative power of his music that, given conditions at all favourable, devas of coeval vibration-type are drawn toward his mighty vortex and are able to materialize, if not quite in densest physical matter, at least in etheric, and thus become visible to any who possess the very slight degree of clairvoyance necessary for etheric vision.[1] It is quite a common occurrence to meet persons of utter integrity who declare that they have made this experience. No student of even my lowly standing could fail to note that the master contacted the Buddhic plane of which he gives such a wondrous paraphrase in the *Charfreitagzauber*. He is less concerned here, however, with the glories of the devic manifestations upon that plane, than with the human vibrations which may be contacted there; but he shows us these through the *ambience* of clouds of elemental and nature-spirit vibrations proper to the burgeoning of Spring.

The foregoing information—merely a tiny scrap germane to our present subject—from a body of real teaching of greater bulk, is, I am aware, highly controversial in its nature. It is, however, the result of at least a modicum of first-hand experience of the realms under consideration, and some measure of contact with the life that informs them.

When applying this knowledge, however scanty and incomplete it may be, to the world of music and musicians,

[1] The etheric portion of the aura can be seen by anyone who makes use of Dr Kilner's apparatus.

and to the interplay between certain types of deva and artists who are responsive to the vibrations of their worlds, it is surely better to proceed to reason *a priori*—acquainting ourselves so far as is possible with the causes that manifest in our mundane world as effects—rather than *a posteriori*—attempting to educe from the effects with which we are familiar, a speculative, nebulous theory of causes; a timid and unhelpful theory, of the ' it may possibly be ' order.

Thus, acquainting ourselves with this unique type of vibration, whose characteristics are so strong that they are instantly recognizable by one who has sympathetically studied them, we notice how clearly it shows in the work of certain composers toward whom we may now more profitably turn our attention.

I do not assert that these composers (with perhaps one or two exceptions) were aware of the sources of their inspiration in any such objective way as that sketched out in the foregoing. They do not know and do not need to know, for genius can accomplish much more than learning can attain to. But, even so, progress takes the form of rendering overt the workings of natural law which were formerly occult—as we have previously seen—and among these I take the present aspect to be one of real importance in the world of music.

We are now in a position more accurately to review the grandest effort made by any musician since Palestrina to convey some of these deva-vibrations to us through music.

Chapter Fifteen: Vignettes Continued

Scriabin — Debussy — Delius — MacDowell — Sibelius. — A Vignette Tailpiece.

THE lack of any balanced evaluation of, or satisfactorily definitive judgment upon the work of ALEXANDER NICOLAS SCRIABIN (Russian; born 1871) up to the present time, is not difficult to understand.

All musicians, all music-lovers, all critics, are sharply divisible into two categories: those who concentrate more naturally upon the technical, and those who gravitate more easily toward the inspirational sides of the art. Hitherto there has not appeared, so far as I am aware, a critical estimate of this composer's work which holds the balance at all fairly between these two opposing tendencies; and certainly none showing in addition to an adequate musical equipment, any grasp of occultism, experience of actual occult experiments, or even one that betrayed a reasonably wide course of study in those fields of occult lore, tradition and experience, whence Scriabin drew so much of his inspiration (That L. Sabaneiev fulfils the latter but not the former condition in his book *Scriabin* (Moscow 1916) I have upon good authority, though only at second hand, as I cannot read Russian.)

At one time, so great was his hold upon the second type of listeners that his fame grew at extraordinary speed, spread far and wide, and culminated in a veritable Scriabin-worship of such ardency and such unquestioning acceptance as is properly due only to the loftiest souls that incarnate in the human kingdom. Scriabin was emphatically not of these. Upon the other hand, his detractors, persons of our first type, finding plenty of 'holes in his technique' and congenitally unable to respond to his 'philosophic ideations' have roundly abused him as a pseudo-occultist, have described his music as Chopin-and- (theosophic) water, and have endeavoured to consign him and all his works to the limbo of things best forgotten.

Of specific opinions upon his work published in this country, four will serve to indicate the divergences noted above. A. Eaglefield Hull, in a book of some three hundred pages devoted to Scriabin, dismisses the one motive-force that dominated his life, the creative urge behind all his greater works, the *raison d'être* for *Prometheus, Poème de l'Extase*, the *Mystery*, etc., the illuminating power of his whole make-up, mental, moral, spiritual, psychological and creative—I mean his theosophy; in a few apologetic lines. As thus: " This is where I am very much at sea. I am not a theosophist, and cannot ' function on the astral plane ' as they put it. Scriabin would hardly expect one to judge of theosophy by his music. Still less is one able to estimate his music in terms of theosophy. I am keenly sympathetic and appreciative of Scriabin's outlook in life and art "; (what a claim to make, by the way, by one who denies having either theoretical or practical knowledge of the occult teachings on which Scriabin founded both his life and his art) " I can at any rate judge of the effect of Scriabin's music on myself, and Scriabin certainly wrote his music for the general public, and not for the Theosophists in particular.

" I can well imagine that when Scriabin joined the Theosophists he would eagerly welcome a system of

A Series of Swift Vignettes

Philosophy which fitted in so well with what musicians are ever trying to express more clearly. For no philosophy has systematized the scale of the emotions . . . so well as have the Theosophists."

As well might a book be written about Blake by one who should know nothing of Mysticism. Interesting up to a point it might be; hardly informative, definitive, or satisfactory could it possibly be if it omitted a consideration of the mainspring of his creative work.

A more recent writer, W. J. Turner, opines that Scriabin's work in the musical field " represents the chief advance in musical consciousness since Beethoven's time." Against which we may set the opinion of C. Gray in an essay on Scriabin, that " he initiated an era of charlatanism in music, and it is on this account alone that he will be remembered." [1] To anyone with an ounce of *savoir-vivre* who ever met Scriabin, even the juxtaposition of the word charlatan with his name would be impossible. Like or dislike his music as you may, he was a man of transparent sincerity of purpose, of utter integrity of aim and of an almost naïve simplicity. To be antagonistic to his views—antipathetic to his music; that is understandable; but . . . " initiated an era of charlatanism in music "—what train of thought, what odd angle of contact, what crooked bye-alley of misapprehension could lead to such a conclusion? . . . Well, well; it is a wonderful world!

Upon the other side again, E. Newman writes to the effect that " no amount of criticism of the work " (*Prometheus*),

[1] This writer by the way, speaking of ' second-rate artists,' pays them quite unintentionally this compliment, that ' they are not satisfied with the limited range of their own personalities.' I should think not indeed! Considering what a very limited field his ' personality ' covers he would be a mole-like microcosm indeed who should be so satisfied.

" in details can diminish the wonder of such an achievement as this." And " listening to it solely as music only a congenitally unimaginative dullard or a musician sodden with the futile teaching of the text-books and the conservatoires, could help feeling that here is music that comes as near as is at present possible to being the pure voice of Nature and the soul themselves."

The information presented in the foregoing digression and similar ' occult ' research alone can give us a key to the enigma of Scriabin and enable us to suggest, it may be, a point of view from which some at least of these diverging and conflicting opinions may be brought into relation, if not into agreement.

In his natural desire to avoid the implication that he composed to a system (which every serious composer would understand), Scriabin denied that his music grew out of theosophy and claimed, on the contrary, that his theosophy grew out of his music. In a sense this may have been so, but it undoubtedly reinforced, refreshed and made more articulate in physical-plane terms his previous acquaintance with occult and psychic matters, and led him to a clear realization of the possibility of the co-operation already posited.

His natural temperamental bias is shown in the Chopinesque character of all his works up to and including the *First Symphony* (op. 26). Tchaikovsky had been a big enough musician to see the possible danger of over-emphasizing national characteristics and had indeed shown marked hostility toward any such idea. Scriabin benefited by this. Another influence which helped to mould his musical equipment—as also that of Rachmaninof and Medtner—was that of Taneiev. And to this influence Scriabin was obedient all his life. Let it be said at once that he never freed himself

A Series of Swift Vignettes

from the strict, old-fashioned four-bar, eight-bar, sixteen-bar fetters; nor from the habit of imposing upon all his larger works the Sonata design. This latter, a very real fetter upon his imagination, is one to which a good many composers of our day unthinkingly submit, as it seems to me. Their matter and manner may be fresh and vital; the matrix in which these are shaped is too often an outworn one which should also be outgrown. The two different and opposed styles which we may describe as the closed symphonic and the free rhapsodical style offer us a categorical division. Take Brahms as exemplar of the former and Wagner of the latter and you clearly see the directions in which they lead. Subtle as the distinction may seem, the reality of it is realized at once if we compare the logical design of any of the symphonic first movements (which are closed-symphonic in style) with the apparently non-logical but equally satisfactory *Siegfried Idyll* (which is freely-rhapsodic in style).

In 1921, when conducting the chorus for Safonov for a performance of Rimsky-Korsakov's *Sadko*, I took the opportunity of questioning him upon certain points which were still obscure to me regarding Scriabin, who had been his pianoforte pupil at the Moscow Conservatoire in 1888. Safonov, at any rate, made no bones about the source of Scriabin's inspiration. The lessons took the form of a series of improvisations played by the pupil to the teacher. " He has more than once played me into a trance," said the old man in effect, " and his music was not *composed*, it was ' free ' music of pure magic." And again, " But he told me it was impossible to put down on paper the music *that he heard*." That Safonov followed this up by remarking that Scriabin had formed an immoral *liaison* with

Music To-day

Tatiana Feodorovna which had "resulted in all his mad new music," was just another instance to add to the many, of the frequent confusion between human-moral judgments, and artistic values.[1] Such confusion, however, is easier to understand and excuse in the case of the peasant-born rough Cossack with his conservative musical outlook than with some others who could be named.

It was soon after the completion of his first symphony that Scriabin reached the important turning-point in his creative work. He now began consciously to contact the great deva evolution, and to attempt to translate these contacts into music. Under this influence his old-fashioned harmonic system was gradually remoulded until it was able to afford us such superbities as we see in the *Tenth Piano Sonata* and *Prometheus*.

Yet, although his latest works show a clear approach to ultra-chromaticism, he never achieved complete freedom in his harmonic system. Certainly he gradually forsook the tonal system and worked in that of upper-partial-tone harmonies, thus breaking away from the old fetters and creating such remarkable things as the opening of the *Eighth Piano Sonata*, opus 66:

[1] Cf. p. 188.

A Series of Swift Vignettes

But that even under the tremendous impulsion of the deva life he fell short of complete harmonic emancipation we may ascribe to two causes. First; the insufficiency of his sheer musical personality: second; his lifelong, and from this point of view unfortunate devotion to the pianoforte. This tempered instrument helped to 'step down,' as an electrician would say, the devic vibrations of much of Scriabin's inspiration and, useful and admirable as it is, the sincere musician cannot help but agree with Beethoven that in several ways " it is and always will be an unsatisfactory instrument."

But in spite of these personal and technical imperfections, unavoidable as they were, the creative impulse fostered in Scriabin by this new type of contact raised his work at once from a merely local into a world-wide significance. For a realization of the glory and power of the inexpressible magnificence of devic realms henceforward pervaded the whole of his life and work.

The first composition in which was demonstrated the new force at work in Scriabin was the *Divine Poem* for orchestra, op. 43, which, however, still exhibits more of the theosophic influence in its 'programme' than devic influence in its presentation. 'Luttes,' the first movement, shows the conflict between man (of the first, second, and 'lower' third planes of our plan) and Man (the 'higher' mental, intuitional, and spiritual being). The latter prevails. 'Voluptes,' the second movement, depicts the delights of the sensual world (as have many other works) and somewhat less finely than, for example, the *Venusberg* music in *Tannhäuser*. 'Jeu Divin,' the last movement, shows the greatest proportion of devic inspiration in an endeavour to depict the liberated spirit of the 'higher' mental (Causal), intuitional (Buddhic), and spiritual (Atmic) realms. The musical world of the West had heard nothing like this before.

It was about this time (1905) that he came into close touch with the leaders of theosophic thought, with whom he continued to correspond for the remainder of his life. And it seems to me (who am no theosopher) only fair to say that it is probably due to their guidance, their advice and experience that no such tragedy overtook Scriabin as those already mentioned in connection with Schumann, Smetana, Jullien and others.

Jean Delville, the famous Belgian painter (who was a close friend of the musician and designed the cover for some of his works), told me that at this period Scriabin was an omnivorous reader of the Upanishads and other early Eastern scriptures, as well as a close student of modern glossarial comments thereon. This study undeniably clarified his thoughts, crystallized his aims and elucidated his inner aspirations.

Le Poème de l'Extase, op. 54, clearly shows the results of this expansion and definition of Scriabin's perceptions. Thus, contrarily to the *Divine Poem*, it exhibits more of the devic realization and much less indication of working to a theosophic 'programme.' Here he attempts to parallel upon the physical plane the utter joy, the unrestrained ecstasy, the inexhaustible activity which a glimpse of deva life reveals to us. No wonder this music was said (even by admirers) to be as baffling as it was stimulating. It achieves a degree of sonorous beauty hitherto unheard from a modern orchestra.

Now Scriabin became completely imbued with the devic fire and under its influence his incandescent spirit flamed

A Series of Swift Vignettes

out in the blinding inspiration of *Prometheus: The Poem of Fire*, op. 60. This is, beyond question, his greatest work and one of outstanding importance in the progress of modern music.

Writing to A. N. Briantchaninov after a performance in London in 1913 he says: " The public is particularly moved by the performance of works which have philosophical [mystical?] ideas as a basis, and combine the elements of various arts." [1] If one is unable to agree—amazing, staggering though the work may be, nay, is—that it is a complete success, the reasons would seem to be several. First: he was attempting to pour new (deva) wine into old (classical-sonata) wine-skins. Second: his personal *karma*, his stage in evolution, precluded a greater measure of perfection. It may be, too, that the gods in their wisdom deem the time not yet ripe to unloose upon a but-partly-evolved mankind vibrations of the extreme rapidity and potency of the ' shining ones' and their supernal realms. Again, his tentative employment of the colour-organ in this work [2] (which has already been mentioned as an attempt towards a synthetic presentation of a plurality of arts) confuses those of his audience who are lending a purely musical intelligence to the work, whilst those who bring to bear also a true psychic perception are positively thwarted by the inaccuracy of the instrument and its false correspondences, as already pointed out.

Now a characteristic trait to be noticed as resulting from contact with devas, is the establishing of a *rapport* with the Causal sphere, the sphere (see page 168) of Unity, of Archetypes, of undifferentiated ideations. What is con-

---
[1] Cf. p. 349, *A Synthesis of Arts*.
[2] Cf. p. 95, *Colour and Music*. Also p. 350, *A Synthesis of Arts*.

Music To-day

tacted in those realms as a single, undifferentiated ideation, manifests in this world of Diversity in a multiform expression—diverse in time and in space.

From his deva-contacts emanated the Mystery idea which dominated Scriabin's thoughts to the end of his life. He performed prodigies, was capable of undreamed-of efforts, lived a few wonderful years in the lambent flame of this lofty vibration, composed work after work under its direct inspiration; and finally summoning to his aid all his resources, inspirational and expressional, in one mighty effort to give to the world a glimpse of the divine Unity which can be reached even from this realm of bewildering Diversity, he set his hand to the 'Initial Act' of the *Mystery*.

It was as daring a conception as ever gleamed like a *Fata Morgana* before the inner eye of a St Germain, a Jacob Boehme, a William Blake, a Wagner, or a Gregoriev. Scriabin well knew that mankind was far from ready to respond to such a concept, but regardless of all but the inner compulsion to express to less happy mortals his joy and his exaltation, he laboured on till kindly *karma* intervened and shining devas welcomed him to happier worlds than this, his life-work uncompleted, his Mystery unexpressed, his great plan unachieved.

Still, he remains the grandest composer of this type save Palestrina, and by far the greatest exemplar in modern times of the many who have been touched by the creative deva-fire and have glimpsed a faint and muted adumbration of the ineffable glories of devic life.

It occasionally happens in the evolution of music that a single work, even one of small dimensions, is ultimately seen to be a veritable landmark in the art: is recognized as

A Series of Swift Vignettes

either a marvellously succinct epitome of, or a profoundly pregnant forecast of vital tendencies. Such a work was *L'Après-midi d'un Faune* of CLAUDE DEBUSSY (French; born 1862). His supernormal sensitivity, early impressed by the great Bayreuth master, caused later in his development a revulsion against the Classics (especially Beethoven) and a characteristically French *volte-face* regarding Wagner. His Latin penetration of perception and Gallic appreciation of niceness of balance between means and end simply would not permit this descendant of Couperin and Rameau to depict unrestraint of any kind. That of Beethoven in his ' unbuttoned ' mood distressed him. Wagner's eroticism in, for example, *Tristan und Isolde* nauseated him. Examples of ' raciness ' or anything ' redolent of the soil ' jarred his aristocratic soul. Upon the technical side the piling up of ponderous masses of sound, and the loss of the special individual characteristics of all the instruments save brass and percussion which this involves, seemed to him the nemesis of a sentimental, heart-upon-sleeve attitude, savouring of vulgarity and lack of breeding.

Harmonically he was not so much an innovator (as has frequently been supposed) as an exploiter. Whole-tone music to which he applied himself and which he erected into a system [1]—which however, he well knew when to forsake, unlike so many of his immediate followers—is now, thanks to his labours, a pawn in the game which every composer of our day may play when it suits his purpose. It had been foreshadowed by Liszt and Mussorgsky as well as by Debussy's compatriot Satie. Usually spoken of as the ' whole-tone scale,' it cannot properly be considered a scale at all. Neither as a mode.[2] It occupies a place between

[1] Cf. p. 43.   [2] Cf. 43.

modal music (properly so-called) in its widest sense, and absolutely ' free ' atonal music. In this respect it resembles chromaticism. Its vagueness arises as we noted in a previous section on Modes, from the absence of a dominant, and useful as it undoubtedly is as a device for the expression of shifting, nebulous, unrelated states, and strikingly liberating as it must have seemed to musicians of Debussy's time, we cannot fail to find it as unsatisfactory a system upon which to erect a musical edifice of any size, as we have seen the modal system, the quarter-tone system, the atonal system, the purely chromatic, or indeed any *one* device in our technical equipment.

His very frequent use of the pentatonic formula has sometimes been pronounced inexplicable and his affinity with musical systems which he was not known to have studied, and of distant countries which he was not known to have visited has likewise puzzled many a commentator. Our previous studies have, however, shed some light upon this usually obscure branch of the subject and we have seen that when the consciousness of the creative thinker is raised to Causal or ' higher ' levels, he is able to contact ideations which are the same for those of any nationality, however they may be coloured by the personality, etc., on their way through to physical-plane expression.[1]

In Chapter XIV (p. 289) it was noted " that composers who work along these lines are naturally prone to greater inequalities than the non-devic type." And it was surely at a time when his devic contact was temporarily out of gear that Debussy constructed the very unconvincing—the incredibly forced—movement whose bones were perhaps rather unkindly laid bare upon page 118.

[1] Cf. p. 223.

A Series of Swift Vignettes

It was because he allowed his consciousness to work by intuition rather than by reason that he was able to contact those deva-vibrations which are so clearly traceable in so many of his works. This is not to say that his technical equipment was other than highly advanced. Putting this at the disposal of his inspiration it is little to be wondered at that it took on novel and wondrous attributes, harmonic, rhythmic and formal, and dominated the art in Europe for nearly a quarter of a century. For his inspiration, when in its full plenitude, completely informed his musical style and in nothing is this more clearly to be seen than in his orchestration. Instead of mixing all the orchestral tones in one massive and muddy *tutti* in which certain of the *timbres* nullify others, he disengages the separate and highly distinctive *timbres* of the instruments, causing one to *rapelle* another in the most delightful and exquisite manner.

But it is particularly by his choice of subjects, by the subtle qualities he exhibits, and by the special characteristics of those nature-spirit and devic vibrations which he so admirably translates into perfect sound-pictures, that he has imposed himself upon modern musical thought in a unique and ineffaceable manner. The adorable *Ariettes oubliées*; the *Nocturnes* (*Nuages: Fêtes: Sirènes*) for orchestra; *La Cathédrale engloutie, La Terrasse des audiences du clair de lune,* and *Ce qu'a vu le vent d'ouest* from the *Préludes*; *L'Après-midi d'un Faune; La Mer;* the ballet *Jeux;* and the opera *Pelléas et Mélisande,* all these are full of passages which abundantly show forth all the qualities categorically examined in our Third Part, excepting those of the sublimest type. When he essays these, as in *Martyre de Saint Sébastien,* he cannot be said to have succeeded. It is therefore pre-eminently as a devic musician, exquisitely sensitive to certain ranges of their influence, masterly in his creation of novel technical means of expression by which only could they adequately be paraphrased, and, most of all, as an exemplar of perfect balance between artless and artistic in his externalizations of these rare and beautiful vibrations, that we may most fittingly regard Claude Debussy. Innumerable must be those who, when they think of him, will find this precious devic echo ' creep i' the ear.'

In the year 1906 I first met FREDERICK DELIUS (English; born 1863) at a festival at Essen. His *Sea Drift* was fairly adequately presented and he was, I remember, greatly encouraged.[1] A little later, meeting at a concert which included his *Appalachia* variations we had a long and interesting talk on the constitution of orchestras. In the same programme was included I think, a Schubert symphony, Mendelssohn's *Ruy Blas* overture, a Wagner excerpt and various other works. Naturally the same orchestra, a large one of some eighty players, had to cope with the whole programme. Now Mendelssohn calls for one alto, one tenor and one bass trombone: Schubert writes for two tenor and one bass trombone. The whole programme was played through with two tenor trombones, one bass, and one bass tuba. But Delius was adamant in his opinion that

[1] The words are taken from Walt Whitman and the composer creates an effective choral background by use of a reiterated motif to the words: " Two, together; two, together." In this performance, of course in German, " Zwei, zusammen; zwei, zusammen," its sibilants multiplied by 350 (the number of the chorus) sounded anything but euphonious.

A Series of Swift Vignettes

no self-respecting orchestra should contain other than three of four tenor trombones, and no tuba.

Anything like ponderosity in the brass section obviously caused him real pain. The 'small' trumpets in C whose volume is notably less than that of the old F instruments demanded by the 'classical' composers was also one of his *desiderata*. In short, subtlety was the one quality of which he was avid. That he has not altered but rather intensified this trend with the passage of time is self-evident in his works.

His Dutch (father) and German (mother) descent accounts for the 'pull' which Germany has exercised over him and, to a certain extent, for the recognition which his work has received in that country. Why is his work almost totally neglected in France where he has lived for nearly forty years? A witty Frenchman to whom I posed the question epitomized that country's reaction to Delius in the phrase, "Il est un homme crée dans l'image de son maître . . . Debussy." Witty, maybe, but hardly profound. For there is a world of difference between, say, the French composer's chief work *Pelléas* and Delius' *Mass of Life*.

In England also, but for some early performances by Bantock and Wood, his work went unrecognized until taken up, repeatedly played, and eventually popularized by Beecham. This part of his propaganda has now been well done indeed so far as England is concerned. That of his personal proponent Philip Heseltine equally well done also, and I therefore confine myself here to a few personal sidelights upon his views and aims, and a suggestion (which may be helpful to those who can accept it), as to the extent to which he has responded to his undoubted contact—conscious or subconscious—with the realms and vibrations already discussed in the foregoing digression.

Music To-day

That he is an amateur of music is a critcism sometimes levelled against Delius by persons who are not in sympathetic accord with his personal idiom. Many and conspicuous are his lapses from a certain mean level of accomplishment upon the technical side, and I can well see that it is perfectly justifiable, from this point of view, to dub him amateur. Also, in the nature of things, his type of inspiration, as I mentioned in page 288, is more liable to a wide pendulum-swing between best and worst than is that of your typical 'professional' composer. That he is amateur in the sense of having 'taken up' music in the midst of a life-career devoted to other avocations is a notion completely untenable. He is a lifelong devotee to Cæcilia.

Wilhelm Bauerkeller, of whose quartet I was a member in my youth, told me a story of Delius, to whom he taught the violin when the composer was a lad, which clearly substantiates this statement. Being set to learn a trifle of Dancla, "I can make better music than that *of my own*," said the boy, and promptly began to improvise, beautifully.

Clearly then he was a sensitive artist of the creative type from his early years, and himself recognized his inner bent—his egoic urge. I would hazard the guess, it is no more than that, that it was during his self-imposed exile, amid the giant palm trees, fragrant magnolias and scented orange-groves of Florida, where, as his biographer says, his "vision was no longer blurred by the artificialities of modern life," that he first contacted those vibrations which the *cognoscenti* recognize *a prima vista* as the veritable voice of deva. Certainly, in all his works which show traces of this influence increasing mastery of expression is manifested as the composer becomes more and more familiar with it and better able to paraphrase it in physical-plane terms.

A Series of Swift Vignettes

By no means so constantly indicating the deva influence as does Scriabin, nor perhaps able to give concrete expression to such vibrantly ecstatic states as the Russian master, he is far more concerned to give us his comments upon the more purely human aspects of the emotion world. And that sense of utter and complete detachment so often noticed as being one of his most frequent moods results almost automatically when an artist reaches the 'higher' levels of the emotion-world and translates them in physical-plane terms with as little gross admixture as does Delius. We may remember also that the Buddhic (intuitional) realm is, as it were, reflected in the Desire (astral) world.[1] And at his most exalted moments of comparatively complete unity, he would seem to touch levels of the Buddhic world, rarely reached indeed by ordinary mortals, and utterly unrecorded by them.

It is true that a curious sense of impotence sometimes seems to imbue his music with weariness and decay. Something in his nature seems almost to welcome these moods, which are as far removed as possible from the terrific grapplings with fate of a Beethoven, or those temporary lapses into a baffled sterility of a Scriabin. They resemble neither the luxurious melancholy of a Chopin nor the howling self-pity of a Tchaikovsky. But they are of the same nature as those all-too-frequent passages whose depressing exhalations becloud some pages of Brahms. "Who will console me?" Brahms asks in music, and "let me know all my frailty, ere death overtake me."

Delius similarly occupies himself in his *Requiem* with affirmations of man's mortality and of the transitoriness of life; with denials of the soul's immortality; and even with emphatic denial of the possibility of the human con-

[1] Cf. p. 176.

sciousness surviving what is commonly called ' death.' We are all more than familiar with the type of mind that still wallows in a shuddering and inverted enjoyment of the idea of a material Hell, and visualizes as complement to that an equally material Heaven. ' Their number is legion: their affirmations null.' And it is a matter for astonishment that a mind such as that of Delius could lend itself to the task of underlining with music this sort of stuff. For he is no somatist. We need not be surprised therefore to find that in this work he has supplied some unsatisfactory, indeed some downright mediocre music.

In a former section defining Beauty it was said "We must be careful to avoid the common notion that beauty implies only charm, suavity, and suchlike sunny characteristics;" but in a still earlier section regarding the Vital Principle "Any music which discloses weariness . . . of psyche *in the composer*, has parted with its magical spell." And upon this test could most reasonably be based any argument against Delius' value as a living force in the musical world to-day. It may not be denied that these periods of comparative deadness do occur in his works and many are they who could sympathize with the writer in the *Sunday Sun* years ago, who after a three-and-a-half hour Delius programme unburdened himself thus: "Oh! if he could be persuaded to look on the brighter side of things, to give us music that would cheer us . . . It is much more easy to be a pessimist than an optimist . . . I want to be cheered by music, not depressed." Superficial as this sort of thing may be (it is, after all, only journalism and not in the least preteptious), there is an urge back of it. And it is only necessary to remind ourselves that of course, drama, tragedy, sadness, even morbidity when finely expressed by a great artist do

A Series of Swift Vignettes

not give rise to sadness or morbidity in ourselves. Quite the contrary. Were it not so, what of Lear, Hamlet, Othello, Manfred, Faust, Hippolytus, Trojan Women, and the thousand and one other works of such sort? It is only when the creative artist has disclosed " fatigue, or deadness of psyche " *in himself*, that we are infected, as it were, with vibrations of sadness and depression. And, say what we will, certain pages of some of Delius' works are open to this indictment.

Against these lapses we may oppose the glories of the *Mass of Life* with its virile ' yea-saying ' text from Nietzsche's *Zarathustra*: the mysterious suggestiveness of the choral (wordless) commentaries in *Appalachia*, Florida recollections with many hints to those whose ' ears are opened ' of deva influences: the rapt ecstasy of soul-contemplation, almost trance-like in result, of *A Song of the High Hills*:[1] the lower earth-elemental life portrayed in *Brigg Fair*; the first *Dance Rhapsody* whose vertiginous rhythms induce a climax which reaches its apotheosis not upon this plane at all but at a high level of the second plane (the ' Earthly Paradise ' of Dante) whose beauty is of a poignancy so searching as to have rightly been described as ' wounding.'

Lesser devic, *i.e.*, nature-spirit vibrations, pervade *In a Summer Garden*; *On Hearing the First Cuckoo in Spring*; *Summer Night on the River;* and *A Winter Landscape* and *The March of Spring* in *North Country Sketches*. That I am not alone in this view may be realized from the fact that his biographer says, it is true somewhat vaguely, " Delius is indeed a pantheistic mystic."

In the opera *A Village Romeo and Juliet* ' successful ' though it may never become, are to be found many of

[1] Cf. musical example, p. 81.

Delius' finest moments. Something was said in Part Two, Chapter V, as to the possibility or impossibility of a perfect wedding of words and music. The grandest function of music in connection with words and action, as in opera, is to create a psychic *ambience* through which the actions (having themselves taken their rise in the psyche of the *dramatis personæ*) take on a greatly increased significance. Music thus does not illustrate the subject or the action (save in rare cases) but it images forth the soul-states of the participants in the drama, which ultimately give rise to the action. Failures—artistic not 'popular' failures—may thus occur either by reason of faulty co-ordination between imagined psychic states and their portrayal in action (*i.e.*, a fault on the part of the dramatist), or an inapposite parallelism between the music and the inner soul-states. Inability to at-one themselves with the psychic content of proposed libretti has caused many composers to attempt the dual task themselves. Many have been the failures; a fine librettist like Boito lacking sufficient power as musician pure and simple, a fine musician like Delius lacking the literary-imaginative gifts. Thus the latter's two operas *Irmelin* and *The Magic Fountain* must be accounted failures.

Such is not the case with *A Village Romeo and Juliet*. And if one cannot persuade oneself that even this beautiful work is completely satisfactory, in spite of the wealth of superb music it contains, the reason is (for me) that the soul-states of the participants, arresting and touching though they be, and marvellously heightened by the composer's contribution, do not give rise to equally arresting and moving *action*. If you do not aim at this result, and some of our greatest works of art, of course, do not—then play your work in the concert-room, not on the theatre-stage. One

A Series of Swift Vignettes

hears a great deal of nonsense about 'lack of action' in *Tristan und Isolde*. I will not digress into a rehearsal of the masterly way in which Wagner brings action constantly into his glorious drama. Suffice it that he translates all those psychic interactions which will bear it, right into physical representation.

Where there is no artistic necessity for this, Delius soars to his supremest moments. The popular concert-room excerpt *The Walk to the Paradise Gardens* is such a moment, 'in linkéd sweetness long drawn out.' There is abundant vitality of thought in his work;—more in melody, instrumentation and harmony than in rhythm ordinarily so-called —of beauty illimitable oceans; of idealism, purity, individuality and mystical inspiration there is evidence in almost every one of his works; and although I have laid stress upon his deva contacts, as being invaluable to a right understanding of his music, it is finally by his human commentaries that we find ourselves remembering him, and with a sense of peace, of interior harmony, of *samadhi*[1] attained by contemplation and meditation ('positive' meditation) that he leaves us becalmed and enchanted; a master of music-magic.

"In all my work there will be found Celtic influence," so said EDWARD MACDOWELL (American; born 1861), and again, "I love its colour and meaning. The development in music of that influence is, I believe, a new field."[2]

By far the larger part of MacDowell's work consists of short and quite slight piano pieces. None of his technical devices is either new or striking. In musicianship and power of mind-co-ordination I should place him below fifty

---

[1] An utterly serene, almost trance-like state.
[2] Quoted in *Edward MacDowell: a Study*. Lawrence Gilman, New York, 1921.

composers whose names and works are completely forgotten. In what then resides the continued vitality of these little trifles? To some small extent, no doubt, to the natural and patriotic pride which a vast new country feels for its 'first very own composer.' But there are other factors.

As with Sibelius and his localized nature-spirits and lesser devas up to and including some reflections from the National Deva, so with MacDowell. The difference being that of venue and type; Irish instead of Scandinavian.

MacDowell's music resembles many of those short, vague, but haunting poems of W. B. Yeats who has responded to some of the same influences as the American composer. Both write of 'old unhappy far-off things' with which everything Keltic (physical, emotional and mental) seems to be impregnated; and the musician's work is compact of wistful tenderness and simplicity, of subtle magic and reticent though all-pervading fragrance.

There is plenty of virility in his works of greater scope such as the *Keltic Sonata* and the symphonic poems, but not inner vitality. And our interest in him here is confined to the realization that the small pieces—" In Deep Woods," " In a Haunted Forest," " Summer Idyll," " Forest Spirits," " Legend," " In Mid-Ocean," " Witches' Dance," " Play of Nymphs," " Dance of Dryads," Suite *From an Old Garden* (Pansy, Myrtle, Clover, Yellow Daisy, Blue Bell, Mignonette), " The Brook," " Moonshine," " Winter," " In the Forest," " Dance of the Gnomes," " Elfin Dance," " March Wind," "Midsummer Lullaby," "The West Wind croons in the Cedar Trees," " In the Woods," " The Sea," " Through the Meadow," *Woodland Sketches* (" To a Wild Rose," " Will-o'-the-Wisp," "In Autumn," "To a Water-lily," " By a Meadow Brook," " Told at Sunset "), " To

A Series of Swift Vignettes

the Sea," "From a Wandering Iceberg," "Starlight," "From the Depths," "From a German Forest," "Of Salamanders," "An Old Garden," "With Sweet Lavender," "To an Old White Pine," "The Joy of Autumn"—have resulted from a close contact with, and a ready response to the elemental and devic life which informs most of them.

These are not mere labels affixed to jejune effusions after the manner of the green-sick adolescent. They are records of the composer's contacts with veritable realities. They exhibit all the salient characteristics which any penetrating study of devic and nature-spirit life would lead us to expect. The utter *naïveté* so often mentioned in this connection; buoyant inconsequence; nothing whatever of the 'lower' sublevels of the emotion-world—no sex-obsessions, psyche-fevers, erotic languors and what not.

Like many Kelts and Scandinavians he was swiftly and intimately responsive to those comparatively humble types of nature-spirit whose realms of activity are indicated in so many of his titles: elves, nymphs, forest-spirits, dryads, flower-elementals and so on. Beyond this he did not go, and contact with those devas whose aura is so extensive as to ensoul a whole mountain-side or an entire forest was utterly beyond his power to achieve, as indeed it would have been beyond his artistic scope even faintly to adumbrate in music.

Yet, although a German musical upbringing succeeded in muddying some of his expressions of the life he chose to depict, exactly as it did with Grieg who was his great prototype, his work shows vitality, beauty, utter purity (and *naïveté*, as ever present in this type of work), a measure of individuality and originality, and mystical inspiration in conformity with the characteristic devic vibrations.

It would be easy to exaggerate his greatness as a musician

and his influence upon the progress of the art, but the inner vitality which informs his miniatures is a comparatively rare and a valuable quality, and it is this which has sufficed to preserve them when the works of much abler music-makers has been completely forgotten.

A vivid impression remains in my mind, of meeting in a cold concert-room one morning in 1903, a lone unhappy shivering nervous creature who was waiting for his turn to rehearse. With the *camaraderie* which a similarity of profession and aims naturally confers, as well as the esteem which one rehearsal and a glance through the scores of *En Saga* and the *Second Symphony* gave rise to, I paid him my respects. This was JEAN CHRISTIAN SIBELIUS (Finn; born 1865). He was, even upon a first impression, of a type very far removed from the Teutonic musician whose hand had been laid so heavily upon English music throughout the Victorian epoch. So far from exhibiting an overbearing, unsympathetic, even though undeniably imposing exterior as did so many musicians of that type and period, he appeared sensitive to the point of extreme shyness; nervous almost to the point of physical uncontrol. But, whereas in the former type you were likely to encounter, once you had pierced the surface personality, an amiable sentimentalism and a not too dynamic intelligence; in the case of Sibelius, once the personality was dealt with and one was face to face with his individuality, a granite strength, a powerful intellect, and an inviolable reserve became apparent, frequently lightened however by a charming *fantasie* of an unusual kind.

And these are the qualities that inform all the work of Sibelius.

A Series of Swift Vignettes

An assimilation of the point of view concerning nationalism in music which was put forward in a previous section,[1] would help to clear up a good deal of confusion in many persons' minds as to the Finnish nationalism in Sibelius' music. Shortly, and without re-traversing the ground already covered, it may be said that Sibelius, whilst his personal idiom is, of course, coloured by heredity and environment, is able to draw his inspiration from sources which far transcend mere nationalism, and almost never has recourse to Finnish folk-melodies in his work.

As to the environment which so greatly influences his music—*A Saga, The Swan of Tuonela, Finlandia, Karelia,* etc., and which in its higher aspects colours all his most characteristic work in such a forceful way as to make every favourable listener a worshipper, and every other a positive antagonist; this is largely that of the nature-spirits and the national devas of his native and the adjacent countries.

I would not say that this is the sole, or even a constant influence in Sibelius' music; but it is a frequent one, and sufficiently so as to justify his inclusion in the present category.

It would appear, by all accounts, that the lesser devas of Scandinavia are a dullish lot. Grey, cold, weird, eerie and forbidding. As they ' like me not,' I write of Sibelius with a distinct personal bias and know it.

As with Scriabin, Delius, and other composers dealt with in this section, so with Sibelius; and in almost everything he has written there is the sense of aloofness, remoteness, a-humanity, which, though shot through from time to time with a delightful *naïveté* and faëry dalliance, is clearly traceable by the experienced, to deva vibrations. And

[1] Cf. p. 220, *et seq.*

Music To-day

biassed though one may be against his choice of *what* he will report to us, there is no excuse for mistaking the significance of his reports. For this is a man of genius.

Composing as he so clearly does under these influences, Sibelius loves to sack-clothe his ideas in gloom. No doubt everything in this world is open to a depressing as well as a cheering interpretation, but, to one 'of my kidney' it seems a gratuitous affair to render springtime as *La Tristesse du Printemps*. There is nothing here, read it and render it how you may, of the glorious burgeoning of Spring, not even of that underlying mystical aspect of the re-birth of the Solar year which Wagner so magically shows in the *Charfreitagzauber*.

Dark and sombre as are so many of this master's works, restrained and subdued as is so much of his orchestration, austere, even ascetic as is his harmonic style, it is not at all surprising that its acceptance has been a slow matter. What will be surprising will be any general or widely diffused popularity of his *serious work*, should that ever come about.

Because of the popularity of *Finlandia* and the *Valse Triste* many years ago, the absurd notion has spread that, starting with such ephemeral trifles Sibelius has gradually taken to more serious work, and that it is a shame that the 'great' composer should be pursued by the spectre of his youthful indiscretions. Now this is nonsense. The question of 'light' music has already been discussed (page 127 *et seq.*) and truer proportions in this matter indicated. One of his apologists (Skörgen I think he spelled himself) was translating the master to me in 1923. His line of approach was something like this: "Ah, you people in England only know his early works like *Finlandia* and *Valse Triste*, but

A Series of Swift Vignettes

he has grown since then and become quite classical! He now writes *real* music and is worthy of serious attention."[1]

A glance at a list of his works shows, what indeed we might have expected, that he no more grew from 'light' to serious than from male to female. Opus 4 is a String Quartet; op. 7 *Kulluvo* is a symphony for solo, chorus, and orchestra; op. 9 *En Saga*; op. 12 a Piano sonata . . . (sufficiently 'serious,' one would have thought). Opus 110 three compositions for violin and piano are entitled respectively, *Scène de Danse*; *Danse caractèristique*; *Rondeau romantique*. Does the point now become clear?

Throughout his life-work in fact you find things which have cost him prodigious efforts, interspersed with pieces in lighter *genre*: valses, novelettes, humoresques, impromptus, dances, rondes, harlequinades, and so on. The *Musette* from the incidental music to *King Christian II* is a perfect example of this type of his music, and is worth twenty symphonies I could name.

. . . But not symphonies of the calibre of his own. The Second, wherein he reverses the orthodox process of stating the themes in full and dissecting them afterward in the course of the 'working-out' section: (here he first offers us the *disjecta membra* of his chief melodies, afterwards assembling them more and more convincingly; finally overwhelming us with the creative logic of his intellect); the 'little' Third, so understandable, so serene; the Fourth, which upon its technical side always seems to me to owe much to the Beethoven of the late quartets, so spare is it, so economical of sheer notes, so suggestive harmonically, yet so unlike that master in its atmosphere of

---

[1] Quaintly enough, exactly the same kind of apologia was offered for the present writer in the 'Musical Opinion' in 1924. Save us from our friends!

settled gloom and unrelieved tragedy; the Fifth, which might be said to bear some such relation to the Fourth as does Schubert's Seventh to the *Unfinished*, so copious, so at-ease in its presentation compared with the precious terseness of the earlier work; the admirably balanced, eminently sane Sixth—not destined perhaps to become the most familiar of them; lastly, the prodigious Seventh— prodigious, that is to say, in completeness of conception and presentation, not, I think, in loftiness of ideation, for there are many moments when the giant (make no mistake about the giant) seems to turn his back on the world to which, nevertheless, he is addressing himself, and thus, instead of carrying us with him permits us to slip altogether out of the magic of his *ambience*.

What can be the reason of his restricted appeal? Chiefly, I think, this: The majority of persons (of whom I am one) are not temperamentally of the order of those who delight in breaking the Serpentinean ice of a biting Christmas morn. We do not join heartily in the chorus: " Welcome, wild North-easter: Welcome, black North-easter," *à la* Kingsley. For us, the warmer seas, the bluer skies of farther south; for there is something forbidding, something contra-human in many of the nature-vibrations of the bleak North-land. Artists and art-loving folk are happier in more genial climes, and for a real reason. Anything which tends to focus the consciousness in the physical body and thrust it back there, willy-nilly, as does a rigorous (however 'healthy') stark, and inimical climate, is just another enemy to be combated and overcome before the spirit, free of earthly entanglements, can soar into the spaceless Empyrean and there commune with the gods. There is, we know, a method of facilitating the so-desired escape from mundaneities, in-

A Series of Swift Vignettes

volving the elevation of the right elbow! A good sherris-sack, said one who knew, " ascends me into the brain . . . makes it apprehensive, quick, forgetive, full of nimble fiery and delectable shapes." But I have never heard that it could bring a creative artist in tune with the higher gods.

Having little affinity with those who—like Tchaikovsky—must wail of their unhappiness and their perfectly natural mortal disappointments and difficulties upon almost every occasion of putting pen to paper; nor with Sibelius when he finds himself moved to emphasize the *sadness* of spring; I naturally find Blake with his ' jocund spring ' more congenial. Even Beethoven, when he descends to self-pity is less than admirable, but, whatever may be the case in his letters, he very seldom allows this to appear in his music. As an artist I well know, of course, the curiously inverted joy of the reflections of sadness at some remove. This is a different matter altogether, and does not depress us.

Music should transport us in a trice, out of our physical consciousness into the ' Garden of the Hesperides ' 'mid " the Apple-trees the Singing and the Gold " rather than emphasize the ' old unhappy far-off things ' which, after all, are better forgotten. Is it not Bridges who says: " For howsoe'er a man may hug his care the best of his art is gay."

The ' nature-vibrations of the bleak Northland ' creep into a great proportion of Sibelius' work. I well remember the impression of wraiths, goblins, sub-human elementals and so on, which a performance of *En Saga* thirty years ago gave me. Acquaintance with the *Second Symphony* served to confirm this impression. The *Swan of Tuonela*, a ' legend ' for orchestra, tells of the nether regions (called in Finnish folk-stories Tuonela). The Swan (a popular physical-

Music To-day

plane figure in mythic literature to denote denizens of the inner realms) floats upon the waters of the Finnish Lethe, singing. Again one is aware of the nature-spirit vibrations of a not very high order expressed in this music. Without being exactly deleterious, they yet deplete the listener with their foreboding, mysterious sorrows, and their strange quasi-hypnotic spell-binding. The veriest neophyte in the magic arts, even an ordinarily sensitive artist, could not mistake this.

Upon its technical side the work is a marvel, and when one admits its construction and handling to be on a level with the *Lohengrin* vorspiel, one has paid a compliment hard to surpass.

His is not the large Jupiterean grandeur of the serene gods. And he is sometimes, it must be admitted, somewhat slow to start. But once let him make contact with however tiny a fragment of Truth—let him but lay hands on such scraps as

and you will 'hear of something to your advantage.' His tenacity of mind is titanic and he will 'grow' any such tiny tendril into a veritable forest before he is through.

One of his greatest gifts is this ability to grow a 'seed'-motive in the way Nature teaches us. Acorn; oak tree; thousands of trees; millions of leaves; all oak-tree leaves

A Series of Swift Vignettes

but no two exactly alike. The power to make a seed-motive grow, put forth leaves, blossom, flower and fruit, is a gift which has only shown itself (in Western music, *videlicet*) in recent times. Beethoven, Berlioz, Liszt, Schumann, Brahms, Wagner, Strauss, Bartók, and some others have it; Franck, Bruckner, Mahler, and many moderns have it not. Much of our modern music fails from lack of this gift, for when it is not the real but the simulated, not the imagined but the imitated, it is as arid and as easily detected as the love-sick adolescent's recourse to the Rhyming dictionary in his versifications.

Pohjola's Daughter, a symphonic fantasia (which is a favourite work in the *répertoire* of Sibelius' friend and fellow-countryman Kajanus, whose conducting of it I have heard several times), is another work in which the same influences are traceable. In *Tapiola*, a tone poem, the presence of the same mysterious Forces is clearly discernible, and rightly so, for the printed score is prefaced:

Widespread they stand, the Northlands dusky forests,
Ancient, mysterious, brooding savage dreams,
Within them dwells the Forest's mighty God
And wood sprites in the gloom weave magic secrets.

these Forces being the vibrations of sub-human devic type and somewhat inimical to man in so far as they can affect him.

To confirmed city-dwellers, perhaps more especially in this country, such notions may seem fanciful, far-fetched, worthy only of the nursery, even utterly untrue. They seem less so when surrounded by the magic hills and lakes, the ' little men ' and leprechauns of Erin; still less so amid the mighty mountains and wind-swept fjords of Scandinavia; and acceptable as realities among Sicily's almond-blossomed slopes or the scented orange-groves of Magna Græcia where still the Greek gods may be communed with as of old.

Had but Scriabin, with his immensely lofty devic contacts, possessed the sheer intellectual musical power of Sibelius; had but Sibelius the soul-force to shake off the lower devic vibrations and transcend those of even country, continent, hemisphere; and with consciousness ego-free range the glorious devic-worlds which Scriabin contacted, what unimaginable splendours would have then been ours.

It is the province of poets, musicians, artists, seers all, to keep clear and undefiled such avenues 'twixt gods and men, and to nourish in our hearts and minds a grander concept than the omnipresent egocentricity of the *hoi polloi* which ever threatens to o'erwhelm us.

§ 1. A VIGNETTE TAILPIECE

In glancing through the swift sketches of composers and their characteristics which have made up this Fourth Part, I am conscious that the 'lights seem a little turned down.' It almost seems that a niggardly measure of praise has been meted out even to those of whose work the writer is admittedly in close sympathy and to whom none but the warmest expressions of love and admiration would be adequate. Had it been my thesis that composers have already scaled all the heights and plumbed the depths of human experience this would have been a severe and an unanswerable indictment. It is not so. Still remain many of the inexhaustible marvels of the Causal and Buddhic realms, and the transcendent vibrations of the Atmic sphere to be contacted and translated for millions yet unborn.

One loves the gentle hills of Albion, and the delectable

A Series of Swift Vignettes

rivulets and trout-streams of the Lowlands; but how shall one exhaust superlatives in their praise when the giant scarps of Everest and the cataracts of mighty Amazon are our standards of comparison.

Again, it may have seemed that too great a value is placed upon technical modernities in evaluating composers' works. Of Scriabin and Delius, for example, we said that they never achieved complete harmonic freedom, whereas of Hindemith and Honegger that (as any tyro may perceive) they have done so. This is not automatically to place the latter above the former. The immortal works of any art are expressed in terms which were current at the time of their creation; they are universal in their appeal by reason of the fact that they embody ideations contacted at Causal, Buddhic, or Atmic levels, and not in the evanescent, impermanent, lower worlds; also by reason of the fact that they are/were clothed in appropriate expression upon the physical plane.

The reason why a little more stress may legitimately be laid upon the forward-moving musical technique of our day than upon say that of the literary world is because it is so much the younger art. For ages the literary art—in many of its forms just as we know it to-day—has flourished; music, so far as the Western world is concerned, is the infant of the arts, still cutting new teeth, still learning to coordinate its reflexes. If it is able to comprehend the fact 'two and two make four' and to state a simple equation, it is still far from any real contact with Intuitional, Causal, Spiritual, and many Devic vibrations. Indeed even if its protagonists were able to establish such contacts and bring the results across irrefragably into the brain, our present musical technique would be ludicrously unable to body forth the faintest real correspondence to them. Hence the stress rightly laid upon all forward-leading technical methods.

Long ago Debussy said, in effect, that the premature attempt to 'place' and 'label' young composers, and the too early discussion of their as yet immature technical equipment, not to mention their aims and general individual trend, is a hindrance rather than a help to them and 'is, in fact, little short of criminal.' Cordial agreement with this view explains why I have refrained from discussing at length certain young composers whose works are of great interest, noteworthy as achievement, and of splendid promise.

But, fresh as I am from a lengthy and intensive study of the works of all the composers mentioned in the foregoing, and many more, I am impelled to reassert, with all the emphasis at my disposal, that until composers pay to the rationale of inspiration a degree of attention which is more commensurate with its importance in relation to that which they pay to their technical studies; just so long will they continue to court the danger of pouring out 'new' works which are dead before they are born; flimsily draped lay-figures; desiccated cerebral chaff, 'without value—null and void.'

PART FIVE
NEW VISTAS

CHAPTER SIXTEEN: TECHNICAL

The Perfect Orchestra—Counterpoint of Timbres—'Just' Intonation—Auralizing Music—Improved Listeners.

THERE is a school of thought which is attracting a good deal of attention in musical circles at the moment. It opines that the end of the world (musical) is at hand, that the ultimate sun has indeed already set, and that we have seen the last of the great composers. It is no new thing.[1] More than forty years ago my godfather, a worthy Italian bassoon-player named Raspi, told me that my aspirations as a composer were doomed to failure because " all the best melodies had already been used! " It is extremely unlikely that he had been reading John Stuart Mill, or had heard of his assertion that new melody will some day be impossible to invent.

Certain musicians who must be suffering the last stages of mental myopia, assert that greatness ended with Schubert;[2] a poet,[3] in thrall to Dante's immense genius, as well he might be, opines that no poetry as good as his can be written again.

Perhaps the attitude of the above-mentioned musicians is the most pessimistic—for they are dealing with the youngest of the arts, an art, as we know it in the West, barely three hundred years old. Well, well; there are others of us who still entertain hopes for the baby's future.

---

[1] Spengler, " The Downfall of the West."
[2] *E.g.*, Schnabel in *Schubert: The last of the Great Composers.*
[3] T. S. Eliot.

And speculation upon the future of the art need not necessarily be either vapid, uninteresting, or unhelpful.

Making no claim whatever to seership; assuming no familiarity with those realms or states of consciousness whence (so we are told) it is possible to see what *has* happened in the future; let us more humbly pursue lines of thought arising out of our examination of what has recently occurred and is to-day taking place in the world of music.

§ 1. THE PERFECT ORCHESTRA

We have already spoken of the modern symphony orchestra as "by far the grandest, most subtle, most varied and characteristic instrument known to us at present." It is not, of course, perfect. In what respects then can we visualize practical forward-steps?

I have a predilection for completing each family of the orchestral ensemble.

Piccolo, Flute, Bass Flute already complete this department.

Oboe, Corno Inglese, Bassoon,[1] leave a gap which might be filled with good results by the addition, or rather the restitution of the Tenoroon. This instrument possesses certain characteristics of *timbre* which clearly differentiate it from the Oboe and Bassoon in some such way as those of the Viola distinguish it from Violin and Violoncello.

Clarinets become a complete family with their characteristic tone-colour unbroken, if we add to those normally in use a D or an E flat instrument, and a Bass Clarinet.

The Horn family is complete.

Trumpets in C, universally used nowaday, might be

---

[1] Of true oboe-family quality. See Ante, p. 86.

The Perfect Orchestra

supplemented by at least one in F; and 'speciously' by the addition of Bass Trumpet as in some Wagner scores.

Trombones should be granted the status of a quartet by inclusion of the noble bass instrument in G; for the common use of a Tuba with three Trombones in four-part soli chords is never quite satisfactory to a sensitive ear, however passable it may be in full *tutti*.

The Tuba however, should not be excised. It might be augmented into a complete quartet as suggested for Oboe, Flute, Clarinet, Horn, Trumpet and Trombone. And certainly two tenor, one bass in F, and one contra-bass instrument in BB flat would give a grand tone-colour addition to this department of the orchestra.

If each department were completed in this way there would be no need for Bassoon to attempt to match Horns, or Tuba, Trombones, as has hitherto been the case. Each could then preserve its true characteristics.

There is room also for the introduction of numerous beautiful and novel *timbres* which, if and when musicians in general have developed their sensitivity in this respect to a higher pitch, will be readily forthcoming from inventors working under their guidance. The instrument exhibited by M. Terepnine at the Opera in Paris in 1928, by use of which he externalized musical sounds from *les ondes éthèriques*, was of great interest to musicians as introducing a new and 'legitimate' tone-colour. The sounds resembled those of the *celesta* with this important difference: The *celesta* and all analogous instruments are percussive. After they are struck there is an immediate *diminuendo*, sometimes greater sometimes less. With this instrument however, the bell-like *timbre* was sustained, was capable of a great range of dynamic—from subtlest *ppp* up to, I compute, a very tolerable *f*—and was adjustable as regards pitch and intensity, in a manner not unlike the human voice. One could imagine a group of these instruments adding a rare and matchless beauty to the orchestra as it is at present constituted.

In the department of percussion there is great scope for development. From the Orient again we may learn much about such instruments. Burmese and Chinese gongs; Indian drums (male and female!); instruments of the extraordinary delicacy and subtlety of Tambura, Vina and Saranghi, or the so-called *Chapeau Chinois* to which my own instrument, the *Sistrum*, is in some ways an approximation. Needless to say, the multiplication of mere noise-creating toys such as abound in jazz-orchestras is not what is meant here. Hence the necessity, as above remarked, that these new instruments should be made under the immediate co-operation of artists with a finely trained sensitivity to pure *timbres*.

Ears may so easily be debauched and come to accept as desirable (or at least not to cavil at), qualities of tone which, to fresh or finely sensitive ones, are highly obnoxious.

Whilst Radio retains its present characteristics it is quite a breach of artistry to use an orchestra of the same constitution as that for the concert-room. Of course it is expedient to do so. But from the point of view of what is desirable, *qua* artistry, special orchestrations are necessary for transmission by this medium.

Most important of all questions connected with this branch of the art, is the need for a re-estimate of the values of *timbre*. Perhaps the most magical thing in music, it should be raised from the thraldom of sensuous appeal to the emancipation of the creative appeal.

Counterpoint of 'Timbres'

§ 2. COUNTERPOINT OF 'TIMBRES'

From the persistency with which I have introduced considerations of *timbre* throughout this book, it will have been gathered that I attach more importance to this aspect of the art than is perhaps usual. It is one of the most important, because one of the most magical of our elements, and its uses are sure to be more clearly realized in the future.

Counterpoints have always hitherto been (as the name implies) movements of *lines of melody* the one against the other.

A natural extension of this idea in modern music is the movement of *blocks of harmony* the one against the other.

Remains almost entirely unexplored the possibility of a counterpoint of *changing timbres*. A chord of arresting beauty might remain static spatially, but by use of voices and/or instruments of dynamic and rainbow-changing *timbres* a complete picture might be painted upon that single chord.

Sustained *timbres*; changing *timbres*; percussive *timbres*; these are our media.

We know something of these in our orchestral instruments of to-day, but it is not generally realized that the human voice is capable of all of them to an extent at present undreamed of.

§ 3. 'JUST' INTONATION

There is room for further intensive study and practical experimentation in the matter of what we might call natural tuning. The overtones, the upper partials, are not, of course, 'in tune' with each other from the point of view of our tempered scale-tuning. Trumpets, Horns, etc., can play these intervals resulting from their fundamental tone (this, in its turn depending upon length of tube) in 'just intonation.' Advantage has been taken of this by certain composers, quite tentatively, and I am bound to say without very satisfactory results hitherto.

Still, this fact in nature remains, and it is certainly one which will not go unexploited in the future development of the art. It would seem that its employment would rule out modulation—would necessitate remaining in one key—and could only exist by reference to one fundamental key-note. To those typical modern musicians who put all their eggs in the one basket of free chromaticism, this may appear a retrograde step. That I do not think so (and why I do not think so) has been stated in an early chapter dealing with Modes. Diatonality, as well as Polytonality and Atonality, is a necessity in the equipment of any composer who has both deep and wide contacts to express. Natural tuning is congenitally affiliated with Diatonality. And it is surprising that, notwithstanding the enormous preponderance of tempered tuning to which the modern musician is subjected, the appreciation of 'just intonation' has not disappeared. Yet no string player with a fine ear plays in tune with the tempered pianoforte. Szigeti, for example, plays the leading note much sharper, the minor third (in a common chord) much flatter than the same notes on a piano. And the subtleties of intonation that arise during the performance of any extended, or any modern work, may be imagined. These enharmonic differences, subtle though they be, are no mere academic hair-splitting niceties, but distinctions of real importance in the presentation of a composer's ideas, and absolutely vital to the faithful conveyance of his message.

'Just' Intonation

So firmly does the present writer believe this that he has not hesitated to 'modulate' from A flat major to G sharp major in an extended movement which indicates a transition from the 'form' side to the 'life' side. Fully convinced of the potency of this difference before utilizing it, and fully satisfied of its efficacy after many performances, he is here merely preaching what he practises:

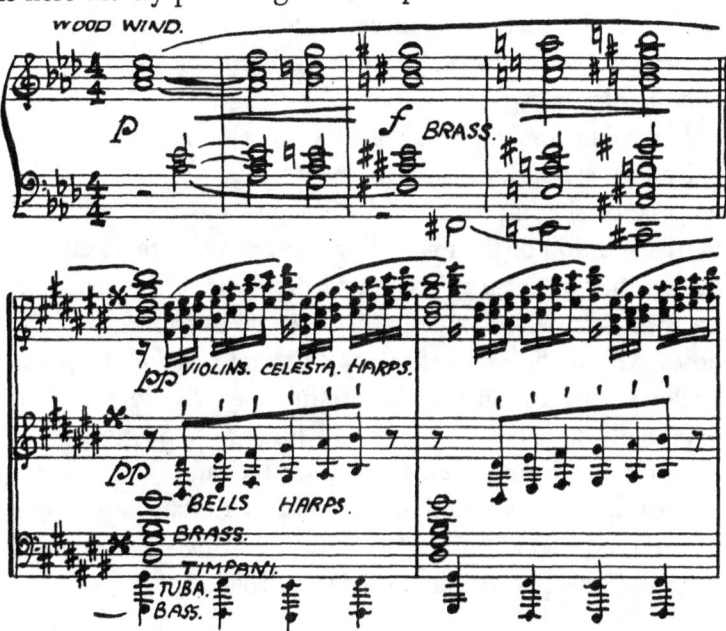

Busoni's tertia-tones are open to the objection that they are not working towards those natural divisions of the octave we are discussing. The same is true of my quarter-tonal essays already referred to. Still, these are useful steps, perhaps necessary ones in our enforced attempts to enlarge our powers of expression—powers which are taxed to the uttermost in any endeavour to parallel those soul experiences so often referred to in these pages.

Music To-day

Modes having been reduced to two; tempered tuning having been exploited; complete chromatic freedom having been achieved, thanks to these; it is now time we came full circle and readopted 'just intonation' as one feature in our equipment. It is thus possible to conceive of a work which might make use of both 'tempered' and 'just' intonation as contrasted idioms, in the same way as it might contain polytonal as contrasted with unitonal, diatonal contrasted with atonal, and block-harmonic with linear polyphonic passages.

Musical history shows a logical progress. Beginning with unison music or that sung in the octave; followed by the practice of singing in parallel fifths and fourths; followed by the addition of the major third and its use; there ensued the practice of music with natural divisions of the octave in unequal parts. Bach stabilized the equal distribution of the notes within the octave, an un-'natural' but useful step. Follows now the utilization of still finer divisions of this admittedly unnatural 'tempered' tuning. And possibly a return to just intonation as laid down by nature—which can be heard, measured and tabulated, as resultants from any given fundamental tone (see countless text-books)—will round off this part of the Musician's Progress.

§ 4. AURALIZING MUSIC

In many ways the ability to read music and, as it were, to auralize it in imagination may be a source of great delight to the fortunate possessor of the faculty.[1] Just as it is possible to enjoy a silent reading of poetry even more than a recitation; in the same way it is possible—by repetition

---

[1] I have occasionally met instances of this faculty being confused with clair-audience. The two experiences are quite dissimilar.

Auralizing Music

of chosen themes or phrases, by a slowing of the *tempo* here and there, by a judicious pause whilst the imagination takes flight (things which are impossible when listening to a performance)—to get closer to the heart of certain compositions in the study than in the concert-room. Probably increasing numbers of persons will cultivate this faculty. Possibly, in the far distant future, there may be as much silent reading as audible performance of music—and ears will thus be spared which nowaday are frequently debauched.

Everyone who possesses the faculty of auralization will have made the experience that many passages read better than they sound in performance.

Here is one, for example:[1]

[1] From the *Gurre-Lieder*. Schönberg, cf. p. 251.

Music To-day

which, however clear and indeed eminently satisfying to the eye, instantly becomes a muddy meaningless noise in performance when other instrumental counterpoints are added to it.

Modern composers especially are prone to turn out quantities of 'paper' music. Work after work, concert after concert, reveals a concentration on the manufacture rather than the creation of musical edifices. Many of them are undeniably interesting 'on paper' (even enthralling), but when translated into physical-plane terms as sound, they fail lamentably either to charm the ear, move the heart or interest the mind, not to mention those realms of Fancy and Imagination, of the Sublime and Transcendent, to which we are transported by the great masters.

The limits of ability to auralize music vary greatly. Many excellent musicians do not possess the faculty at all and there are some among them who deny that anyone can possibly read a full orchestral score comprising, say, thirty lines of music to be read simultaneously. I have seen it done so frequently, and known so intimately of its being done, that I must disagree with them.

Another important factor, however, affects this question. Well able to read him, I was unable really to get to grips with Shakespeare until (as a youth) I had seen one or two representations of his work. Professor Tovey—an astounding score-reader by the way—records an analogous experience in regard to Palestrina. Thus a wide experience of heard music and much eclectic musical practice are necessary before the stage is reached when real enjoyment can ensue from perusal and auralization of musical scores. Still, from intimate experience of the joys of this kind of musical adventure, one may easily embrace as a fact what the poet

Improved Listeners

told us long ago, that though " heard melodies are sweet," those unheard of the mortal ear may be " sweeter still."

§ 5. IMPROVED LISTENERS

It must not be thought that the attainment of the still, meditative attitude of the 'inner' bodies spoken of on page 209 is of interest and importance only to creative artists. Listeners too could well benefit by a little self-training along similar lines. How frequently one may notice in our concert-halls to-day the grand entry of a party some fifty seconds or so before a masterpiece is to be played. Bustle and commotion of settling in seats; business of programme-buying, staring around casually to make sure that others are staring too—at them! greetings to and from friends, and so forth—a physical commotion that is as nothing to that going on in their brains; a veritable pandemonium which I will not attempt to describe. Small wonder that after a Berlioz, a Sibelius, or a Bartók has painted a wonderful picture in marvellous colours, the most they can admit is to have found it ' amusin'.' (A ' sin ' with all recognition of the ' muse ' omitted).

We are, most of us, so mighty busy doing nothing in particular that we have no minute to devote to the nourishment of our souls. Beyond question, until we can gain this quiet mind and meditative attitude, the greatest of great works will be, to us, as pearls cast before swine.

Without some measure of this positive-negative attitude it is impossible to detect the mysterious but unmistakable presence of the ' divine afflatus.' Many years ago I wrote: I well know that it is not the fashion of the moment to talk of inspiration in the arts. It is an age of the deification of the mechanical and I say nothing about that here. But when Mozart, Goethe, Shelley, Beethoven, Keats, Berlioz, Scriabin and, thank heaven, a thousand others, tell of the visitation of the divine creative Dionysiac frenzy, it is not mere rodomontade, romanticism, or the cloudy vapourings of pseudo-mysticism. It is a matter of the highest importance, and I would to God that every music-lover would try to learn to recognize the signs of the living inspiration in new as well as old works, instead of, as is too often the case, losing himself in vain speculations on the relative cleverness of the works he hears.

Chapter Seventeen: Non-Technical

Simplicity—Complexity—Synthetic-Simplicity—Orientalities—Improvization—Music and Magic—'Nature'-Pitch—A Synthesis of Arts.

Just as, in our survey of the world of music to-day account was taken of the inspirational as well as the expressional aspects of the art, so, in glancing at certain possibilities in the future evolution of the art, equal attention must be given to the non-technical as to the technical sides.

§ 1. SIMPLICITY—COMPLEXITY—SYNTHETIC-SIMPLICITY

The old axiom of the simplicity of the finest art has been attacked recently, and one sees reason in the arguments of Kaikhosru Sorabji upon this point. His diatribe against simplicity betrays the Oriental's natural tendency toward extraordinary elaboration of detail. The true simplicity of which I speak here as synthetic-simplicity more nearly approaches the archetypal conception—which is one-ness. This is far indeed from the simplicity of inanity for which I have as little love as the above-named writer. It is easy, unfortunately, for the unpenetrating mind to mistake for inanity the simplicity which is only the result of immense refinement, rejection and condensation.

Not so long ago a work was spoken of as 'glib and facile' which I happen to know had been worked over with incredible labour; condensed, refined and every inessential completely burned out. But, thank heaven, there are still those who prefer one drop of pure attar of roses, to the making of which thousands of blooms have yielded their quota, to an ocean of cheap, alcoholized 'perfume.'

What may be noticed as happening in the work of individual artists will, I believe, also happen in the evolution of the art. Its three stages are noted at the head of this section. First you had the infantilities of the early practitioners of the art. Second, a period of increased and increasing complexity (in which stage most musical activities are labouring at present; certainly those of creative artists). Third, a type of work which, whilst exhibiting a superficial appearance of simplicity, bears, upon examination, so illuminating and suggestive a connotation, and potentialities so rich and so synthetic in type, that only the vast and detailed experience of the second period could have furnished it forth.

Compare the works of Beethoven's nonage with those of his maturity—these in turn with the sparse, but infinitely fertile idiom of the late quartets, and the point becomes clear. A similar process may be traced in the work of Sibelius. It shows clearly too in Scriabin's harmonic evolution.

In early years this was of Chopin-and-water simplicity. In the second phase he evolves the 'mystic,' 'Promethean' chord resulting from the first thirteen of the upper partial tones arranged in fourths, thus:

Orientalities

These, he develops still further as his style becomes more and more complicated. In the Sixth and Seventh Piano Sonatas he deforms the 'Promethean' chord by lowering the ninth partial, the D. In the Eighth Sonata he lowers the tenth partial tone, the E, thus bringing us to a point (the Tenth Sonata) where complexity merges into simplicity. Not, however, the simplicity of his comparatively undeveloped early style, but a synthetic simplicity which carries all the implications of (and even more than) his middle-period style.

Certainly the beauty and the magic of music can be enshrined in factors far more simple and at the same time more potent than we of this complicated age are apt to assume.

And when I said on page 22 that 'I have seen far greater effects produced by a single note of a certain *timbre* than by whole symphonies comprising uncountable thousands of notes' it carried the above as well as other connotations.

§ 2. ORIENTALITIES

I anticipate that the influence of Sanskrit literature will not be less profound than the revival of Greek in the fourteenth century. To the person even slightly acquainted with a few facets of that literature, the above dictum of Schopenhauer's demands not merely enthusiastic concurrence, but its extension into many other activities than literature. For the ancient Easterns have also something to teach us of the profoundest importance to music. The Indian musical system, for example—a completed and settled tradition centuries before our Western system began to evolve—can probably teach us as much as it can learn from us. Whereas in all our music we employ but one system

Music To-day

of dividing the notes within the octave, namely, into equal half-tones, they employ several different tunings according to the type of ideation they desire to express. Rhythmic patterns attain a degree of subtlety undreamed of here; the most admired of our jazz rhythms, for example, being quite infantile by comparison. They can teach us something too about *timbre*; certain of their instruments, as vina and tambura, I have never heard equalled in evocative power and sensitivity. In its metaphysical aspects too and those allied to its magical uses, as well as in its natural correspondences to other arts in the manner spoken of in a previous section on Colour and Music, they possess priceless teachings a thorough study of which would fertilize the whole of Western musical thought.

There has been an enormous amount of imitation-oriental music written during the past twenty years or so. In former days, when the world was so much larger than it is now, Mozart and Beethoven were quite content, and quite justified too, in sprinkling their score liberally with triangle and cymbal and calling it 'Turkish' music! This was a convention accepted by the West at that period as standing for oriental music (much as a Shakespearean 'prop' would be accepted as representing a castle, though it resembled one not at all). None but the most ignorant would have accepted it as a faithful transcription of Eastern music written down for our instruments.

Nowaday, when abundant information is available regarding oriental musical systems, no musician need lack first-hand experience of Indian, Chinese, Japanese, Burmese, Javanese and other types of oriental music, and the pseudo-oriental pinch-beck so frequently foisted upon the public nowaday is indefensible. Few things in music can make

Improvisation

the artist quite so quickly quite so sickly as those inane 'orientalities' of some of the composers who should know better. Your oriental suites, song-cycles (Persian, Chinese, Greek, etc.), love lyrics ('Indian' and what not), settings of Omar Khayyám, instrumental *intermezzi*, Egyptian suites, Eastern ballets, etc., exist and become popular by other means than by being true to their titles. For they are no more truly Eastern in conception and execution than my piano is African because of its ivory keys. They employ drone fifths in the bass, tam-tam and other percussive effects, avoid to a certain extent the baldest of everyday occidental musical *clichés*, and attempt to conjure up visions of the languorous dreams or phrenetic dances of the Orient. It is surprising that a modern artist of the eminence of Rimsky-Korsakov should have perpetrated such an egregious example of this sort of thing as he has done.

There do exist, however, a number of *bona fide* transcriptions of oriental music. I have had the inestimable advantage of a close acquaintance with a great deal of Indian music in this way, hence the claims I have made at the beginning of this section for a study of it, and the importance of the results which seem to me certain to follow.

§ 3. IMPROVISATION

The Indian musician sets less value than we upon 'ready-made' music. Just as he dislikes to eat foods which, having already been prepared and cooked, are now rehashed and served up again and again. Food must be freshly prepared and cooked especially for immediate consumption. Similarly, music must be new-created here and now for his delectation; and from this point of view all our artist performers are not 'musicians' at all, properly speaking. He regards them as something like second-hand dealers in other persons' ideas.[1]

It must not be supposed, however, that the Indian musician's improvisation is either the spineless sprawl so frequently offered by our Western improvisers, or a cut-and-dried affair of rigid obedience to inelastic rules. Within certain fixed limits both of Raga (roughly Mode) and Tala (roughly basic-rhythm) there is apparently illimitable scope for free emotional play, for mental-constructive skill, and pre-eminently for those efforts to bring both creator and participator into *rapport* with 'higher' states of consciousness which so much of our Western music makes, and so small a proportion achieves.

Here—in Improvisation, individual and collective—is a fertile field for the creative musician of the West, in future years.

§ 4. MUSIC AND MAGIC

Many times throughout these pages I have spoken of the magical use of music. Deep-seated in the nature of many persons is a horror of this word, of all it implies, and much that it does not imply. Sympathetically to these persons, let us temporarily substitute a word which covers many (though not of course all) of its connotations; the word 'alterative'—having power to change.

Humanity, leading in the main a drab existence, acknowledges a common need for alteratives. Drugs, alcohol, tobacco—love, certainly the greatest and most powerful—and all the arts upon one side of their operations; these are magical in their results; they are alteratives.

---

[1] Cf. the relative importance of composer and performer, p. 243.

'Nature'-Pitch

The irrational but no less real antipathy which some persons feel toward the magical aspect and operation of certain of the arts, is probably a deep-seated racial recollection of grave consequences of misuse in the distant past. Such dangers no longer existing, it is best frankly to recognize that music stands or falls by its possession of magic power. It is nothing beside the point that the vast majority of persons are susceptible only to quite inferior music—jazz, comic or sentimental songs and the like. They seek its ministrations as an alterative. Among the more cultured, musically, are some who derive their principal enjoyment from an intellectual appreciation of the beauties and subtleties which abound in any fine composition. Remain a few, who, whether or not they possess the requisite technical knowledge to evaluate a work upon its 'art' side, are able to respond to the magical power of the loftiest works in the art, and permit these to evoke in them a reaction which is among the rarest of human experiences.

Music will become much more self-conscious, definite and accurate in all these properly so-called magical aspects and applications in the future, far less nebulous and tentative. And the effects will be produced, as I have said elsewhere, by immeasurably simpler means than those we use at present which all too often, alas (despite the employment of hundreds of instruments and countless thousands of notes), completely fail to cause the slightest change of vibration in any part of the listeners' make-up.

§ 5. 'NATURE'-PITCH

The pitch at which we choose to play our instrumental music is not an inescapable and unadjustable fact laid down

Music To-day

by nature such as is, for example, the length of our days and nights, or the duration of our seasons. It is a purely arbitrary choice. We have agreed to make our music at a pitch at which middle A will give 435·4 double vibrations per second. A useful and indeed a necessary agreement.

Is this final, unchangeable, pre-eminently desirable? Is it possible more nearly to approach nature in this matter? What is meant by the designation at the head of this section?

It will be remembered that in a previous chapter we studied mystical inspiration, and in an elucidation of some aspects of the rationale of inspiration we examined certain operations of the consciousness and certain super-normal contacts made by it when in an exalted state. In such a condition it is sometimes possible to become aware of the never-ceasing music of that 'nature-symphony of the circumambient air' so marvellously indicated in *The Tempest*. This music 'made without hands,' as real as (more real indeed than) that of ' violins and harps,' is always heard *at a certain pitch*. This is not the pitch at which we make our music ordinarily. But (speaking from some practical experience) music played at what I have ventured to call ' nature '-pitch produces greater effects than at the ' normal ' pitch. Again, as I said in a section on the therapeutic effects of music, the musical tones to which the various plexuses correspond, more swiftly and more powerfully affect these nerve-centres when they are sung at ' nature '-pitch than at any other.

We need a new interpretation of our ideas of pitch. No longer would it be possible to toy with pitch,[1] as do con-

---

[1] which has varied in different countries at different times between C=512 and C=548. At the present time our orchestras play at about C=522; our military bands at C=538.

A Synthesis of Arts

temporary musicians, if once the relation between pitch and the forces of Nature had begun to be recognized.

§ 6. A SYNTHESIS OF ARTS

The tendency of modern life is toward the co-operation of hitherto severed functions. The statesman-educationist looks to the artist for re-creative stuff; the creative artist, no longer remaining at lofty altitudes on the level of imagination, tends to offer the fruits of his artistic labours to the statesman-educationist.

The comparative failure of music hitherto, in education, therapeutics and scientific research, is ultimately traceable to a lack of co-operation between the creative musician in the free and untrammelled exercise of his power with the teacher, the doctor and the scientist. Thus it is that we find musical education often devoid of inspiration, musical therapeutics degraded to the level of mere crankism, and musical science bereft of dynamic power. Scientists no doubt admit sound as a force in Nature, but in practical research they devote themselves in the main to electricity, heat, light, any natural force but sound.[1] And research into the mysteries of the sound-art is scarcely regarded as coming under the category of accepted scientific subjects at all. Now, the creative artist, responding on his own level to this main tendency toward co-operation, has sensed an ancient truth [2] which should have far-reaching consequences upon the next generation, namely, the synthesis of the arts themselves.

There have been rare souls in every age who have reached a state of consciousness in which the Archetype has been

[1] Among the exceptions the foremost name is that of Helmholtz.
[2] 'In the beginning is the Sound,' etc. Cf. p. 105.

perceived, and who have endeavoured to give it expression in a synthesized art-form. When an Æschylus makes Music with Drama; when a Blake gives out a unified conception as music-poem-picture; when a Wagner synthesizes Music, Action, Poem, Scene; when a Scriabin attempts a music-colour-scent, or a Boito a musical, poetical, pictorial presentation of one ideation, these artists are merely showing that they have contacted the ideation in a state of consciousness where Unity is, and have shown it forth in a synthesis of art-forms.

Many other instances of attempts at a synthetic presentation of the arts occur to one. Each and all these efforts are foredoomed to failure unless founded upon the *true* correspondences of the arts and their true inter-relationship which have yet to be fully discovered and demonstrated, and unless given adequate presentation in physical-plane terms. To this end an all-round education for artists is called for; a specialized training in all the arts. For, obviously, a synthetic training is necessary for artists who would give a synthetic presentation of their concepts.

Chapter Eighteen: Conclusion

THE musical revolution of the past thirty years or so has concerned itself almost entirely with technical matters. But the time is ripe for experiment and investigation—combined investigation by creative artists and scientists, of powers and forces which have been much talked and written about in the past, but scarcely investigated at all.

As to the methods of co-operation in research between the creative artist and the scientist, I assert that it is impossible to go far along this line without adventuring into the fields of psychology, psychic investigation and the like. In creative music, for instance, we are dealing with the intangible, albeit the intangible must always be tested by definite results. Two methods then suggest themselves, both scientific, equally important, and (like the inspiration and technique of an art) to be followed concurrently. The one is that of physical and analytical investigation of musical effects, carried out in a purely scientific manner; the other is that of psychical investigation carried out with equal care, and entirely severed from the methods of the crank. No investigation of the forces used in sound-art can go beyond a first step without plunging into what may truly be called the occult.

A small group of artist-scientists has glimpsed by use of these methods certain possibilities which will serve, together with the many instances already given in this volume, to indicate the possibilities.

It has been found that the human voice under certain

Music To-day

conditions of training (which differ widely from those of the accepted training of the modern concert artist, and are not intended to compete with or supplant that training in any way) is an organ, the proper use of which in meditation or concentration, will induce definite psychological and physiological states. It has been found that such states may be re-induced by various persons, by repetition of the same processes, and moreover that, given sufficient spiritual power in the generator, the condition induced in him- or her- self may be imparted to others in greater or lesser degree according to their sensitivity. The possibilities for research along this line are immense, and the fact that such possibilities are perceived through the intuition rather than justified by philosophy, ought no longer to have such exaggerated weight as formerly. One has but to consider the intricacies of the subconscious and unrevealed self, and of its physical instrument the brain and nervous system; the infinite varieties of tonal action and reaction between these; the fascinating subject of pitch in relation to them, and the effects of *timbre* upon the whole to realize the field that is before us.

Close correspondences have been discovered or indicated by means of this method between notes, forms, colours, psychological states, elements, vowels, etc. It is a field of experiment in which the testing instrument is man himself and the force employed that of the creative imagination. One might call it the esoteric aspect of the art of music.

The possibilities are immense, and intensive study and experiment along these lines would result in a revolution upon the expressional side of the art commensurate with that which has already taken place upon the technical.

· · · · ·

Conclusion

It is time—after these irruptive divagations into so many fields where the most sympathetic of readers will hardly fail to find, at times, a greater degree of curiosity and inquiry than succinct and detailed knowledge—to terminate our studies. Upon the whole we have divided them fairly between the Form side and the Life side. And if I choose to end as I began by emphasizing the Spiritual rather than the Mundane—the Inspiration rather than the Expression—it will be upon some such *apologia* as that of Amiel:—

O Plato! O Pythagoras! ages ago you heard these harmonies,
      Surprised these moments of inward ecstasy,
      Knew these divine transports.
If music thus carries us to heaven, it is because
      Music is Harmony,
      Harmony is Perfection,
      Perfection is our Dream,
         and
      Our Dream is Heaven.

Postscript

Since the completion of the foregoing I have received permission to be more explicit upon the source and derivation of those portions which refer to occult and oriental matters. In acknowledging my indebtedness to Maud MacCarthy, whom I met in 1915 and to whose guidance in these unfamiliar realms of the art I owe the little I know, it is but fair to say that I alone am responsible for the opinions I have put forward. Most of the occult and oriental information in this volume is ascribable to my memory of her unpublished MSS. As my work along occult lines has of necessity been sporadic, it is unreliable by comparison with that of my mentor whose life has been devoted to studies and achievements in this field. The teacher does not always agree with the methods and statements of the pupil.

I know no one else who is doing this important work. For this reason I pass on her comments as follows: "(1) Psychism is not necessarily spiritual or inspired: the depth of life-experience alone determines the height to which genius may soar. (2) There is grave danger in 'practices' of any kind—*e.g.* concentration on the *chakras*—without the help of a teacher. (3) Knowledge of the true nature of sound, form, colour and number is alone possessed by the Adepts, but it may be apprehended and practised by those who have great simplicity and whose egotism is dispersing. Such knowledge is given from individual to individual and is not to be found in cliques, academies, or

Music To-day

'isms' of any kind." As to the source from which she has obtained this knowledge, she goes so far as to assert that it could revolutionize the arts and sciences.

It is thus clear that the indebtedness referred to here covers such subjects as microtonal and Indian music; "nature-pitch," which she discovered and revealed to the group mentioned on p. 351; Indian modes (the first 72 of the table, pp. 46–7); etheric breathing, hearing, touch, etc.; correspondences between sounds and cosmic—individual—psychological states, elements, vowels, organs of the body, nerve-centres, *chakras*, etc.; Phono-therapy, of which she is the discoverer and pioneer (*e.g.* the " remarkable cure," p. 110); the processes described on pp. 209–213 and elsewhere.

In short, so far as the statements which I have made may be inaccurate, mine is the responsibility: but insofar as readers find them stimulating and helpful, the above acknowledgments do more than merely indicate a personal indebtedness; they direct anyone sincerely interested to her unique experiences, records and experiments—a veritable treasure-store.

INDEX

A

Academies of Music
  neglect of 'Rationale of Inspiration,' 20, 253
  orthodox musical training, 156
Accentuation, 73
Ādi
  Divine Realm, 159
  man cannot contact, 159
Æschylus
  music with drama, 350
Æsthetic
  schematization of, 14
  standards, 39, 151
  musical, 155
  difficulty of discussion, 155
  presentation and representation, 158
  schematization formulated, 156, 159, 164
  genius defined, 161, 170
  'realms' fron which music is inspired, 163
  toward a musical æsthetic, 164
  schematization, 164
  comprehensiveness of system, 164
  music derived from Physical Realm, 165
  music derived from 'Etheric' Levels, 165
  impressionists and symbolists, 165
  music derived from Emotional Realm, 166
  music derived from Lower Mental Levels, 167
  higher realms unexplored, 166
  technical means inadequate, 167
  higher realms must be explored, 167
  modern tendency to turn from Emotion, 168
  dividing line between ephemeral and permanent, 168
  Causal world, 168
  consciousness in Causal world, 169
  music derived from Causal levels, 166, 169
  ideations contacted, 169

Æsthetic—continued
  ditto : diversified presentation of, 169
  ideations contacted simultaneously, 170
  ditto : supposed plagiarism, 170
  functioning of *Manas*, 169
  music derided, 171
  ineptitude *re* musical evaluation, 171
  music derived from 'five worlds,' 172
  emotional and non-emotional, 172
  Paul Bekker *re*, 173
  ditto : Criticism of Bekker's system, 174
  music derived from Buddhic Realm, 174
  rarity of Buddhic vibrations, 174
  ditto : Supremacy of Palestrina, 175
  music derived from Atmic Realm, 176
  reflections between Realms, 176
  Mantras from *Avatara*, 177
  creative vibrations : contacted and expressed, 179
  varying effect of *Tristan*, 178
  ensouling of Music, 179
  qualities of Inspiration, 185
  'live' music, 186
  the Beautiful in music, 188
  Idealism in music, 190
  Purity in music, 192
  Spirituality in music, 192
  individuality and originality, 193
  originality and novelty, 195
  individuality and personality, 196
  Mysticism and Mystical Inspiration, 198
  ditto : assures immortality, 198
  ditto : as crux of our studies, 198
  inspiration defined, 199
  inspiration and technique, 200
  exaltation of consciousness, 201
  ditto : method of attaining, 209
  materialistic views controverted, 214
  ditto : J. H. Newman quoted, 214
  Busoni's 'Sketch of a New Æsthetic of Music,' 245 and fn.
  craftsmen and artists, 265

355

Index

Africa (Saint-Saëns)
  performances by Busoni, 243
African Types
  folk-music, 223
Albe, Fournier D'
  Optophone, 99
Albéniz, Isaac
  Spanish folk-tunes, 259
  Iberia, 260
Alchemists
  re psycho-physiological effects of music, 109
Alexander
  Torrey and, 175 fn.
Alfano, Franco
  completed Puccini's *Turandot*, 278
Allen, J. B.
  Scales in Music and Colours, 101 fn.
Also Sprach Zarathustra (Strauss), 229, 230, 231
  use of Flute in, 79
  use of Trumpet in, 83
  dance in, 129
  influence on Bartók, 254
Amateur
  position in time of Haydn, 14
  difficulty in bridging gap, 47
  importance of, 149
  influence of radio on, 149
  Berlioz, Delius, Boito, 263
  Delius, 308
Amen Chorus (Handel's *Messiah*), 70
America
  attitude to modern composers, 25
  MacDowell, 313 et seq.
American Types, 58, 221
  folk-music, 223
  Negro folk-music, 274
  question of national music, 274
  American group of composers, 273
Amiel
  quoted, 188, 353
Amor Quando Floria: Death of Laura (Petrarch)
  Palestrina's setting, 175, 214
Anakreon's Grab (Wolf), 250
Angel Chorus (La Damnation de Faust—Berlioz), 286
Angels, 215, 280, 291
  See also under *Deva*
Animal Kingdom
  reaction to music, 108, 237
Anima Poetæ (Coleridge)
  quoted, 16 fn.
'Anna'
  episode in Strauss' *Don Juan*, 230

Anupādaka
  Monadic Realm, 159
  man cannot contact, 159
Apostles, The (Elgar), 236
Appalachian Types
  folk-music, 223
Appalachia Variations (Delius)
  a performance of, 306
  wordless choral commentaries, 311
Appreciation of Music
  cult of, 156
Apprenti Sorcier, L' (Dukas)
  Double-bassoon solo, 82
Arab Types
  Bartók's contact with, 255
'*Arabella*' (Strauss), 232
Archetypes, 198, 223, 341, 349
  echoes of, 35
  in Causal world, 168
  Plato's *Dialogues* refer to, 168
Ariettes Oubliées (Debussy), 305
Aristotle
  re Sound-Colour correspondences, 99
  re psycho-physiological effects of music, 109
  re educative value, 188
Art of Mobile Colour, The (Remington), 101 fn.
Arts
  presentative and representative, 158
  peasant, 261
  magical aspect of, 346
  as alteratives, 346
  synthesis of, 349
Aryan Race
  India as cradle of, 45
  inception of, 159, 279 fn.
Assumpta est Maria. Mass (Palestrina), 175
Astral Realm or 'World'
  See under *Emotional Realm or 'World'*
Atma, 324, 325
  Spiritual Realm, 159
  consciousness can contact, 159
  music inspired from, 164, 166, 176
  largely unexplored by composers, 166
  reflected in Physical Realm, 176
  Mantra from *Avatara*, appertaining to, 177
  qualities of Atmic music, 193
  mystical inspiration, 199
  contact with, 212
  Atmic realm, 223, 246
  Scriabin's *Divine Poem*, 299
Atonality, 33, 41, 56, 334

Index

Atonality—*continued*
  modern composers free from 'key-consciousness,' 42
  a necessary item in modern technique, 42
  defined, 42
  as opposed to Diatonality, 42
  difficulty in defining, 51
  resulted from Polytonality, 56
  described, 57
  a real addition to means of expression, 57
  exclusive use deprecated, 57
  use and abuse, 57
  non-nationalistic character, 58, 221
  necessity of, 58
  Busoni's disapproval of, 244
  Schönberg, 250 *et seq.*
  Bartók, 255
  Hindemith, 262 *et seq.*
  Honegger, 268
  Milhaud, 269
  Szymanovski, 271
  Cyril Scott, 277
  use of in '*A World Requiem,*' 281 fn.
  relation to whole-tone 'scale,' 303
A Travers Chants (Berlioz)
  Quoted, 40
Audion (de Forest), 99
Augustine, Saint, 188 fn.
Aura, Human, 213, 225
  auric disturbances seen in terms of colour, 101 fn.
  Dr Kilner's apparatus, 291 fn.
Auralization, 336
Auric, Georges, 274
  one of *Groupe des Six*, 266
Aus Holberg's Zeit Suite (Grieg), 270
Aus Italien Suite (Strauss), 228
  'light' music in, 129
Avatara
  Mantras from, 177
Ave Maria (Verdi)
  use of 'Enigmatic scale' in, 50 and fn.

B

Bach, Johann Sebastian
  Bach-Brahms period, 26
  technique, 30
  Die Kunst der Fuge, 37, 127
  two-modal system adequate for, 44
  Bach-Strauss period, 45
  revival, 52
  pre-Bach revival desirable, 52

Bach, Johann Sebastian—*continued*
  stabilization of Equal Temperament, 60, 336
  development since, 66
  use of Sequence, 116
  Double Concerto: Example from, 116
  dances by, 127
  his best work, 128
  his linear work broadcasts better than modern scoring, 149
  musical output since, 166
  Wohltemperirte Klavier as musicians' 'daily bread,' 176
  chorales played by Busoni, 181
  studied by Schumann and Mendelssohn, 194
  daily application to work, 201
  polyphonic mastery, 212
  Mass, 214
  'light' jigs and gavottes, 234
  influence on Stravinsky, 239
  works performed by Busoni, 244
  as typical professional musician, 263
  rarity of lapses, 263, 271, 289
  movement of blocks of harmony contrapuntally, 275
  absence of devic influence, 283
Baird
  television apparatus, 100
Bakst
  founded Russian decorative school on Fra Angelico, 53
Ballads, Shop-
  source, 163
Ballet
  Le Sacre du Printemps (Diaghilev-Stravinsky), 237
  Daphnis et Chloé (Diaghilev-Ravel), 249
  Le Train Bleu (Diaghilev-Cocteau-Milhaud), 269
  Sylph ballet in Berlioz' *La Damnation de Faust*, 285
  Jeux (Debussy), 305
  Eastern ballets, 345
Balzac, 228
Bande Mataram
  performance by Military Band, 181
Banner of Saint George (Elgar), 234
Bantock, Granville
  Choral Symphony: performance of, 67
  copious output, 276
  championship, long ago, of Sibelius and Delius, 276 fn.
  early performances of Delius, 307

Index

Barque dans l'Océan, Une (Ravel), 247
Bartók, Béla, 339
  Second Quartet, 138
  properly belongs to several categories, 227 fn.
  Kossuth, 235
  Vignette, 254 *et seq.*
  name coupled with Kodály, 258
  started with Hungarian folk-music, 258
  ditto : further development, 258
  has grown beyond folk-music, 261
  power to create ' seed '-motives, 323
Bass Clarinet, 330
Bass Drum
  example of use of, 84
Bass Flute, 330
  example of use of, 80
Bassoon, 330, 331
  examples of use of, 81
  use of four in Berlioz' *Faust*, 82
  Schubert's use of, 86
  German, 86
  French, Belgian and English, 87
  demands of new French school, 88
  duets with Clarinet, 92
  via Radio, 149
Bass Trombone, 331
Bass Trumpet, 331
Bass Tuba, 331
Bat-Squeak
  high note of, inaudible to some, 65
Batterie
  example of use of, 85
'Batti Batti' (*Don Giovanni*-Mozart), 284
Battle Symphony (Beethoven), 128
Bauerkeller, Wilhelm
  Delius as pupil of, 308
Bax, Arnold
  Keltic types, 248, 275
  often compared with poet W. B. Yeats, 276
B.B.C.
  quoted *re* Reduction of Dynamic *via* Radio, 142 fn.
  See also under *Radio*
Beauty and the Beast (*Mother Goose Suite*—Ravel), 247
Beauty, Musical, 310
  theory of, to be formulated, 155
  spiritual transcends intellectual, 163, 197
  Schelling quoted *re*, 281
Beecham, Sir Thomas
  as Conductor, 94
  brought about recognition of Delius, 307

Beethoven, 224, 309, 321
  technique, 30
  two-modal system adequate for, 44
  use of Lydian mode, 44 fn.
  Leonora in the prison house, 68
  clarinet-bassoon duet passages, 92
  violin Concerto, 92, 235
  translated *sights* into music, 97
  tonal imitation (Cuckoo), 98, 165
  C Minor Symphony, 121
  ' light ' music by, 127, 234
  Scottish and German Dances, 128, 234
  Battle Symphony—Schlacht bei Vittoria, 128
  Rûle Britannia!, 128
  tune in *Ninth Symphony* jazzed, 134 fn.
  symphonies played by Hallé Orchestra, 141
  correspondence with publishers *re* ' expression ' marks, 141
  Equali, 181
  Cavatina from Quartet, 181
  Grosse Fuge, 185
  ditto : as an ideation contacted in Causal Realm, 185
  claim *re* moral value for music, 188
  study of Haydn and Mozart, 194
  studied by Brahms, 194
  conviction of superiority, 194
  quoted, 195 fn.
  mystical inspiration, 199
  attainment of condition of ' raptus,' 201
  sketch-books, 207
  dramatic-logic, 212
  Coriolanus, 214
  contrasted with Piccini, 220
  German nationality, 223
  influence on Berlioz, 223
  ' little joke,' 226
  pianoforte Concertos, 242
  influence of, on Bartók, 256
  Fortissimo passages contrasted with Honegger's, 267
  quoted, 268
  Devic influence, 288
  ditto : *Pastoral Symphony*, 288
  Pastoral Symphony : Grove quoted *re*, 288
  quoted *re* unsatisfactory nature of Pianoforte, 299
  Debussy's revulsion against, 303
  Influence of, on Sibelius, 319
  power to create ' seed '-motives, 323
  re ' divine afflatus,' 340
  his development, 342
  ' Turkish ' music, 344

Index

Bekker, Paul, 265
  champions non-emotionalism in music, 173
  Organische und mechanische Musik, 173
  criticism of his system, 174
Bel Canto, 70
Belgian Types, 58, 220, 221
Bell, Graham
  Photophone (1880), 99
Bennett, Arnold
  quoted, 16, 178
Bennett, Sterndale
  Devic influence, 287
Berceuses des Chat (Stravinsky), 238
Berg, Alban, 253
  name coupled with Webern, 258
  Wozzeck, 272, 273
Berlioz, 339
  found Beethoven's technique inadequate, 30
  À travers Chants quoted, 40
  book by, on orchestration, 79, 236
  use of Oboe (*Roi Lear* Overture), 80
  use of four Bassoons in *Faust*, 82
  use of French horn, 87
  a piece by, 90
  use of recognition thrill, 119
  Symphonie Fantastique, 119, 197, 237, 285
  Faust: *Cor anglais* 'recollection' of Marguerite melody, 119
  starved to unproductiveness, 125
  Memoires, 126
  the waltz, 132
  quoted *re* use of Harps, 146
  Queen Mab scherzo, 181, 237
  study of Gluck, 194
  conviction of superiority, 194
  influence of Harriet Smithson, 197
  mystical inspiration, 199
  quoted *re* his own inspiration, 208
  Sanctus, 214
  contrasted with Schumann, 221
  French nationality, 223
  ditto: Weismann quoted *re* influence of Beethoven, 223
  Grand Traité d'instrumentation et d'orchestration modernes, 236
  influence on Strauss, 236
  Symphonie Fantastique and *Romeo et Juliet* compared with Elgar's *Falstaff*, 236
  influence on Hugo Wolf, 250
  as amateur, 263

Berlioz—*continued*
  lapses, 263, 289
  living inspiration of, 274
  quoted *re* Gluck, 284
  harmonic and melodic *gaucheries*, 285
  Devic influence, 286
  ditto: impossible fairly to evaluate his work without understanding of above, 285
  ditto: *Symphonie Fantastique*, 285
  ditto: *La Damnation de Faust*, 285
  ditto: *Romeo et Juliet* symphony (Scène d'Amour), 285
  ditto: *Queen Mab* Scherzo, 286
  ditto: *Ronde du Sabbat*, 286
  ditto: Angel Chorus (*La Damnation de Faust*), 286
  ditto: *Messe des Morts* (*Sanctus*), 287
  ditto: *Les Troyens*, 287
  Saint-Saëns quoted *re*, 287
  power to create 'seed'-motives, 323
  re 'divine afflatus,' 340
Berners, Lord
  satirical note in music, 27 fn.
Bertrand, Louis, 247
Bizet
  a piece by, 90
  performance of *Carmen*, 181
  Busoni's Fantasy on *Carmen*, 241
Blackwood, Algernon
  The Bright Messenger, 288 fn.
Blake, William, 205, 225, 295, 302, 321
  quoted, 124
  inspiration from 'Causal world,' 169
  ditto: diversified-presentation of, 169
  sang many of his poems, 169
  quoted, *re* his own inspiration
  unified conception as music-poem-picture, 350
Blavatsky, H. P.
  Secret Doctrine quoted *re* Sound-Colour Table of Correspondences, 103
Bliss, Arthur, 276
Bloch, Ernest
  a modern work by, 90
  Hebrew types, 248, 269, 274 and fn.
  Schelomo, 274 fn.
  Trois Poèmes Juifs, 274 fn.
  Devic influences, 274 fn., 287
Bluebeard (Bartók), 256
Boehme, Jacob, 302
Bohemian Types
  Smetana's use of, 260
Boito, 312
  inspiration from 'Causal world,' 169

359

Index

Boito—*continued*
  ditto : diversified presentation of, 169
  as amateur, 263
  lapses, 263
  synthesis of arts, 350
Bolero (Ravel), 129, 249
  basic rhythm, 137
Bose, Sir Jagadish
  quoted *re* effect of Sound on plant life, 108
Boughton, Rutland
  Devic influence, 287
  ditto : *The Immortal Hour*, 287
Braga
  Serenata, 184
Brahmarandra Chakra, 213 fn.
  crystallization of ideas through, 213
Brahms, Johannes, 127, 309
  quoted, 17
  Bach-Brahms period, 26
  found Bach's technique inadequate, 30
  Brahms-Schönberg period, 30
  case of conversion to, 38
  imperfections, 38
  beauties, subtleties and grandeurs, 38
  two-modal system adequate for, 44
  unsatisfactory accompaniments to old modal songs, 49
  art-songs, 67
  use of Flute (*First Symphony* : Finale), 80
  use of Piccolo (*Pianoforte Concerto*), 80
  horn theme in *finale* of first symphony, 87
  orchestral progress since, 95
  use of recognition thrill, 120
  ' light ' music by, 128, 234
  Hungarian Dances, 128
  hack work by, 131
  the waltz, 132
  a Brahms symphony on gramophone, 147
  violin concerto : performances by Kreisler, 180
  study of Beethoven and Schumann, 194
  studied by Strauss, 194
  conviction of superiority, 194
  Schicksalslied, 214
  violin concerto, 235
  pianoforte concertos performed by Busoni, 242
  growth of themes, 262
  Pfitzner derivative from, 272
  as exemplar of closed symphonic style, 297

Brahms, Johannes—*continued*
  ditto : symphonic movements contrasted with *Siegfried Idyll*, 297
  power to create ' seed '-motives, 323
Brass Band
  inferior to orchestra on gramophone, 142
Brautwahl, Die (Busoni)
  use of Clarinets in, 81
Briantchaninov, A. N.
  letter from Scriabin quoted, 301
Bridges, Robert
  quoted, 321
Brigg Fair (Delius), 311
Bright Messenger, The (Algernon Blackwood), 288 fn.
British Broadcasting Corporation
  See under *B.B.C.*
Broadcast Music
  See under *Radio*
Brodsky, Adolf
  quoted, 17
Browne, Sir Thomas, 127
Brownies
  Stevenson's, 204
Browning, 127
Bruckner
  aural powers and limitations, 64
  inability to create ' seed '-motives, 323
Brunet
  Columbine by, paraphrased by use of Quarter-Tones, 59
Buddhi, 166, 174, 324, 325
  Intuitional Realm or ' World,' 159
  consciousness can contact, 159
  music inspired from Buddhic levels, 163
  largely unexplored by composers, 167
  rarity of composers who can adequately translate vibrations from, 174
  ditto : supremacy of Palestrina, 175
  reflected in Emotional Realm, 176, 309
  Mantra from *Avatara*, appertaining to, 177
  Buddhic aspect of *Tristan and Isolde*, 178
  ditto : contacted by Wagner during composition, 178
  expression of vibrations in Buddhic realm, 179
  qualities of Buddhic music, 193
  mystical inspiration, 199
  contact with, 212
  Buddhic realm, 223, 246
  Buddhic contacts by Bartók, 256

Index

Buddhi—*continued*
  contacted by Wagner in *Charfreitagzauber* (Parsifal), 291
  Scriabin's *Divine Poem*, 299
  Delius' contact with, 309
Bugles
  re Brass Band Gramophone records, 142
Bülow, Von
  as Conductor, 92
Bunyan, 279 fn.
Burmese Gongs, 332
Burmese Music, 344
Burns, Robert, 248
Busoni, Ferruccio
  quoted, 32 fn.
  proposed scales against 'foreign' chords, 49
  use of Clarinet (*Die Brautwahl: Pezzo Mistico*), 81
  quoted, 168 fn.
  in some Bach chorales, 181
  Vignette, 257 *et seq.*
  Tertia-Tones, 335
Byrd, William
  quoted *re* vocal and instrumental music, 66
Byron, 224
  Manfred, 311

C

Cadman, John, 274
Capablanca, 37
Cardillac (Hindemith), 266
Carlyle
  quoted, 107
Carmen (Bizet)
  Zelie de Lussan in, 181
  Busoni's Fantasy on, 242
Carpenter, J. Alden, 274
Caruso
  in a Neapolitan street song, 181
Casella, 277
Castanets, 260
Castelnuovo-Tedesco, 277
Castel Sant' Angelo
  Beethoven's *Equali* from towers of, 181
Cathédrale Engloutie, La (Debussy), 305
Causal 'Body,' 170
  See also under *Causal Realm* or '*World*'
Causal Realm or 'World,' 301, 304, 324, 325

Causal Realm or 'World'—*continued*
  higher sub-planes of mental world, 166 fn., 168
  music derived from, 166, 168
  largely unexplored by composers, 167
  Plato's Archetypes inhere in, 168
  functioning of consciousness in, 168
  translation of ideations from, 168
  Mozart, 169
  Blake, 169
  Wagner, 169
  Scriabin, 169
  Boito, 169
  music from, accused of coldness, 172, 189 fn.
  reflected in Lower Mental Realm, 176
  Mantra from *Avatara*, appertaining to, 177
  expression of vibrations in, 179
  Beethoven's *Grosse Fuge* contacted in, 185
  causal presentation is complete, 189 fn.
  qualities of music emanating from, 193
  mystical inspiration, 199
  Einstein's inspiration, 202 fn.
  contact with, 212
  characteristics of, 212, 223
  glimpses of, in Strauss' work, 230
  Stravinsky, 240, 246
  Scriabin's *Divine Poem*, 299
Cavatina (Beethoven Op. 130)
  performance by Joachim, 181
Celesta
  example of use of, 86
  characteristics of, 331
  resemblance to, of M. Terepnine's new instrument, 331
'Cello
  See under *Violoncello*
Celtic Types
  See under *Keltic Types*
Ce qu'a vu le vent d'ouest (Préludes—Debussy), 305
Cerebro-Spinal System, 279
  response from, 39
Cervantes
  in translation, 69
Chabrier
  a piece by, 90
Chadwick, George W., 274
Chakras, 207
  Scriabin's meditation upon, 203
  each *chakra* responds to musical vibration-rate, 210
  operation on, *re* musical composition, 210

Index

Chakras—continued
 Brahmarandra, 213 fn.
 ditto: crystallization of ideas through, 213
Chamber-Music
 receiving increased attention, 75
Chanson Hindou (Rimsky-Korsakov), 128 and fn., 345
Chapeau Chinois, 332
Charfreitagzauber (*Parsifal* - Wagner), 214, 291, 318
Chatterton
 starvation of, 125
Chess
 Capablanca plays 20 games simultaneously, 37
 Paul Bekker's system and, 174
Chinese Gongs, 332
Chinese Music, 344
Chopin, 309
 a Nocturne by, 128 fn.
 the waltz, 132
 studied by Scriabin, 194
 Nocturnes, 197
 ditto: influence of George Sand, 197
 influence on Scriabin, 294, 296, 342
Choral Music, 309
 lags behind orchestral, 67
 Symphony of Bantock, 67
 Hallelujah and *Amen* Choruses, 70
 community singing, 71
 pre-eminence of English choral singing, 71
 effectiveness of communal song, 72
 decline of interest in choral activities, 75
 broadcasting considerations, 146
 large scale works *via* Radio, 149
 See also under *Songs ; Vocal Music*
Chord-Progressions, 29
Chromaticism
 comparatively restricted field of, 42
 chromatic scale, 42
 Greek chromatic system, 44
 unsatisfactory chromatic harmonization of diatonal melody, 49
 Spohr's harmonic style, 50
 as end of all forward movement, 51
 pictorial (Brunet's *Colombine*), 59
 Scriabin and ultra-chromaticism, 298
 resemblance to whole-tone ' scale,' 304
 chromatic freedom, 335
Church Ritual
 Gregorian modal system, 44
 Palestrina's settings, 175
 modal vestiges, 275

Cinema
 See under *Kinema*
Clair-Audience, 210, 336 fn.
Clair-Voyance, 210
Clarinet
 example of use of, 81
 duets with Bassoon, 92
 via Radio, 148, 330
Cocteau, Jean, 269
Coleridge
 Anima Poetæ quoted, 16 fn.
 attainment of condition of ' raptus,' 201
Colleges of Music
 See under *Academies*
Colombine
 picture by Brunet, paraphrased by use of Quarter-Tones, 59
Colour and Sound : Correspondence, 102 *et seq.*, 352
 association of, 97 *et seq.*
 correspondence between pictorial and musical sense, 97
 correspondence between pictorial and musical art, 99
 many persons always associate sound with colour, 99
 claims that exact correspondence is a fact in Nature, 99 and fn.
 experimentalists, etc., 99
 transmutation of light into sound, 100
 Remington Colour-Organ, 100
 Rameau and Grétry, 101
 Scriabin's *Prometheus*, a Symphony of Sound and Colour, 101
 ' Tastiera per Luce ' used in Scriabin's *Prometheus*, 101, 301
 ditto: false correspondence, 101, 301
 Scriabin's scheme, 102
 Rimsky-Korsakov's scheme, 102
 observation of, due to use of psychic faculty, 102
 suggested tables, 102
 Madame Blavatsky's table, 103
 Cyril Scott's *Philosophy of Modernism* 103
 discrepancies, 103
 discrepancies explained, 103
 occult lore *re*, 105
 Indian teachings, 344
 Scriabin's attempted synthesis, 350
 investigations, 352
' Colour-Hearing ' Sense, 102
Colour Music (Jameson), 101 fn.

Index

Colour-Organ (Remington), 100 *et seq.*
  adopted and used by Scriabin in *Prometheus*, 101, 301
Columbus, Christopher, 61
Combarieu, Jules
  Music, Laws and Evolution quoted, 34 fn.
Common Chord
  potential dynamic of, 35
Community Singing, 71
  effectiveness of, 71
  potentialities and limitations, 72
Complexity, 341 *et seq.*
  not a desirable end, 53
Concertina
  unsatisfactory quality of tone, 78
  as substitute for full brass chord *via* Radio, 147
Conducting and Conductors, 90 *et seq.*
  performance of old works possible without conductor, 91
  performance of post-Spohr works impracticable without conductor, 91
  ability to beat undeviating *tempo* essential, 91
  team-spirit in orchestras, 92
  necessity for 'magnetic personality,' 92
  Von Bülow, 92
  Wagner at Philharmonic concerts, 92
  Richter at ditto, 92
  Mahler, 93
  Nikisch, 93
  Richter and Toscanini compared, 93
  Albert Wolff (Concerts Lamoureux), 93
  Sir Thomas Beecham, 94
  conducting from memory, 94
Conservatoires of Music
  See under *Academies*
Consilium Angelicum, 181 fn.
Contra-Bass Tuba, 331
Cor Anglais
  See under *English Horn*
Coriolanus (Beethoven), 214
Cornet
  unsatisfactory quality of, 78
Corno Inglese
  See under *English Horn*
Correspondences
  colour and sound, 97 *et seq.*
  postulated series embracing Colour—Sound—Form—Vowels—Psychological states—Elements—etc., 99 fn.

Correspondences—*continued*
  Grétry's postulated Emotion—Colour—Sound correspondence, 101
  Remington Colour-Organ, 100 *et seq.*
  Scriabin's use of 'Tastiera per Luce,' 101
  Indian teachings, 344
  importance of, *re* Synthesis of Arts, 350
  investigations, 352
  See also under *Colour and Sound: Correspondence*
Cosmic Symphony, 285
Counterpoint
  ability to follow, 37
  of Rhythm: use of drums in, 84
  movement of lines of Melody, 333
  movements of blocks of Harmony, 333
  of changing *Timbres*, 333
Couperin
  Debussy as musical descendant of, 303
Cows
  reaction to music, 108
Cuckoo
  Beethoven's imitation of, 98, 165
Curwen
  publisher, *The Reed Player*, 71 fn.
Cymbal
  in 'Turkish' music, 344

D

Dalle tre Commedie Goldoniane (Malipiero), 278
Damnation de Faust, La (Berlioz), 285
  use of four Bassoons in, 82
  Cor anglais 'recollection' of Marguerite melody, 119
Dance, 190
  by Bach, 127
  Beethoven's Scottish and German dances, 128, 234
  Brahms' Hungarian Dances, 128
  in *Also Sprach Zarathustra* (Strauss), 129
  waltzes in *Rosenkavalier* (Strauss), 129
  jazz as music of negroid origin, 132
  evaluation of jazz, 132 *et seq.*
  music as erotic stimulant, 178
  Wein, Weib und Gesang waltzes (Johann Strauss), 185
  Bach's jigs and gavottes, 234
  Schubert's waltzes, 234
  Smetana's polkas, 234

Index

Dance—*continued*
  Delius' *Dance Rhapsody*, 311
  Sibelius' 'light' music, 319
  Pseudo-oriental, 344
  See also under *Waltz*
Dance Rhapsody No. 1 (Delius), 311
Dancla
  a trifle by, 308
Danse Caractéristique (Sibelius), 319
Dante
  in translation, 69
  his realm of Divine Intelligence, 168
  The Vision of Dante (Choral work), 232 fn.
  his 'Earthly Paradise,' 311
  T. S. Eliot quoted *re*, 329
Daphnis et Chloé (Ravel), 249
Da Vinci, Leonardo
  See under *Vinci, Leonardo da*
Death of Laura (Petrarch)
  Palestrina's setting of *Amor quando floria*, 175
Debussy, Claude
  quoted (from *Revue Blanche*), 26
  found Rameau's technique inadequate, 30
  addicted to whole-tone 'scale,' 43
  use of voice apart from words, 70
  use of French horn, 87
  a piece by, 90
  type of orchestration, 95
  use of sequence, 117
  string quartet: Finale—analysis of (see also 328A), 117
  music from 'etheric' levels, 165
  canker of 'personality,' 198
  poignant harmonic *nuances*, 212
  harmonic sense, 233
  L'Après midi d'un Faune as work of epoch-indicating character, 237
  name coupled with Ravel, 258
  living inspiration of, 274
  Devic influence, 287
  Vignette, 303 *et seq.*
  alleged influence over Delius, 307
  Pelléas et Mélisande his chief work, 307
  ditto: contrasted with Delius' *Mass of Life*, 307
  quoted, 326
Defence of Poetry (Shelley)
  quoted, 162
De Forest
  Audion, 99
Delius, Frederick, 224
  use of voice apart from words, 70

Delius, Frederick—*continued*
  use of English horn (*Song of the High Hills*), 81
  a modern work, 90
  Deva-touch, 212
  Song of the High Hills, 214
  A Village Romeo and Juliet, 256
  Fennimore and Gerda, 256
  name coupled with Elgar, 258
  as amateur, 263
  lapses, 263, 289
  championed by Bantock, 276 fn.
  Devic influence, 287, 317
  Vignette, 306 *et seq.*
  harmonic freedom, 325
Delville, Jean
  quoted *re* Scriabin, 300
Demarquez, Suzanne
  quoted from *Revue Musicale re* modern English music, 225
Demon Chorus (*La Damnation de Faust*—Berlioz), 285
Dent, E. J.
  quoted *re* English music, 224
De Quincey
  attainment of condition of 'raptus,' 201
Deva, 205, 300
  Deva-touch of Grieg, Delius, Sibelius, 212
  influences on Bloch, 274 fn.
  part four, chapter xiv, 279 *et seq.*
  etymology, 279 fn.
  parallel evolution of devas and humans, 280
  Gandharvas, 280
  interaction between devas and world of music, 281
  ensouling of music, 281, 290
  co-operation with composers of certain type, 281
  human and devic types of artist, 281
  attempted simulation of deva-music in '*A World Requiem*,' 282 fn.
  Wagner's *Ring*, 282, 290
  Bach a non-devic composer, 283
  Palestrina essentially a devic composer, 283, 292
  Haydn under influence of, 283
  Handel's attempt to paraphrase music of *Gandharvas*, 283
  Handel's conscious contact, 283
  ditto: Handel quoted *re Messiah* 'raptus,' 283
  influence on following composers:
    Gluck, 284

Index

Deva—*continued*
  influence, etc.—*continued*
    Mozart, 284
    Schubert, 284
    Schumann, 284
    Smetana, 284, 287
    Schumann, Smetana and Jullien unbalanced, 204
    Berlioz, 285
    Grieg, 287
    Sterndale Bennett, 287
    Mendelssohn, 287
    MacDowell, 287
    Dvořák, 287
    Debussy, 287
    Franck, 287
    Sibelius, 287
    Delius, 287
    Holst, 287
    Bloch, 287
    Szymanovski, 287
    Boughton, 287
    Beethoven, 288
    Wagner, 290
  Gandharva Music, 288
  inequalities of devic composers, 289
  methods of devic composers, 289
  ditto: Wagner's methods, 290
  ditto: *Meistersinger, Ring* and *Parsifal*, 290
  ditto: evocative power of *Parsifal*, 291
  Devic type instantly recognizable, 292
    inspiration mostly unconscious, 292
  Vignettes of devic composers:
    Scriabin, 293 *et seq.*
    Debussy, 302 *et seq.*
    Delius, 306 *et seq.*
    MacDowell, 313
    Sibelius, 316
  Scriabin's conscious contact, 298
  contrast between Scriabin and Delius, 309
  lesser devas of Scandinavia, 317
  contrast between Scriabin and Sibelius, 324
  Devic vibrations, 325
Dhyana, 209
Diaghilev
  ballet wedded to Stravinsky's *Le Sacre du Printemps*, 237
  ballet wedded to Ravel's *Daphnis et Chloé*, 249
  ballet wedded to Milhauds' *Le Train Bleu*, 269
Dialogues (Plato)
  re Archetypes, 168

Diatonal Music, 41 *et seq.*, 334
  defined, 42
  as opposed to Atonality, 42
  Greek system, 44
  extended by adoption of 90 modal system, 48
  unsatisfactory chromatic harmonization, 49, 334
  'natural tuning' affiliated with, 334
D'Indy, Vincent, 274
  pupil of Franck, 274
  founded Paris Schola Cantorum, 274
Di Salo, Gasparo
  See under *Salo, Gasparo di*
Divine Poem (Scriabin), 299, 300
Divine Realm or 'World' (Ādi), 159
  man cannot consciously contact, 159
Dodecaphony
  Josef Hauer's system, 56
  Schönberg, 250 *et seq.*
Dogs
  reaction to music, 108
Don Giovanni
  'Batti batti,' 284
Don Juan (Strauss), 229
  use of Horns in, 82
  'Anna' episode in, 230
  composed at age of twenty-four, 232
Don Quixote (Strauss), 98, 229, 230
  'light' music in, 129
  antics of Sancho Panza, 129
Dorfmusikanten-Sextett (Mozart)
  whole-tone 'scale' as joke, 43
Double-Bass, 89
  via Radio, 149
Double-Bassoon
  example of use of, 82
Double Concerto (Bach), 116
Downfall of the West, The (Spengler), 329 fn.
Drama
  Æschylus' synthesis with Music, 350
  Wagner's synthesis of arts, 350
Dream of Gerontius, The (Elgar), 232, 236
Drum
  unique use of, 84
  Indian drums (male and female), 332
Dryads, 315
Dukas, Paul, 274
  double-bassoon solo (*L'Apprenti Sorcier*), 82
Duparc
  use of voice apart from words, 70
Dupré, Marcel
  in Hindemith's *Concerto*, 262

Index

Durey, 274
  one of *Groupe des Six*, 266
Dvořák
  use of Slav folk-tunes, 260
  Devic influence, 287
Dynamic
  varying indications of, 86
  improvement in Hallé orchestra, under Richter, 141
  one of most potent means in a composer's equipment, 141
  meticulous observance of, 141
  Beethoven *re* above, 141
  enormous reduction in, *via* Gramophone or Radio, 141 *et seq.*
  B.B.C. admission *re* above, 142 fn.
  control of, in Radio, 144
  ditto: under control of official, 144
  example of working of above, 143
  range of M. Terepnine's new instrument, 331
Dynamic Triptych, 51 fn.
  basic rhythm from, 137

E

Ear, Human
  more highly evolved than eye, 34
  ability to detect Quarter-Tones, 38, 60 fn.
  ability to distinguish small intervals, 60 fn.
  aural vagaries, 64, 151
  usually in advance of musical intelligence, 64
  Hyperacusis, 64
  case of Bruckner, 64
  and high note of bat-squeak, 65
  and upper partials, 65
  and resultant tones, 65
  sensitivity to *timbres*, 77, 331
  ditto: easily debauched, 332
Edison
  Kinetophone, 99
Education, 349, 350
Ego
  as 'pure Activity,' 196
Einstein, Professor Albert
  inspirational method, 202
Elektra (Strauss), 229, 230
Elementals, 205, 280
  Berlioz' music, 285
  Wagner's *Ring*, 290
  Wagner's *Charfreitagzauber* (*Parsifal*), 291
  Delius' *Brigg Fair*, 311

Elementals—*continued*
  flower-elementals, 315
  Scandinavian, 317
  Sibelius, 317
  See also under *Nature-spirits : Deva*
Elgar, Sir Edward
  use of sequence, 116
  Enigma Variations: example of sequence, 116
  'light' music by, 128
  Salut d'Amour, 128
  Vignette, 232 *et seq.*
  name coupled with Delius, 258
Eliot, T. S.
  quoted, 329
Elves, 315
Emotion 'Body,' 111
Emotional Realm or 'World,' 166, 239, 315
  (*Kama*), 159
  consciousness can contact, 159
  realm of Desires and Emotions, 160
  music emanating from, 160
  range of vibration-numbers, 163
  masses respond to vibrations of, 163
  music from, alone considered as worthy of attention, 166, 171
  emotional and non-emotional music, 172
  Buddhi reflected in, 176, 309
  expression of vibrations in, 179
  reflection of Buddhic aspect of *Tristan*, 178
  Johann Strauss' *Wein, Weib and Gesang*, 185
  contact with, 212
  post-Bach music directed from and to, 239
  Stravinsky's repudiation of music from, 238 *et seq.*
  Reger's repudiation of music from, 241
  Ravel's contacts with, 249
  Hugo Wolf's contacts with, 250
  spiritualistic 'Summerland,' 276
  Dr Eaglefield Hull quoted *re*, 294
  Delius, 309, 311
  ditto: *Brigg Fair*, 311
  Dante's 'Earthly Paradise,' 311
'Emperor' Concerto (Beethoven)
  performances by Busoni, 242
Enfant et les Sortilèges, L' (Ravel), 247
England
  Brahms quoted *re*, 17
  Adolf Brodsky quoted *re*, 17
  stylistic traditions of, 17
  attitude to modern composers, 25

Index

English Horn, 330
  example of use of, 81
  demands of new French school, 88
  in Berlioz' *Faust*, 119
English Types, 58, 221, 224
  founding national music on folk-art, 259
  Vaughan Williams' use of, 260, 275
  English group of modern composers, 275 *et seq.*
Enharmonic System
  Greek employment of, 44
  potency of enharmonic differences, 335
Enigma Variations (Elgar), 116, 232, 233 fn., 235
En Saga (Sibelius), 316, 317, 319, 321
Ensouling of Music, 179 *et seq.*
  by devas, 281
  Wagner's music, 290
Entwurf einer neuen Ästhetik der Tonkunst (Busoni), 245
Equali (Beethoven)
  from Castel Sant' Angelo, 181
Equal Temperament, 334,
  stabilized by Bach, 60, 336
  ditto: Bach's *Das Wohltemperirte Klavier*, 60
  quarter-tones as offspring of, 60 336
' Er . . . bide with me '
  accentuation and word-stress, 73
Esplá, Oscar
  modal work, 55
Essais sur des Modes
  See under *Essays in the Modes*
Essays in the Modes, 45 and fn., 52
' Etheric ' Music
  M. Terepnine's instrument, 331
Etheric Realm or ' World '
  ' higher ' portion of Physical World, 160
  only recently exploited through 'Wireless,' 160
  music derived from, 165
Euphonium
  unsatisfactory quality of, 78
Euripides
  Hippolytus and *Trojan Women*, 311
Evocation des Ancêtres (*Sacre du Printemps*—Stravinsky)
  use of Bassoons in, 82
Exotic
  title of one of *Essays in the Modes*, 52
Expressionism, 173, 226
  term redundant *re* Music, 226

Expressionism—*continued*
  music has always been Expressionist, 226
  Schönberg, 251
' Expression ' Marks
  importance of, 141
  Beethoven's correspondence with publishers *re*, 141

F

' Fables ' (Stevenson), 204
Fairies, 280
Fairy Song (*The Immortal Hour*), Fiona Macleod-Boughton, 287
Falla, Manuel de
  use of repeated rhythmic patterns, 135
  music from ' etheric ' levels, 165
  Vignette, 260 *et seq.*
' False Relation '
  use of in *A World Requiem*, 282 fn.
Falstaff (Elgar), 236
Falstaff (Shakespeare's)
  quoted, 321
Familiarity and Contempt, 114 *et seq.*
' *Farewell* ' Symphony (Haydn)
  finale: Radio alterations of Dynamic, 144
Farjeon, H.
  quoted *re* Modes, 55
Fascist *régime*, 111
Fauré, 274
Faust (Berlioz)
  See under *Damnation de Faust, La*
Faust (Goethe), 311
Fennimore and Gerda (Delius), 256
Feodorovna, Tatiana, 298
Fêtes (*Nocturnes*—Debussy), 305
Fétis
  inability to discern melodies in Tannhäuser Overture, 36
Fiancée du Timbalier, La (Saint-Saëns), 119
Finlandia (Sibelius), 235, 317, 318
Finnish Types
  Sibelius, 317 *et seq.*
Fixed Pitch, 31 fn., 210
Florentine Nights (Heine), 97
Florida
  influence of, on Delius, 308
  recollections in Delius' *Appalachia*, 311
Flos Campi Suite (Vaughan Williams), 276
Flower-Elementals, 315

367

Index

Flower-Maidens
   in Wagner's *Parsifal*, 290
Flute, 330, 331
   examples of use of, 79
   via Radio, 148
Folk-Music, 17, 238, 255, 257, 258, *et seq.*, 274, 296, 319
   founding national music on folk-art, 17, 221
   by modern composers, 128
   Neapolitan folk element in Strauss' *Aus Italien* Suite, 129
   Russian folk-tunes used by Stravinsky, 238, 258
   Hungarian folk-tunes used by Bartók, 254
   influence of, on many composers, 254
   modal vestiges, 254, 275
   Arab contacted by Bartók, 255
   Hungarian used by Kodály, 258
   Oriental influences, 259
   Spanish: Moorish influence, 259
   Spanish: Spanish composers' use of, 259 *et seq.*
   Negro: American composers' use of, 274
   English: Vaughan Williams' use of, 275
   Finnish, 317
Folk-Song
   See under *Folk-Music*
Forest, De
   Audion, 99
Forsyth, Neils W.
   book by, on orchestration, 79
Fournier d'Albe
   Opto-phone, 99
Four Russian Songs (Stravinsky), 238
Fourth Dimension
   Hinton's accounts of, 172
Fra Angelico
   Russian decorative school founded upon work of, by Bakst, 53
France
   stylistic traditions, 17
   attitude to modern composers, 25
Franck, César
   two-modal system adequate for, 44
   orchestral progress since, 95
   use of Recognition Thrill, 120
   harmonic sense, 233
   influence on Elgar, 236
   d'Indy as pupil and devotee of, 274
   living inspiration of, 274
   Devic influence, 287
   inability to create 'seed'-motives, 323

Frau ohne Schatten, Die (Strauss), 229
French Horn
   See under *Horn*
French Types, 58, 221
   French group of modern composers, 266 *et seq.*
Friml, 132
Fuge, Die Kunst der (Bach)
   See under *Kunst der Fuge, Die*

G

Galsworthy, John
   inspirational method, 203
Gandharva Music, 288
Gandharva
   music-devas, 280 *et seq.*
   Handel's attempt to paraphrase music of, 283
   Schumann, Smetana and Jullien unbalanced through contact with, 284
   See also under *Deva*
Gaspard de la Nuit (Ravel), 247
Genius, 194 *et seq.*
   defined, 161 *et seq.*, 170
   misuse of word, 161
   rarity of, 162
   case of Einstein, 202
   Sibelius, 318
German Types, 58, 221
   folk-music, 222
   German group of modern composers, 272 *et seq.*
Germany
   stylistic traditions, 17
   attitude to modern composers, 25
Gerontius (Elgar)
   See under *Dream of Gerontius, The*
Gershwin, 132, 274
Gibet, Le (Ravel), 247
Gilbert, Henry F., 274
Gilman, Lawrence
   book on MacDowell quoted, 313 and fn.
Glockenspiel
   varying quality of, 89
Gluck
   studied by Berlioz, 194
   attainment of condition of 'raptus,' 201
   Devic influence, 283
   Berlioz quoted *re*, 284
Gnomes, 280
Godowsky
   as performer and composer, 243

368

Index

Goethe
  in translation, 69
  quoted, 189
  quoted, 191
  poems set by Hugo Wolf, 250
  Faust, 311
  re 'divine afflatus,' 340
Gongs
  Burmese and Chinese, 332
Good Friday Music (*Parsifal*—Wagner)
  see under *Charfreitagzauber*
Götterdämmerung (Wagner)
  Trauermarsch, 120
  Trauermarsch jazzed, 134 fn.
Gramophone, 15, 220
  limitations: analogy from mechanically reproduced pictures, 140
  limitations discussed, 140
  loss in Dynamic, 141
  loss of variety of Tone-colour, 142
  brass band records satisfactory, 142
  H.M.V. quoted *re* above, 142
  epoch-making improvement not yet reached market, 147
  distortion of orchestral *timbres*, 148
Granados
  Spanish popular music, 260
Grand Traité d'instrumentation et d'orchestration modernes (Berlioz), 79, 236
Gray, Cecil
  quoted *re* Scriabin, 295
  quoted *re* 'second-rate artists,' 295 fn.
Greek Gods, 324
Greek Modes
  diatonic, chromatic and enharmonic Greek system, 44
  Lydian Mode used by Beethoven, 44 fn.
Greek Types, 221
Gregorian Modes, 44
Gregoriev, 302
Gregory the Great, *Saint*, 44
Grétry
  re Emotion-Colour-Sound correspondence, 101
Grieg
  chromatic harmonization of diatonal melody, 50
  quickly *en rapport*, 182
  Deva-touch, 212
  contrasted with Leoncavallo, 221
  Aus Holberg's Zeit, 270
  Devic influence, 287, 315
  lapses, 289
  as prototype of MacDowell, 315
  Devic expression muddied, 315
Griffes, C. T., 274

Groupe des Six, 266
Grove
  quoted *re* Beethoven's *Pastoral Symphony*, 288
Gurre-Lieder (Schönberg), 251
  example quoted, 337 and fn.

H

Hába, Alois
  string quartet in quarter-tones, 62
  quarter-tone signs, 61 *et seq.*
Hadley, H. K., 274
Hadow, W. H.
  quoted *re* Cyril Scott, 277
Hafiz
  set to music by Szymanovski, 271
Haire, Dr Norman
  quoted, 112
Hallé Orchestra
  as trained by Hallé, 141
  after coaching by Richter, 141
Hallé, Sir Charles
  studied *Symphonie Fantastique* with Berlioz, 236
  ditto: illuminating rendition, 236
Hallelujah Chorus (Handel's *Messiah*), 70
Hamlet (Shakespeare), 311
Hamsa, 112
Handel
  two-modal system adequate for, 43
  Hallelujah and *Amen* choruses, 70
  use of sequence, 116
  Devic influence, conscious contact and musical imitation, 283
  ditto: quoted *re* conscious devic contact, 283
  ditto: quoted *re Messiah* 'raptus,' 283
Hari Janos (Kodály), 258
Harmonic System
  gap between past and present, 47
  new systems, 54
Harmonics
  increasing numbers able to hear upper partials, 65
Harmonics of Tones and Colours (Hughes), 101 fn.
Harp
  example of use of, 86
  Berlioz on use of, 146
  Wagner's writing for, in *Rheingold*, 146 fn.
Hauer, Josef
  modal system of 44 (Greek) tropes, 56
  Wandlungen, 56

Index

Haydn
  two-modal system adequate for, 44
  'Farewell' Symphony: finale via Radio, 144
  studied by Beethoven, 194
  daily application to work, 201
  attainment of condition of 'raptus,' 201
  quartet-tune as Austrian National Anthem, 254
  ditto: *fugato* upon, in Bartók's *Kossuth*, 254
  Devic influence, 282
Healing
  see under *Therapeutic Effects of Music*
Hebrew Types
  Bloch's use of, 248, 269, 274 fn.
  Milhaud and Schönberg, 269
Hebridean Types
  folk-music, 223
Heine
  association of picture and music, 97
  Florentine Nights, 97
  Rhapsodie nach Heine, 97 fn.
Heldenleben, Ein (Strauss), 26, 228 fn., 229, 230
  love-song in, 230
Helmholtz, 349 fn.
Henry IV (Shakespeare)
  Falstaff quoted (Part 2), 321
Henry VIII (Shakespeare)
  incidental music in the period, 270
Henry, O., 121, 127
Heseltine, Philip
  as proponent of Delius, 307
Heykens, 132
'Highbrows,' 107, 122
  'Highbrow' music, 131
  attitude to Jazz, 139
'Higher' *Manas*
  see under *Manas*
Hiller
  Reger's *Variations and Fugue upon a Merry Theme of Hiller*, 240
Hindemith, Paul
  example from *Suite für Klavier*, 34
  use of repeated rhythmic patterns, 134 230
  name coupled with Křenek, 258
  Vignette, 262 *et seq.*
  addicted to fugal exposition, 271
  harmonic freedom, 325
Hinton
  re Fourth Dimension, 172
Hippolytus (Euripides), 311
Histoires Naturelles (Ravel), 247

Holbrooke, Josef, 31, 277
Holst, Gustav
  use of voice apart from words, 70
  use of repeated rhythmic patterns, 135
  Perfect Fool Ballet, 138
  addicted to fugal exposition, 271
  influence of Vaughan Williams, 276
  ditto: *Somerset Rhapsody*, 276
  The Planets, 276, 287
  Devic influence, 287
  ditto: end of *Neptune* in *The Planets*, 287
Homer
  in translation, 69
Honegger, Arthur
  use of trombones (*Pacific 231*), 84
  tonal imitation of locomotive at speed, 165
  tonal imitation: psychological reactions also emphasized, 226
  Vignette, 266 *et seq.*
  one of *Groupe des Six*, 266
  addicted to fugal exposition, 271
  harmonic freedom, 325
Horace Victorieux (Honegger), 268
Horn, 330, 331
  use of four in Wagner's *Meistersinger*, 82
  examples of use of, 82
  Schubert's use of, 86
  discrepancy between French and German, 87
  demands of new French school, 88
  unsatisfactory brass chord effect *via* Radio, 147
  via Radio, 148
  re 'Just Intonation,' 333
Horn, English
  see under *English Horn*
Horses
  reaction to music, 108
Housman, A. E.
  quoted, *re* his own inspiration, 206 *et seq.*
Hughes, F. J.
  Harmonics of Tones and Colours, 101 fn.
Hugh the Drover (Vaughan Williams), 276
Hull, Dr Eaglefield
  book on Scriabin quoted, 294
Humperdinck
  contrasted with Puccini, 220
Hungarian Dances (Brahms), 128
Hungarian Types, 220
  Brahms' *Hungarian Dances*, 128
  Kodály's use of, 248, 258

Index

Hungarian Types—*continued*
  folk-tunes used by Bartók, 254, 258
  Oriental origin, 259
  founding national music on folk-art, 259
Hy Brāsil, 245
Hyperacusis, 64
Hypnotic Effect of Music
  case discussed, 39

I

Iberia (Isaac Albéniz), 260
Idealism in Music, 190
Illuminare Jerusalem (Palestrina), 175
Immortal Hour, The (Fiona Macleod-Boughton), 287
Impressionism, 165, 226
  Schönberg, 250 *et seq.*
Improperia (Palestrina), 175
Improvisation
  collective, in jazz, 139
  Indian musical system of, 345
  as fertile field for future, 346
India
  as cradle of Aryan race, 45
  as mother of Aryan languages, musical and verbal, 45
  re rhythm of Ravel's *Bolero*, 137
  influence on European folk-music, 259
  see also under *Indian Music*
Indian Music
  ancient Indian musical tradition, 45, 343, 346
  constructed on 72 modal system, 45
  Indian and European musical systems, 45, 343
  Maud MacCarthy's labours in bringing to Western world, 60 fn.
  ditto: sings 23 notes (*srutis*) within the octave, 60 fn.
  ditto: and practicability of Quarter-Tones, 60 fn.
  Rimsky-Korsakov's *Chanson Hindou*, 128
  Tala quoted, 138
  folk-music, 222
  Indian instruments, 332
  musical system, 343
  ditto: improvisation, 345
Individuality
  and Originality, 193 *et seq.*
Individuality, Immortal
  Atma-Buddhi-'Higher' *Manas*, 159, 196 *et seq.*
  Scriabin's *Luttes* (*Divine Poem*), 299

Ingenuous
  title of one of *Essays in the Modes*, 52
Inspiration, Rationale of, 14
  unstudied in Academies, etc., 20, 253
  data available, 20
  influence of women, 112
  love and condition of 'raptus,' 113
  sources of Inspiration—Part III, Chapter 10
  Shelley quoted *re* poetic composition, 162 fn.
  qualities of Inspiration, 185 *et seq.*
  Mysticism and Mystical Inspiration, 198 *et seq.*
  Mystical Inspiration assures immortality, 198
  ditto: as crux of our studies, 198
  inspiration defined, 199
  inspiration and technique, 200
  exaltation of consciousness: attainment of, 201 *et seq.*
  ditto: a method of attaining, 209 *et seq.*
  materialistic view controverted, 214
  ditto: J. H. Newman quoted, 215
  sporadic behaviour of inspirational faculty, 249
  protean quality of creative impulse, 250
  craftsmen and artists, 265
  importance of attention to, 326
  'divine afflatus,' 339
  Amiel quoted, 353
Instrumental Music
  see under *Orchestral Music*
Instruments
  see under *Orchestral Music* and under the various instruments
Intellect
  see under *Manas*
Intermezzo (Strauss), 229
Introversive
  title of one of *Essays in the Modes*, 52
Intuitional Realm or 'World'
  see under *Buddhi*
Ireland, John, 272, 276
Irish Types
  folk-music, 222
  Stanford's use of, 260
  MacDowell, 313 *et seq.*
  Yeats' poems, 314
Irmelin (Delius), 312
Isolde (Wagner)
  swan-song of, 68
Italian Types, 58, 220, 221
  Neapolitan folk element in Strauss' *Aus Italien* Suite, 129

371

Index

Italian Types—*continued*
 Italian group of modern composers, 277 *et seq.*
Italy
 stylistic traditions, 17
 attitude to modern composers, 25

J

Jameson, D. D.
 Colour Music, 101 fn.
Japanese Music, 344
Javanese Music, 344
Jazz
 new shades of orchestral tone-colour and *timbres*, 78
 decadent jazz tunes, 127
 good jazz tunes, 131
 evaluation of, 132 *et seq.*
 dance music of negroid origin, 132
 sponsored by some serious musicians, 132
 legitimate scope of, 133
 limitations of, 133, 136
 jazzing the classics, 134 fn.
 examination of constituents, 135
 rhythmic patterns, 136, 139, 344
 reason for widespread popularity, 136
 its failure with more serious artists, 136
 example of jazz basic rhythm, 137
 elements worthy of attention, 139
 basic rhythmic formulæ, 139
 new tone-colours, 139
 collective improvisation, 139
 source, 163
 obscenities, 185
 instruments, 332
 as an alterative, 347
Jekyll and Hyde (Stevenson), 203 fn., 204
Jeu Divin (Scriabin)
 third movement of *Divine Poem*, 299
Jeux (Ballet by Debussy), 305
Jeux d'Eau (Ravel), 247
Jewish Types
 see under *Hebrew Types*
Joachim
 in Beethoven's Violin Concerto, 92
 in *Cavatina* from Beethoven Op. 130, 181
Joyce, James
 quoted, 29
Jullien
 contact with *Gandharvas*, 284, 300
Junge Magd, Die (Hindemith), 267

' Just ' Intonation, 333 *et seq.*
 voice can easily cope with, 74

K

Kajanus
 as conductor of Sibelius, 323
Kalidasa
 in translation, 69
Kama
 see under *Emotional Realm or ' World '*
Karelia (Sibelius), 317
Karma, 233
 Scriabin's, 301, 302
Keats, John
 Nightingale ode: attempts to enhance by music, 68
 Lines in imitation of Spenser, 271
 quoted, 339
 re ' divine afflatus,' 340
Kelley, E. Stillmann, 274
Keltic Sonata (MacDowell), 314
Keltic Types
 folk-music, 222
 Bax's use of, 248
 MacDowell's use of, 314
 Yeats' poems, 314
Key-Consciousness
 modern composers free from, 42, 52
 see also under *Atonality*
Keynote
 re Diatonal music, 42
Kilner, Dr
 apparatus, 291 fn.
Kinema
 Silent films *v.* ' talkies,' 68
Kinetophone (Edison), 99
King Christian II (Sibelius)
 Musette, 319
King Lear (Shakespeare), 311
Kingsley
 quoted, 320
King, Yeend, A.R.A., 35 fn.
Kingdom, The (Elgar), 236
Kodály, Zoltan, 274–276 (twice)
 Hungarian types, 248
 Vignette, 257
Korngold, Erich, 273
 quoted *re* Puccini's *Tosca*, 273
Kossuth (Bartók), 235, 254
Kreisler
 performances of Brahms' Violin Concerto, 180
 re passage-work in Elgar's *Violin Concerto*, 235
 as performer and composer, 243

Index

Křenek, Ernst, 230, 253
  has sponsored Jazz, 133 fn.
  name coupled with Hindemith, 258
  Symphonic music, 272
Kulluvo (Sibelius), 319
Kunst der Fuge, Die (Bach), 37, 127

L

Lalande
  his bassoon, 92
Land of Hope and Glory (Elgar), 234 and fn.
Landor, 224
L'Après midi d'un Faune (Debussy), 303, 305, 306
  of epoch-indicating character, 237
La Tristesse du Printemps (Sibelius), 318
La vie de Bohème (Murger), 99
Leading Motifs
  see under *Motifs, Leading*
Lear, King (Shakespeare), 311
Leblanc, 127
L'Enfant et les Sortilèges (Ravel)
  see under *Enfant et les Sortilèges, L'*
Leoncavallo
  contrasted with Grieg, 221
Leonora
  in the prison house, 68
Leprechauns, 323
Les Noces (Stravinsky), 238
L'Heure Espagnole (Ravel), 248
'Light' Music, 127 *et seq.*, 318
  contumelious use of term, 127
  Bach's Dances, 127
  Beethoven's Scottish and German Dances, 128
  Beethoven's *Battle Symphony* (Rûle Britannia !), 128
  Schubert's 'light' music, 128
  Brahms' Hungarian Dances, 128
  Sibelius' *Valse triste*, 128
  Ravel's *Bolero*, 128, 129
  Rimsky-Korsakov's *Chanson Hindou*, 128
  by modern serious composers, 128
  Elgar's *Salut d'Amour*, 128, 234
  folk-music by modern composers, 128
  Poulenc's idiom, 129
  Strauss' 'light' music in major works, 129
  adroit introduction of, in *Rosenkavalier*, 129
  Strauss quoted, 130
  and 'Serious': abuse of terms, 130
  Rossini's dictum, 130

'Light' Music—*continued*
  hack work by serious composers, 131
  term, in opprobrious sense applied to Jazz, 135
  Sibelius, 318
Linke, 132
Liszt, 242
  use of Recognition Thrill, 119
  influence on Strauss, 236
  comparison with Busoni, 242
  foreshadowed whole-tone 'scale,' 303
  power to create 'seed'-motives, 323
Liturgy, Roman
  Palestrina's settings, 175
'Live' Music
  see under *Vitality in Music*
Loeffler, Charles, 274
Loge
  in Wagner's *Ring*, 290
Lohengrin (Wagner)
  Vorspiel, 322
London Public
  Scriabin quoted *re*, 301
Londonderry Air
  unsatisfactory transcriptions, 49
Lord Bateman's Daughter, 261
'Lowbrows'
  'Lowbrow' music, 131
'Lower' *Manas*
  see under *Manas*
Lussan, Zelie de
  in *Carmen*, 181
Luttes (Scriabin)
  first movement of *Divine Poem*, 299
Lydian Mode
  used by Beethoven, 44 fn.

M

MacCarthy, Maud
  introduced term 'Microtone,' 60 fn.
  labours in bringing Indian music to Western world, 60 fn.
  singing 23 notes within the octave, 60 fn.
  bearing of above feat on practicability of Quarter-Tones, 60 fn.
Macdonald, J. D.
  Sound and Colour, 101 fn.
MacDowell, Edward
  Devic influence, 287
  Vignette, 313 *et seq.*
Maclean
  experimentalist *re* Colour-Sound correspondence, 99

Index

Macleod, Fiona
   The Immortal Hour, 287
Madrigali Spirituali (Palestrina), 175, 176
Magic
   magical effects of music, 21, 346
   definition, 21
   ensouling of music, 179 *et seq.*
   magical operations *re* musical composition, 203 (Scriabin); 209 *et seq.*
   Delius, 313
   timbre, 332, 333
   Indian music, 343 *et seq.*
   music and, 346 *et seq.*
   power: music stands or falls by its possession of, 347
Magic Fountain, The (Delius), 312
Mahler, Gustav
   use of voice apart from words, 70 .
   as conductor, 93
   Vignette, 272
   inability to create 'seed'-motives, 323
Major Mode, 44
   nearly all music, A.D. 1700–1900 in major or minor mode, 44
   Palestrina and minor, 55
   H. Farjeon quoted *re*, 55
Malipiero, 277
   pamphlet *The Orchestra* quoted, 20 fn.
   found Palestrina's technique inadequate, 30
   quoted *re* Palestrina, 55
   Dalle tre Commedie Goldoniane, 278
   Variazioni senza Tema, 278
   ditto: comparison with Vaughan Williams' *Pastoral Symphony*, 278
Ma Mère l'Oye (Ravel), 249
Manas
   mental Realm or 'World,' 159
   consciousness can contact, 159
   divided into 'higher' and 'lower,' 160
   Sanskrit derivation, 160 fn.
   lower as realm of ratiocinative principle, 160
   lower, 'raises mankind above brute,' 160
   lower, has brain as instrument, 160, 163
   higher, enables man to 'commune with the gods,' 160
   higher, has psychic faculties as instrument, 160
   dividing-line between 'lower' and 'higher,' 160, 168

Manas—continued
   music emanating from 'below' and 'above,' 160 *et seq.*
   possible to distinguish, 160
   range of vibration-numbers, 162
   present-day busy-ness originates in 'lower,' 163
   music inspired from 'higher,' 164, 166, 168 *et seq.*
   Higher levels largely unexplored, 167
   music from lower levels, 167
   concentration on lower, 167
   plethora of merely cerebral works, 167
   Netherland school of fifteenth century, 168
   Plato's Archetypes, 168
   Higher, as Causal world, 168
   Higher, functioning of, 169
   Lower, functioning of, 170
   Lower, danger of concentration on, 173
   ditto: Paul Bekker and, 173
   Higher, reflected in lower, 176
   Higher, *Mantra* from *Avatara*, appertaining to, 177
   vibrations in Mental World, 179
   Higher, Beethoven's *Grosse Fuge* contacted through, 185
   Causal presentation complete, 189
   music from Higher, accused of 'coldness,' 189 fn.
   music from Higher: qualities, 193
   mystical inspiration, 199
   contact with Higher, 211
   characteristics of Higher, 212
   Higher levels of, 223, 246, 325
   lower, 223
   glimpses of higher in Strauss' work, 230
   Stravinsky's concentration on, 238
   barrenness of music from lower, 239
   Reger's concentration on, 240
   Scriabin's *Divine Poem*, 299
   Higher, 301
   see also under *Causal Realm*
Manfred (Byron), 311
Manfred Overture (Schumann), 91
Mantra
   definition, 117 fn.
   Three Mantras from *Avatara*, 177
March of Spring, The (*North Country Sketches*—Delius), 311
'Marguerite' Melody (Berlioz' *Faust*), 119
Marseillaise, La
   Vougeot singing, 181

Index

Martyre de Saint Sébastien (Debussy), 306
Mass (Bach), 214
Mass (Vaughan Williams), 276
Mass of Life (Delius), 311
   contrasted with Debussy's *Pelléas et Mélisande*, 307
Masses (Palestrina), 175, 271
Mechanical Music, 140
   analogy from painting, 140
   Sir Richard Terry quoted *re*, 143
   see also under *Gramophone* and *Radio*
Mechanized Music
   see under *Mechanical Music*
Meck, Nadeshda von
   re Tchaikovsky's *Fourth Symphony*, 197
Medtner
   use of voice apart from words, 70
   his German heredity, 273
   influenced by Taneiev, 296
Meistersinger, Die (Wagner)
   Overture, 37
   mainly diatonic, 42
   contrasted with chromatic *Tristan*, 42
   use of Horns in, 82
   Overture: example of Sequence, 117
   Walter's *Preislied* in, 119
   Vaughan Williams quoted *re*, 224, 275
   uniformity of idiom: contrast with *Tristan*, 271
   contrasted with *Ring*, 282
   Devic passage in Act 3, 290
Memoires (Berlioz), 126
Mendelssohn, 172
   two-modal system adequate for, 44
   use of 'pommer' oboe, 86
   a symphony of, 90
   study of Bach, 194
   conviction of superiority, 194
   violin concerto, 235
   Devic influence, 287
   Ruy Blas Overture, 306
   trombone requirements, 306
Mental 'Body,' 112
Mental Realm or 'World'
   Manas, 159
   consciousness can contact, 159
   'higher' and 'lower,' 160 fn.
   music emanating from, 160
   range of vibration-numbers, 162
   see further under *Manas*
Mer, La (Debussy), 305
Messe des Morts (Berlioz)
   Sanctus, 287

Messiah (Handel)
   Hallelujah and *Amen* choruses, 70
   composer's 'raptus': Handel quoted, 283
Metaphysic
   limitations of English vocabulary *re*, 156
   Schematization formulated, 156, 159, 164
   see also under *Æsthetic*
Microphone
   see under *Radio*
Microtones
   employed by Eastern musicians, 59
   and Quarter-Tones, 60
Migot, Georges, 65, 274
Milhaud, Darius
   one of *Groupe des Six*, 266
   Vignette, 269 *et seq.*
Military
   title of one of *Essays in the Modes*, 52
Military Band
   playing *Bande Mataram*, 181
   pitch used by, 348 fn.
Mill, John Stuart
   quoted, 329
Milton, 127
Mime
   in Wagner's *Ring*, 290
Minchon (Ravel), 247
Mind ('Higher' and 'Lower')
   see under *Manas*
Mineral Kingdom
   reaction to music, 108
Minor Mode, 44
   or Major, A.D. 1700–1900, 44
   or Major, Palestrina and, 55
   or Major, H. Farjeon *re*, 55
Minuet des Follets (*La Damnation de Faust*—Berlioz), 285
Modes, 41 *et seq.*, 245, 336
   necessary item, 42
   exist by reference to tonic and dominant, 43
   Greek, 44
   Gregorian, 44
   Major and Minor, 45
   72 Indian, 45
   Essays in the, 45, 52
   system of 90, 45 *et seq.*
   value of 90, 48, 55
   dominant and tonic in, 48, 49
   purity of, essential, 48, 50
   unsatisfactory use of, 49
   chromatic accompaniment of, 50
   Verdi's *Ave Maria*, 50

Index

Modes—*continued*
  exclusive behaviour of, 51
  discordant effect of 'foreign' note in, 51
  do not express mood, 52
  simplicity not inanity of, 53
  possible abuse of, 53
  effect of liberation of, 55
  Palestrina's use of, 55
  influence in modern music, 55
  Oscar Esplá's work, 55
  Josef Hauer's system, 56
  exclusive use deprecated, 57
  Busoni's concentration upon, 245
  mild modal tang, 254
  vestiges of, 254
  fundamental roots, 254
  larger aspect of, assimilated by Bartók, 255
  Vaughan Williams, 275
  relation to whole-tone 'scale,' 303, *Raga* (Indian), 346
Monadic Realm or 'World' (*Anupādaka*), 159
  man cannot contact, 159
Moody
  Sankey and, 175 fn.
Moore, Tom, 248
Moorish Music
  and Ravel's *Bolero*, 137
  influence on Spanish, 259
Môrnaunaon (Ravel), 247
Mortal Personality
  see under *Personality, Mortal*
Mother Goose Suite (Ravel), 247
Motifs, Leading
  and Wagner's influence on Elgar, 236
Mouvements Symphoniques (Honegger), 267 fn.
Mozart
  technique, 30
  whole-tone 'scale' joke, 43
  two-modal system adequate for, 44
  clarinet-bassoon duets, 92
  one ducat for concertos, 124
  starvation of, 125
  'light' music by, 127
  inspiration from 'Causal world,' 169
  quoted, 169
  studied by Beethoven, 194
  studied by Tchaikovsky, 194
  quoted, 195 fn.
  mystical inspiration, 199
  quoted, *re* his own inspiration, 205
  imitated by Poulenc, 270
  Devic influence, 284

Mozart—*continued*
  ditto: '*Batti batti*,' 284
  re 'divine afflatus,' 339
  'Turkish' music, 344
Murger
  Schaunard's '*Symphony in Blue*,' 99
Musette (*King Christian II*—Sibelius), 319
Musical Opinion
  quoted, 319 fn.
Music-Hall Ditties
  source of, 163
Music: its Secret Influence throughout the Ages (Cyril Scott)
  quoted, 281 fn.
Music, Laws and Evolution (Jules Combarieu)
  quoted, 34 fn.
Music-Pictures
  use of Quarter-Tones, 59
  Queen's Hall, Hallé Concerts, 59 fn., 98 fn.
Mussolini
  play *Napoleon*, 121
Mussolov
  factory machine-room, 165
  psychological reactions, 226
Mussorgsky
  pictures in music, 98
  whole-tone 'scale,' 303
Mutes (trumpet)
  use of papier-mâché, 83
Mystery, The (Scriabin), 294, 302
Mysticism, 198 *et seq.*
  defined, 198 fn.
  as essential element, 198
  as crux of our studies, 198
  exaltation of consciousness, 201 *et seq.*
  Dhyana and *Samadhi*, 209
  William Blake, 295
  Delius, 313
  MacDowell, 315

N

Napoleon
  re educative value of music, 188
Napoleon (Play by Mussolini), 121
Nationalism, Musical, 220, *et seq.*, 235 238, 255, 257, 258, 274, 296
  founding on folk-art, 17
  absence of, in Atonal music, 58
  Bartók, 254
  Vaughan Williams, 275
  Tchaikovsky, 296
  Sibelius, 317

Index

Natural Tuning, 348
  see under *'Just' Intonation*
'Nature'-Pitch, 210
  therapeutic use of, 110, 348
  potency of, 210 fn.
Nature-Spirits, 205, 280
  in Wagner's *Ring*, 282
  Haydn's music, 283
  Berlioz' music, 285
  Beethoven's *Pastoral Symphony*, 287
  Wagner's *Charfreitagzauber* (*Parsifal*), 291
  Debussy, 305
  Delius, 311
  Sibelius, 314, 317 et seq.
  MacDowell, 313
  Keltic response to, 315
  Scandinavian, 317 et seq.
Nazi *Régime*, 111
Negro Types
  American composers' use of, 274
  American national music and, 274
Neapolitan Song, A
  sung by Caruso, 181
Neo-Classicism, 226
Neptune (*The Planets*—Holst), 287
Netherland School (fifteenth century, 168
Neues vom Tage (Hindemith), 266 fn.
Neue Zeitschrift für Musik (Robert Schumann)
  quoted, 36
Newman, Ernest
  quoted *re* Scriabin's *Prometheus*, 295
Newman, John Henry
  quoted, 214
Niagara Falls
  analogy from, 143
Nietzsche
  quoted, 107
  Zarathustra and Delius' *Mass of Life*, 311
Nightingale Ode (Keats)
  music to, 68
Nijinsky, 269
Nikisch, Artur
  as conductor, 92
Nin, Joaquin
  re Spanish music, 259
Noces, Les (Stravinsky), 238
Nocturnes (Chopin), 197
Nocturnes (Debussy), 305
Norfolk Rhapsody (Vaughan Williams), 276
North American Indian Types
  folk-music, 223
North Country Sketches (Delius), 311

Notation
  quarter-tone signs, 61
Nuages (*Nocturnes*—Debussy), 305
Nusch-Nuschi, Das (Hindemith), 265
Nymphs, 280, 315

O

Oboe, 330, 331
  use of, 80
  'Pommer' type of, 86
  discrepancy between types, 86
  and French school, 88
  via Radio, 149
Occult Aspects of Musical Art, 19 et seq. 198 et seq.,
  ensouling of music, 179, 281
  'Cosmic Symphony,' 285
  Devic influence on composers, 279
  Vignettes of devic composers, 293 et seq.
  Scriabin Vignette, 293
  investigations, 367
  see also under *Physical Aspects*
Ode to a Nightingale (Keats)
  see under *Nightingale Ode*
'*Olalla*' (Stevenson), 204
Omar Khayyám
  settings of, 345
Ondine (Ravel), 247
On Hearing the First Cuckoo in Spring (Delius), 311
Opera
  in unknown language, 68
  decline in, 75
  'Comic,' 190
Optophone (Fournier d'Albe), 99
Oratorios
  by Elgar, 236
Orchestra
  superiority over Chorus, 67
  modern symphony the finest instrument, 75
  ambience of different orchestras, 76
  restricted types, 78
  levelling of tone-values, 89
  team-spirit in orchestras, 92
  Hallé Orchestra under Hallé and Richter, 141
  superiority over brass band, 142
  gramophone reproduction, 142
  Orchestre Straram (Paris), 262
  Delius quoted *re*, 306
  the perfect orchestra, 330
  ditto: additional instruments, 330
  M. Terepnine's instrument, 331

Index

Orchestra—*continued*
  ditto : orchestral possibilities, 332
  new instruments, 331 *et seq.*
  Oriental instruments, 332
  jazz instruments, 332
  radio orchestras, 332
  need for re-estimate, 332
  pitch used, 348 fn.
Orchestral Music
  superiority over vocal, 66
  William Byrd quoted *re*, 66
  Robert Schumann quoted *re*, 66
  Post-Bach German masters on, 66
  the Orchestra, 75 *et seq.*
  receiving increased attention, 75
  appreciation of *timbres*, 76
  novel tone-colours, 77
  greater range possible, 78
  orchestral examples, 79
  clumsy orchestration, 86
  discrepancies, 86
  uniformity of tone-values, 90
  conducting and conductors, 90
  performance of without conductor, 90
  orchestral ' colour,' 94
  ' colour ' at expense of construction, 94
  progress since Brahms and Franck, 95
  superiority of modern scoring, 95
  modern vogue of, 96
  reproduction by Radio and Gramophone, 140 *et seq.*
Orchestration
  Berlioz on, 79, 236
  Forsyth on, 79
  examples, 79 *et seq.*
  adroitness of, 86
  clumsiness in, 86
  modern scoring *via* Radio, 149
  Debussy's, 305
  need for re-estimate, 332
  see also under *Orchestral Music ; Timbre ; Tone-colour and quality*
Organische und Mechanische Musik (Paul Bekker), 173
Orientalities, 343
Originality
  and Individuality, 193
Ornstein, Leo, 274
Ortmann
  quoted *re* ' colour-hearing,' 102
Othello (Shakespeare), 311

P

Pacific 231 (Honegger), 267
  trombones in, 84

Paderewski
  as performer and composer, 243
Paganini
  as performer and composer, 243
Painting, 158
  illustration from, 35 fn.
  paraphrased in music, 59
  ditto : *re* economy of colour, 95
  correspondence between music and, 97
  analogy from, 104
  re limitations of mechanical reproductions, 140
  ' expressionism ' in, 226
  Schönberg, 251
  Whistler quoted, 271
  Blake's synthesis, 350
  Boito's synthesis, 350
Palestrina, 224, 271
  his technique, 30
  revival desirable, 52
  use of modes, 55
  movements of, 65
  his best work, 128
  loftiest name, 175
  ' sacred ' and ' sæcular,' 175
  Masses, 175
  Madrigali Spirituali, 175, 176
  Assumpta est Maria, 175
  Improperia, 175
  Salve Regina, 175
  Illuminare Jerusalem, 175
  Amor quando floria (Petrarch), 175, 214
  Buddhic records, 185
  exemplar of Purity, 192, 212
  devotees of, 192
  pre-Palestrina epoch, 239
  constant devic influence, 283
  Palestrina and Scriabin, 292, 302
  Professor Tovey quoted *re*, 338
Palestrina (Pfitzner), 272
Pan, Kingdom of, 237, 249
' Paper ' Music
  modern composers and, 338
Paracelsus
  re psycho-physiological effects, 109
  Elementals, 280
Parsifal (Wagner)
  Charfreitagzauber, 214, 291, 318
  influence of, on Elgar, 236
  Devic influence, 291
  ditto : Flower-maidens, 290
  ditto : evocative power of, 291
  ditto : contacts Buddhic plane, 291
Pastoral Symphony (Beethoven), 97, 287
  imitation of cuckoo, 98, 165
  Grove quoted *re*, 288

Index

Pastoral Symphony (Vaughan Williams), 275
  comparison with Malipiero, 278
'*Pathétique*' Symphony (Tchaikovsky), 138
Patriotism, Musical
  see under *Nationalism*
Peasant Arts, 261
Pedrell, Felipe
  renaissance of Spanish music, 259
Pelléas et Mélisande (Debussy), 305
  as Debussy's chief work, 307
  ditto : contrasted with Delius' *Mass of Life*, 307
Pentatonic Formula
  Debussy's use of, 304
Percussion Instruments
  varying quality of, 89
  misrepresented, 143, 149
  characteristics of, 331
  ditto : the Celesta, 331
  scope for development, 331
  Oriental instruments, 332
  percussive *timbres*, 333
  tam-tam effects, 345
Perfect Fool, The (Holst)
  ballet, 138
Performers
  demands on technique, 15
  ability to detect quarter-tones, 38
  team-spirit in orchestras, 92
  playing from memory, 94
  interpretative and creative, 243
  professional and amateur, 263
Persia
  influence on Europe, 259
Personality, Mortal, 196 *et seq.*, 295 fn.
  'lower' *Manas*, 159
  'colours' expression of ideas, 223, 304
  Scriabin's *Luttes* (*Divine Poem*), 299
Petrarch
  Death of Laura : *Ballata*, 175
  ditto : *Amor quando floria*, 175
Petrouchke (Stravinsky), 238
Pfitzner, Hans, 272
  opera *Palestrina*, 272
Phædrus (Plato)
  quoted, 168 fn.
Philistines, 196
Philosophy of Modernism (Cyril Scott)
  quoted, 103
Physical Realm or ' World '
  familiarity with, 160
  etheric and dense, 160
  etheric only recently exploited, 160

Physical Realm or ' World '—*continued*
  music emanating from, 160
  range of vibration-numbers, 162
  masses respond to vibrations of, 163
  music derived from, 165
  Atma reflected in, 176
  expression of vibrations in, 179
Physicists
  researches, 109
Photophone (Graham Bell), 99
Pianoforte
  Scriabin's devotion to, 299
  Beethoven *re*, 299
  MacDowell's pieces, 313
  String players with, 334
Pianola, 15
Piatti, Alfredo
  and *Ständchen* of Schubert, 181
Piccini
  contrasted with Beethoven, 220
Piccolo, 330
  example of use of, 80
Pictures
  see under *Painting*
Pierrot Lunaire (Schönberg), 252
Pineal Gland, 213
Pitch
  fixed pitch, 31 fn.
  ' Nature '-pitch, 110, 210, 347
  ditto : effects of, 348
  variations in, 348 fn.
  psycho-physiological effects, 352
Pituitary Body, 213
Pizzetti, 277
Plagiarism
  real and supposed, 169
  Wagner and, 170
Planes of Nature
  and sound-colour correspondences, 104
  women's response to music, 113
  see also under *Realms of Nature*
Planets, The (Holst), 276
  Neptune, 287
Planquette
  contrasted with Sullivan, 221
Plant Life
  reaction to music, 108
Plastic Arts
  ' expressionism ' in, 226
Plato, 353
  re effects of music, 109
  Archetypes in *Dialogues*, 168
  Phædrus quoted, 168 fn.
  re educative values, 188
Platonic Solids, 105

379

Index

Plexuses (in human body)
  correspondences, 105
  re musical therapy, 110, 348
Poe, Edgar Allan
  attainment of 'raptus,' 201
Poème de L'Extase (Scriabin), 294, 300
Poèmes Juifs (Milhaud), 269
Poem of Fire, The (Scriabin)
  see under *Prometheus*
Poetry, 158
  Shelley's *Defence of*, 161 fn.
  Housman re, 206
  'Expressionism' in, 226
  Eliot re Dante, 329 fn.
  silent readings, 336
  Blake's synthesis, 350
  Wagner's synthesis, 350
  Boito's synthesis, 350
Pohjola's Daughter (Sibelius), 323
Polka, 132
  by Smetana, 234
Polytonality, 33, 334
  derivation of, 42
  as genesis of Atonality, 56
  in Strauss, 228 fn.
  Busoni's disapproval of, 244
  Bartók, 255
  Honegger, 269
  Milhaud, 269
  use of in *A World Requiem*, 281 fn.
Pomp and Circumstance Marches (Elgar), 234
'Popular' Music
  see under '*Light*' *Music*
Post-Romanticism, 226
Poulenc, Francis, 269
  idiom adopted, 129
  one of *Groupe des Six*, 266
  Vignette, 270
Powell, John, 274
Prâna, 112, 209
Preislied (Wagner's *Meistersinger*), 119
Préludes (Debussy), 305
Pre-Raphaelite Movement, 52
Presentation, Arts of, 158
Pribaoutky (Stravinsky), 238
Prismic
  title of one of *Essays in the Modes*, 52
Professional Performers
  see under *Performers*
Progress
  cyclic nature of, 52
Prokoviev
  violin concerto, 15
  use of repeated rhythmic patterns, 135

Prometheus (Scriabin), 214, 294, 298, 301
  use of Flute in, 79
  use of 'Tastiera per Luce' in, 101
  performance of in Paris, 181
  E. Newman quoted re, 295
  'Promethean' chord, 342
Proust, Marcel, 171
Psychical Aspects of Musical Art, 13, 19, 198 et seq., 351
  'colour-hearing' sense, 102
  psycho-physiological effects, 108
  'Cosmic Symphony,' 285
  Devic influence on composers, 279 *et seq.*
  Vignettes of devic composers, 293 *et seq.*
  Scriabin Vignette, 293 *et seq.*
  investigations, 351
  see also under *Occult Aspects*
Psychic Faculties
  of 'higher' *Manas*, 160
Psychological Aspects of Musical Art, 13, 351
  investigations, 351
Psycho-Physiological Effects of Music, 109
  investigations, 351
  pitch and *timbre*, 352
Puccini, Giacomo
  use of bassoon, 82
  Tosca: performance of last act, 181
  his music, 182
  wide-embracing tunefulness, 212
  contrasted with Humperdinck, 220
  Erich Korngold re, 273
  influence on composers, 278
  re Wagner, 278
  Turandot, 278
  ditto: completed by Alfano, 278
Purcell, 263
Purity in Music, 192
  Palestrina, 192
  Delius, 313
  MacDowell, 315
Pythagoras, 353
  re psycho-physiological effects, 109
  re value of music, 188
  quoted, 281

Q

Quarter-Tones 59, *et seq.*, 245, 335
  discussed, 37
  ability to detect, 38
  only occasional use advocated, 57

Index

Quarter-Tones—*continued*
  experimental use of, 59
  adoption as item in technique, 59
  Colombine: A Study in Whole-Tones, Half-Tones and Quarter-Tones 59
  Quarter-Tones and Microtones, 59
  defined, 60
  practicability established, 60 fn.
  offspring of equal-tempered scale, 60, 336
  accidental use of, 61
  signs, 61
  example, 62
  by Alois Hába, 62
  Hába's signs, 63
  use and abuse of, 63
  common-sensible forward-step, 65
  voice and, 74
  in *A World Requiem*, 281 fn.
Queen Mab (Berlioz), 237
  in Paris Conservatoire, 181
  Scherzo, 286
Queen of the Pagodas (*Mother Goose Suite*—Ravel), 247
Quincey, De
  attainment of 'raptus,' 201

R

Rachmaninof
  as pianist, 241
  influenced by Taneiev, 296
Radio, 15, 220
  analogy from pictures, 140
  limitations discussed, 140 *et seq.*
  loss in Dynamic, 141
  broadcasting experience, 142
  example of limitations, 143
  control of dynamic, 144
  silent bars *via*, 146
  duplication fails, 146
  loss of *timbre* values, 147
  distortion of *timbres*, 148
  classical music and modern, 149
  large choral works *via*, 149
  importance of, 149
  effect of, 149
  defects, 150
  good results, 150
  Radio orchestras, 332
  ditto: special orchestrations, 332
Raga (Indian)
  mode, 346

Rameau
  technique, 30
  re colour-sound correspondence, 101
  Debussy a descendant of, 303
Rapport, 182
Raspi
  quoted, 329
Rattenfänger, Der (Wolf), 250
Ravel, Maurice
  a piano piece by, 15
  Bolero, 128, 129
  the waltz, 132
  use of repeated rhythmic patterns, 135
  Bolero: basic rhythm of, 137
  canker of 'personality,' 197
  affected by poems, 250
  Vignette, 247 *et seq.*
  name coupled with Debussy, 258
  re Berlioz' gaucheries, 285 fn.
Realms of Nature, 161 *et seq.*, 325
  schematization of, 158
  seven, 159
  man's consciousness and, 159
  music from, 160
  possible to distinguish, 160
  genius can 'realize' higher, 161
  masses respond to lower, 163
  subdivisions of, 164
  higher unexplored, 166
  contacted, 196
  examples of contact with, 201 *et seq.*
  a method of contact with, 209
  music able to make direct effect upon, 239
Recognition Thrill, 116
  sequence, 116
  examples of sequence, 116
  more subtle use of, 119
  abuse of, 120
  defiled, 134 fn.
  effective use of *via* Radio, 149
Reed-Organ
  unsatisfactory tone of, 78
Reed Player, The
  vocal problem in, 71
Reger, Max, 127
  Vignette, 240
  comparison with Hindemith, 262
  as typical professional, 263
  rarity of lapses, 263, 289
  antiquated forms used by, 268
Remington, G. W.
  Colour-Organ, 100
  The Art of Mobile Colour, 101 fn.
  Colour-Organ in *Prometheus*, 101

Index

Renard (Stravinsky), 238
Representation, Arts of, 158
Requiem (Delius), 309
Respighi, 277
  a modern work, 90
  'etheric' music of, 165
Resultants
  few able to detect, 65
  Georges Migot and, 65
Retablo de Maese, El (Falla), 261
Revolution, Musical, 28 *et seq.*
  an unparalleled, 28
  consequent difficulties, 28
  new wine : new bottles, 29
  objections to modern music, 30
  and technical matters, 351
  expressional side, 351
Revue Blanche
  Debussy quoted, 26
Revue Musicale
  Suzanne Demarquez quoted *re* English music, 225
Rhapsodical Style, 297
  in Wagner, 297
Rhapsodie Espagnole (Ravel), 248
Rhapsodie nach Heine, 97 fn.
Rheingold (Wagner)
  writing for Harp in, 146 fn.
Rhine-Maidens
  in Wagner's *Ring*, 282, 290
Rhythmic Formulæ, 29, 30
  Tala (Indian), 346
Rhythmic Patterns
  profundity of effect of, 135
  a primitive device, 135
  use of, 136
  and popularity of jazz, 136
  examples of, 136 *et seq.*
  five- and seven-beat, 138
  Indian, 344
Richter, Hans
  quoted, 17
  at Philharmonic, 92
  quoted, 93
  comparison with Toscanini, 93
  training of orchestra, 141
  re Ein Heldenleben, 228 fn.
  Elgar's *Pomp and Circumstance*, 234 fn.
  mentor to Bartók, 254
Rimsky-Korsakov
  sound-colour correspondences, 101, 103
  Chanson Hindou, 128, 345
  'etheric' music, 165
  Sadko, 297

Ring (Wagner)
  Devic music, 282, 290
  contrasted with *Meistersinger*, 282
Ritual, Church
  see under *Church Ritual*
Rohmer, Sax, 171
Roi David, Le (Honegger), 268
Roi Lear Overture (Berlioz)
  use of Oboe in, 80
Roman Liturgy
  Palestrina's settings of, 175
Romantics, 173
  Schönberg, 250 *et seq.*
Romeo et Juliet Symphony (Berlioz), 237
  Scène d'Amour, 285
Rondeau Romantique (Sibelius), 319
Ronde du Sabbat (*Symphonie Fantastique* —Berlioz), 286
Rosenkavalier (Strauss), 229, 230
  waltzes in, 129
  adroitness of, 129
  third act of on Gramophone, 148
Rossini
  quoted, 130
Roussel, 274
Rubenstein
  as performer and composer, 243
Rugby (Honegger), 267
Rûle Britannia (Beethoven), 128
Russia
  stylistic traditions, 17
Russian Decorative School of Painters, 53
Russian Types, 58, 220, 221
  folk-tunes used by Stravinsky, 238, 258
  Oriental origin, 259
  founding national music on folk-art, 259
Ruy Blas Overture (Mendelssohn)
  a performance of, 306
  trombone requirements, 306

S

Sabaneiev, L.
  book on Scriabin, 293
Sacred Music
  confusion between and sæcular, 175 and fn.
Sacre du Printemps, Le (Stravinsky), 237, 252
  bass Flute in, 80
  '*Evocation des Ancestres*,' 82
Sadko (Rimsky-Korsakov)
  a performance of, 297

Index

Sæcular Music, 44
    confusion between and sacred, 175 and fn.
Safonov
    quoted *re* Scriabin, 297
Saint Augustine, 188 fn.
Saint Germain, 302
Saint-Saëns
    La Fiancée du Timbalier, 119
    Africa, 243
    many-sided art of, 277
    quoted *re* Berlioz, 287
Salamanders, 280, 290
Salo, Gasparo di, 88
Salome (Strauss, 98, 229, 230
    Baptist's music, 129
Salut D'Amour (Elgar), 128, 234
Salve Regina (Palestrina), 175
Samadhi, 209, 313
Sancho Panza (*Don Quixote*), 129
Sancta Civitas (Vaughan Williams), 276
Sanctus (*Messe des Morts*—Berlioz), 214, 287
Sand, George
    re Chopin's *Nocturnes*, 197
Sankey
    and Moody, 175 fn.
Sanskrit Literature
    metaphysical schematization from, 159
    studied by Schopenhauer, 209
    re Dhyana and *Samadhi*, 209
    use of word *Deva*, 279 fn.
    studied by Scriabin, 300
    Schopenhauer and influence of, 343
Saranghi, 332
Sarasate
    as performer and composer, 243
Satie
    use of voice apart from words, 70
    foreshadowed whole-tone 'scale,' 303
Saxophone
    unsatisfactory tone-quality of, 78
Scales
    see under *Modes*
Scales in Music and Colours (Allen), 101 fn.
Scandinavian Types
    folk-music, 222
    Sibelius, 314, 317 *et seq.*
Scarbo (Ravel), 247
Scène d'Amour (*Romeo et Juliet* Symphony—Berlioz), 285
Scène de Danse (Sibelius), 319
'Schaunard'
    (in Murger's *La Vie de Bohème*), 99

Schelling
    quotes Pythagoras, 281
    quoted *re* Beauty, 281
Schelomo (Bloch), 274 fn.
Schicksalslied (Brahms), 214
Schlacht bei Vittoria (Beethoven), 128
Schmitt, Florent, 274
Schnabel
    Schubert: The last of the great composers, 329 fn.
Schola Cantorum (Paris)
    founded by d'Indy, 274
Scholes, Percy
    quoted, 60 fn.
Schönberg, Arnold, 46 fn., 127, 171, 264, 269
    Brahms-Schönberg period, 30
    attracts converts, 125
    hack work by, 131
    canker of 'personality,' 197
    Vignette, 250 *et seq.*
    Gurre-Lieder : example quoted, 337 and fn.
Schools of Music
    see under *Academies*
Schopenhauer
    as Wagner's mentor, 209
    studies in Sanskrit, 209
    re influence of Sanskrit, 343
Schreker, 230
Schröder-Devrient, 252
Schubert, 329
    two-modal system adequate for, 44
    art-songs, 67
    use of trombones, 84
    use of horns and bassoons, 86
    use of bass trombone, 88
    a symphony, 90
    clarinet-bassoon duets, 92
    starvation of, 125
    'light' music by, 127, 234
    Ständchen, 181
    music becomes 'ensouled,' 182
    mystical inspiration, 199
    condition of 'raptus,' 201
    waltzes, 234
    overture *In Italian Style*, 270
    Devic influence, 284
    a symphony, 306
    seventh and *Unfinished* symphonies, 320
Schubert: the last of the great Composers (Schnabel), 329 fn.
Schumann, Robert
    Neue Zeitschrift für Musik quoted, 36
    two-modal system adequate for, 44

Index

Schumann, Robert—*continued*
  quoted, 66
  composed songs in 1840, 66
  art-songs, 67
  Manfred Overture, 91
  Pianoforte Quartet, 116
  recognition thrill, 119
  the waltz, 132
  study of Bach, 194
  studied by Brahms, 194
  conviction of superiority, 194
  exposed Philistines, 195
  contrasted with Berlioz, 221
  Pfitzner derivative from, 272
  Devic influence, 284
  power to create ' seed '-motives, 323
Science of Sound, 349
  neglect of, 349
  Helmholtz *re*, 349 fn.
  proposed investigations, 351
Scott, Cyril, 277
  Philosophy of Modernism, 103
  quoted, 281 fn.
Scriabin, Alexander Nicolas, 264, 309
  use of voice apart from words, 70
  use of flute (*Prometheus*), 80
  type of orchestration, 95
  adapted Remington Colour-Organ, 101
  sound-colour correspondences, 101, 103
  study of ' colour-hearing ' faculty, 102
  and ' Causal world,' 169
  Prometheus, 181, 214
  moral value of music, 188
  study of Chopin, 194, 342
  conviction of superiority, 194
  inspirational method, 203
  inner refulgence, 212
  contrasted with Honegger, 267
  as devic composer, 302
  Vignette, 293 *et seq.*
  conscious devic contact, 298, 318
  contrast with Delius, 309
  contrasted with Sibelius, 324
  and complete harmonic freedom, 325
  re ' divine afflatus,' 339
  harmonic development, 342
  ditto : ' Promethean ' chord, 342
  synthesis of arts, 350
Sculpture, 158
  ' expressionism ' in, 226
Sea Drift (Delius)
  performance at Essen, 306
Secret Doctrine, The (Blavatsky)
  sound-colour Table of Correspondences quoted, 103

' Seed '-motives, 322
Senart, Maurice
  publisher, *Essais sur des Modes*, 45 fn.
Sequence
  provides recognition thrill, 116
  e.g. Schumann's *Pianoforte Quartet*, 116
  e.g. Bach's *Double Concerto*, 116
  e.g. Elgar's *Enigma Variations*, 116
  e.g. Wagner's *Meistersinger Overture*, 117
  e.g. Debussy's *String Quartet : finale*, 117
Serenata (Braga)
  performance of, 184
Sex, 111 *et seq.*
  music and sex, 177
Shakespeare, 225, 338
  in translation, 69
  The Tempest, 268, 348
  Henry VIII, 270
  King Lear, 311
  Hamlet, 311
  Othello, 311
  Falstaff quoted (*Henry IV*, Part 2), 321
  Shakespearean ' prop,' 344
Sharp, Cecil
  and Musical Nationalism, 221
Shaw, George Bernard
  adroitness, 125
  re serious composers, 126 fn.
Shelley
  Defence of Poetry quoted, 162 fn., 224
  quoted, 253
  re ' divine afflatus,' 340
Shepherds of the Delectable Mountains The (Vaughan Williams), 276
Shop-Ballads
  source of, 163
Sibelius, Jean Christian, 339
  use of voice apart from words, 70
  subsidised, 125
  ' light ' music by, 127
  Valse triste, 128
  Deva-touch, 212
  Finlandia, 235
  lapses, 263
  championed by Bantock, 276 fn.
  Devic influence, 287, 314
  Vignette, 316 *et seq.*
  development of 342
Side drum
  example of use of, 85
Siegfried Idyli (Wagner), 297

Index

Signs
  for quarter-tones, 61
Silent Bars
  magical use of, 146
  ineffective *via* radio, 146
Simplicity, 341
  of Modal approach, 53
  not to be eschewed, 53
Sirènes (*Nocturnes*—Debussy), 305
Sistrum, 332
Six, Groupe des
  see under *Groupe des Six*
Sketch of a New Æsthetic of Music (Busoni), 245
Skörgen
  quoted *re* Sibelius, 318
Slav Types
  Dvořák's use of, 260
Smetana
  Polkas, 234
  and Bohemian folk-tunes, 260
  Devic influence, 284, 287
  ditto : unbalance, 284, 300
Smithson, Harriet
  re Berlioz' *Symphonie Fantastique*, 197
Smyth, Dr Ethel
  quoted, 132 fn.
Socrates
  his dæmon, 204
Somerset Rhapsody (Holst), 276
Sonata Form
  the 'repeat' in, 118
  as a fetter, 297
  ditto : Scriabin, 297
  ditto : use of, in *Prometheus*, 301
Song of the High Hills (Delius), 214, 311
  use of English horn in, 81
Songs, 190
  discussed, 67
  enshrine inspirations, 67
  Leonora in the prison house, 68
  Isolde's swan-song, 68
  limitations of language, 68
  wedding of words and music :
    perfection impossible, 68
    not always happy, 69
    W. B. Yeats quoted, 69
    use and abuse, 69
    further discussion *re*, 312
    attempt to solve problem in *The Reed Player*, 71
  community singing, 72
  ditto : effectiveness of, 72
  facile princeps as the social art, 72
  Four Russian (Stravinsky), 238
  Hugo Wolf, 249

Songs—*continued*
  of Many Colours (Hafiz-Szymanovski), 271
  of the Mad Muezzin (Tagore-Szymanovski), 271
  Fairy Song (*The Immortal Hour*—Fiona Macleod—Boughton), 287
  pseudo-oriental, 344
  comic and sentimental as alteratives, 347
  see also under *Choral Music ; Vocal Music*
Songs of Many Colours (Szymanovski)
  words by Hafiz, 271
Songs of the Mad Muezzin (Szymanovski)
  words by Tagore, 271
Sorabji, Kaikhorsu
  re Simplicity in Art, 341
Sound
  occult power of, 21
  and colour : correspondence, 97 *et seq*.
  (see further under *Colour and Sound : Correspondence*)
  effect on mineral kingdom, 108
  effect on vegetable kingdom, 108
  effect on animal kingdom, 108
  effect on human kingdom, 108
  psycho-physiological effects, 109
  therapeutic effects, 109
  range of vibration-numbers, 162
  -vibrations in manifested world, 210
  every object has key-note, 210
  science of, 349
  ditto : neglect of, 349
  ditto : Helmholtz, 349 fn.
  ditto : proposed investigations, 351
Sound and Colour (Macdonald), 101 fn.
Spanish Types, 58, 221
  Ravel's use of, 248
  Oriental origin, 259
  founding national music on Folk-art, 259
  composers' use of, 259
Spengler
  The Downfall of the West, 329 fn.
Spenser, 271
Spheres
  see under *Realms of Nature*
Spiritualism
  negative type of, 199
  'Summerland,' 276
Spirituality in Music, 192
Spiritual Realm or 'World'
  see under *Atma*
Spohr
  chromaticism of harmonic style, 50
  period since, 91

Index

Srutis
  see under *Microtones*
Ständchen (Schubert)
  performance by Piatti, 181
Stanford
  and Irish folk-tunes, 260
'Statement'
  repetition of, 118
Stevenson, Robert Louis
  quoted, 123
  quoted, 201
  Jekyll and Hyde, 203 fn.
  contact with non-human entities, 204
  ditto: his 'Brownies,' 204
  Olalla and other 'Fables,' 204
  quoted, 246
Sthula
  physical Realm or 'World,' 159
  man familiar with, 159
  divided into Etheric and Dense, 160
  see further under *Physical Realm or 'World'*
Stokowski
  difficulty with small intervals, 64
  conducting *via* Radio, 145
Straram, Orchestre (Paris), 262
Strauss, Johann
  Wein, Weib und Gesang waltzes, 185
Strauss, Richard, 241, 249
  Ein Heldenleben, 26
  found Wagner's technique inadequate, 30
  Bach-Strauss period, 45
  revised Berlioz' 'Orchestration,' 79
  use of flute (*Also Sprach Zarathustra*), 79
  use of horns (*Don Juan*), 82
  use of trumpet (*Also Sprach Zarathustra*), 83
  a massive number by, 90
  tonal imitation, 98, 165
  Salome, 98, 129
  Don Quixote, 98
  adroitness of, 129
  Aus Italien Suite, 129
  Till Eulenspiegel, 129
  Don Quixote, 129
  Also Sprach Zarathustra, 129
  Symphonia Domestica, 129
  Rosenkavalier, 129
  Varese quoted *re*, 129
  the waltz, 132
  use of repeated rhythmic patterns, 135
  sheep-bleat imitations, 165
  study of Brahms and Wagner, 194
  conviction of superiority, 194

Strauss, Richard—*continued*
  Vignette, 228
  early recognition of, 232
  appreciation of Elgar, 232
  comparison with Elgar, 232
  Symphonic Poems, 235
  ditto: influence on Elgar, 235
  influence on Bartók, 254
  fortissimo passages, 267
  Tod und Verklärung, 287 fn.
  'seed'-motives, 323
Stravinsky, Igor, 172 fn.
  use of bass flute (*Le Sacre du Printemps*), 80
  use of bassoon (*Le Sacre du Printemps*: 'Evocation des Ancêtres'), 82
  a modern work, 91
  type of orchestration, 95
  has sponsored Jazz, 133 fn.
  music from 'higher' levels, 171
  ditto: derided, 171
  canker of 'personality,' 198
  quoted, 226
  Vignette, 237 *et seq.*
  Le Sacre du Printemps, 252
  use of Russian folk-tunes, 259
  has grown beyond folk-music, 261
Strophic
  title of one of *Essays in the Modes*, 52
Submarine (Honegger), 267
Sub-planes of Nature, 104, 164, 172
Sullivan, Arthur
  accentuation and word-stress, 73
  contrasted with Planquette, 221
Summer Garden, In a (Delius), 311
'Summerland,' Spiritualistic, 276
Summer Night on the River (Delius), 311
Sunday Sun
  quoted *re* Delius program, 310
Swan of Tuonela, The (Sibelius), 317, 321
Sylph Ballet (*La Damnation de Faust*—Berlioz), 285
Sylphs
  in *La Damnation de Faust*, 285
  Flower-maidens in *Parsifal*, 290
Symbolists, 165
Sympathetic-nervous System, 279
  response from, 39
Symphonia Domestica (Strauss)
  baby-in-the-bath episode, 129
Symphonic Music (Křenek), 272
Symphonic Style
  closed, 297
  ditto: Brahms and Wagner, 297

Index

Symphonie Fantastique (Berlioz), 197
  Hallé studied with composer, 236
  an illuminating rendition, 236
  and Elgar's *Falstaff*, 236
  Devic influence, 285
  Ronde du Sabbat in, 296
Symphonie Pathétique (Tchaikovsky), 115
'Symphony in Blue'
  (in *La Vie de Bohème*), 99
'Symphony in White' (Whistler), 99
Synæsthesia
  'colour-hearing' sense so-called, 102
Synthesis of Arts, 105, 349
  Scriabin *re*, 102, 301
  Æschylus, Blake, Wagner, Scriabin and Boito, 350
  necessary training, 350
Synthetic-simplicity, 341
Szigeti
  re tuning, 334
Szymanovski, Karol
  Vignette, 271
  hint of devic influence, 287

T

Tagore, Rabindranath
  set by Szymanovski, 271
Taillefére, Germaine
  one of *Groupe des Six*, 266, 274
Tala (Indian)
  example quoted, 138
  basic rhythm, 346
'Talkies'
  see under *Kinema*
Talleyrand
  quoted, 231
Tambura, 332, 344
Taneiev
  influence on Scriabin, Rachmaninof and Medtner, 296
Tannhäuser (Wagner)
  overture, 36
  use of trombones in, 84
  Venusberg music, 299
Tapiola (Sibelius), 323
Tastiera per Luce
  used by Scriabin, 101, 301
Tchaikovsky, 309, 321
  found Mozart's technique inadequate, 30
  Symphonie Pathétique, 115, 138
  the waltz, 132
  study of Mozart, 194
  conviction of superiority, 194

Tchaikovsky—*continued*
  Fourth Symphony, 197
  ditto: influence of Nadeshda von Meck, 197
  re Musical Nationalism, 296
  influence on Scriabin, 296
Television Apparatus (Baird), 100
Tempered Tuning
  see under *Equal Temperament*
Tempest, The (Shakespeare)
  incidental music by Honegger, 268
  quoted, 348
Tenor Drum
  example of use of, 85
Tenoroon, 330
Tenor Tuba, 331
Terepnine
  his invention, 331
  ditto: characteristics of, 331
Terrasse des audiences du clair de lune, La (Debussy), 305
Terry, Sir Richard
  quoted *re* mechanical music, 143
Tertia-tones, 335
  writer incorrectly accused of using, 60
Theosophy, 300
  Scriabin's, 294
Therapeutic Effects of Music, 74, 105, 107
  psycho-physiological researches, 109
  music in hospitals, 109
  vast potentialities, 109
  writer as witness of, 110
  use of 'Nature'-Pitch, 110, 348
  music-therapy in its infancy, 110
  comparative failure hitherto, 349
Thompson, Francis
  starvation of, 125
Till Eulenspiegel (Strauss)
  'light' music in, 129, 229, 230
Timbre, 35
  effect produced by single note, 21, 343
  vocal-instrumental, 29
  preference for instrumental, 66
  vocal *timbre* contrasts, 70
  contrasts sharply differentiated, 76
  appreciation of orchestral, 77
  dynamic and magic-making, 76
  little attention paid to, 77
  debased new *timbres*, 77
  limited gamut of, 78
  craving for extension of, 77
  lack of discrimination of, 78
  study of, desirable, 76 *et seq.*
  muted trumpets, 83

Index

Timbre—continued
  instrumental discrepancies (see under individual instruments), 86
  lack of unanimity, 86
  demands of French school, 88
  unique features should be preserved, 88
  harmful effect of discrepancies, 90
  orchestral ' colour,' 95
  superiority of modern scoring, 95
  bearing of, on correspondences, 104
  defective in Radio and Gramophone, 145, 148
  loss of *timbre* values, 147
  re ' ensouling of music,' 183
  use of contrasted *timbres*, 282 fn.
  Debussy's use of, 305
  characteristics of oboe, tenoroon and bassoon, 330
  characteristics of violin, viola and violoncello, 330
  numerous novel *timbres*, 331
  characteristics of new instrument, 331
  human ear easily debauched, 332
  need for re-estimate of values of, 332
  counterpoint of, 333
  Indian instrumental, 343
  psycho-physiological effects of, 352
  see also under *Tone-colour and -quality*

Timpani
  examples of use of, 84
  quality constant, 89
  via Radio, 149

Tod und Verklärung (Strauss), 229, 230, 287 fn.
  composed at age of twenty-five, 232

Tone-colour and -quality
  discrimination between pure and impure one of least developed faculties, 78
  greater range possible, 78
  only ' true ' tone-colours should be added, 78
  trumpets C and F, 88
  Gasparo di Salo viola, 88
  violoncellos, bass and baritone, 89
  tubas, 89
  percussion instruments, 89
  timpani, 89
  glockenspiel, 89
  inexhaustible variety of, 94
  contrasts in scoring, 95
  Debussy-Stravinsky-Scriabin orchestration, 95
  increasing selectivity, 95
  see also under *Timbre*

Tone-deafness, 64
Tono-Bungay (Wells), 178
Torrey
  Alexander and, 175 fn.
Tosca (Puccini)
  use of bassoon in Act III, 81
  performance of last Act, 181
  Erich Korngold quoted *re*, 273
Toscanini
  as conductor: comparison with Richter, 93
Tovey, Professor Donald
  Companion to ' Die Kunst der Fuge,' 37
  quoted, 137
  quoted, 271
  as score-reader, 338
  quoted *re* Palestrina, 338
Train Bleu, Le (Milhaud), 269
Trauermarsch (Wagner's *Götterdämmerung*), 120
  jazzed, 134 fn.
Triangle
  in ' Turkish ' music, 344
Tristan und Isolde (Wagner), 313
  almost entirely chromatic, 42
  contrasted with *Meistersinger*, 42
  Isolde's swan-song, 68
  effect on audience, 178
  Buddhic aspect, 178
  ditto : contacted by Wagner, 178
  a memorable performance, 181
  influence of Mathilde Wesendonk, 197, 224
  uniformity of idiom, 271
  Puccini quoted *re*, 278
  contains no devic music, 290
  Debussy's dislike of, 303
Tristesse du Printemps, La (Sibelius), 318
Trois Poèmes Juifs (Bloch), 274 fn.
Trojan Women, The (Euripides), 311
Trollope, Anthony
  daily application to work, 201
Trombone, 331
  examples of use of, 84
  discrepancies, 86
  sonority of German, 88
  Schubert's use of bass, 88
  demands of new French school, 88
  unsatisfactory effect *via* Radio, 147
  Equali for four (Beethoven), 181
  Mendelssohn's *Ruy Blas*, 306
  a Schubert symphony, 306
  Delius, requirements, 306
Tropes (Greek)
  Josef Hauer's system of, 56
Troyens, Les (Berlioz), 287

Index

Trumpet, 330
  example of use of, 83
  muted, 83
  discrepancy between C and F, 87
  demands of new French school, 88
  unsatisfactory effect *via* Radio, 147
  Delius' requirements, 307
  re 'just' intonation, 333
Tuba, 331
  varieties of, 89
  unsatisfactory effect *via* Radio, 147
Tudor School
  Vaughan Williams' affinity with, 275
Turandot (Puccini), 278
  completed by Alfano, 278
Turina
  Spanish popular music, 260
'Turkish' Music
  by Mozart and Beethoven, 344
Turner
  daily application to work, 201
Turner, W. J.
  quoted *re* Scriabin, 295

U

Undines, 280
  in Wagner's *Ring*, 282, 290
Une Barque dans l'Océan (Ravel)
  see under *Barque dans l'Océan, Une*
Unfinished Symphony (Schubert), 320
Unvollendet (Schubert's B minor symphony), 86 fn.
Upanishads
  Scriabin's studies of the, 300
Upper Partial Harmonics
  increasing number able to hear, 65

V

Valse
  see under *Waltz*
Valses nobles et sentimentales (Ravel), 247
Valse Triste (Sibelius), 128, 318
Van Dieren, 245 fn.
Varese, Edgar, 274
  conversation with Strauss quoted, 129
Variations and Fugue upon a Merry Theme of Hiller (Reger), 240
Variazioni senza Tema (Malipiero), 278
Vaughan Williams, Ralph
  and Musical Nationalism, 221
  quoted, 224

Vaughan Williams, Ralph—*continued*
  use of English folk-tunes, 260, 275
  Vignette, 275
  comparison with Malipiero, 278
Vegetable Kingdom
  reaction to music, 108
Venusberg Music (*Tannhäuser* — Wagner), 299
Verdi, 125
  two-modal system adequate for, 44
  modes in *Ave Maria*, 50
  wide-embracing tunefulness, 212
  contrasted with Wagner, 220
  Italian Nationality, 223
'Verism,' 226
Vie de Bohème, La (Murger), 99
Vieuxtemps,
  as performer and composer, 243
Village Romeo and Juliet, A (Delius), 256, 311
Vina, 332, 344
Viola
  timbre of, 88, 330
  by Gasparo di Salo, 88
  via Radio, 148
Violin, 330
  duplication increases effect, 146
  via Radio, 148
  subtle instrument, 289 fn.
  coarseness of, relative to deva-music, 289 fn.
Violoncello, 330
  two types, 89
  via Radio, 149
Vision of Dante, The, 232 fn.
Vistas, New, 329 *et seq.*
Vitality in Music, 186, 310
Vittoria, Schlacht bei (Beethoven), 128
Vivaldi
  tonal imitation, 98
  pieces by, 165
Vocalises, 70
Vocal Music, 312
  discussed, 66 *et seq.*
  superiority of orchestral over, 66
  William Byrd quoted re, 66
  Robert Schumann quoted *re*, 66
  as Nature's perfect instrument, 67
  wedding of words and music, 67
  use apart from words, 70, 73
  'vocalises,' 70
  vocal *timbre*-values, 70, 333
  Hallelujah and *Amen* choruses, 70
  potentialities, 70
  voice least fully exploited of instruments, 70

Index

Vocal Music—*continued*
  attempt to solve a problem, 71
  voice as potent musical instrument, 71
  community singing, 71
  accentuation and quantity, 73
  Ravel's *Histoires Naturelles* for Voice and Piano, 247
  Honegger's voice-leading, 266
  Delius', in *Appalachia*, 311
  see also under *Choral Music*; *Songs*
Voice, the Human
  therapeutic uses of, 110
  investigations into potentialities of, 351
  see also under *Vocal Music*
Voluptes (Scriabin)
  second movement of *Divine Poem*, 299
Von Bülow
  see under *Bülow, von*
Von Meck, Nadeshda
  see under *Meck, Nadeshda von*
Vougeot
  singing *La Marseillaise*, 181

W

Wagner, Richard, 302
  found Weber's technique inadequate, 30
  technique, 30
  Tannhäuser Overture, 36
  Meistersinger Overture, 37
  diatonic *Meistersinger*, chromatic *Tristan*, 42, 271
  two-modal system adequate for, 44
  Isolde's swan-song, 68
  use of horns (*Meistersinger*), 82
  use of trombones (*Tannhäuser* Overture), 84
  imposed his types of instrument, 88
  a massive number by, 90
  dependent on steady *tempo*, 91
  as conductor, 92
  Meistersinger Overture, 117
  Preislied, 119
  use of Recognition Thrill, 120
  Trauermarsch (*Götterdämmerung*), 120
  attracting converts, 125
  quoted, 132 fn.
  jazzing of *Trauermarsch*, 134 fn.
  Wagnerian 'purple patches' *via* Radio, 143
  harps in *Rheingold*, 146 fn.
  etheric music, 165

Wagner, Richard—*continued*
  inspiration from 'Causal world,' 169
  ditto: diversified presentation of, 169
  plagiarism by, 169
  Tristan: effect on audience, 178
  contacted Buddhic Realm, 178
  Tristan: a memorable performance, 181
  his music 'ensouled,' 182
  claim *re* moral value for music, 188
  study of Weber, 194
  studied by Strauss, 194
  conviction of superiority, 194
  exposed Philistines, 196
  Tristan: influence of Mathilde Wesendonk, 197
  mystical inspiration, 198
  quoted, *re* his own inspiration, 209
  Schopenhauer as his mentor, 209
  unifying force of a, 212
  Charfreitagzauber (*Parsifal*), 214, 291, 318
  contrasted with Verdi, 220
  Vaughan Williams quoted *re Meistersinger*, 224, 275
  Tristan, 224, 313
  influence on Elgar, 236
  fortissimo passages, 267
  Tristan and *Meistersinger* contrasted, 271
  ditto: uniformity of idiom, 271
  Pfitzner derivative from, 272
  Puccini quoted *re*, 278
  Devic music in *Ring*, 282, 290
  Ring contrasted with *Meistersinger*, 282
  Devic influence, 290
  ditto: his methods, 290
  ditto: *Meistersinger*, 290
  ditto: *Tristan* contains no devic music, 290
  ditto: *The Ring*, 290
  ditto: *Parsifal*, 290
  Parsifal: failure of Flower-maidens, 290
  Parsifal: evocative power of, 291
  Parsifal: contacts Buddhic Plane, 291
  free rhapsodical style of, 297
  ditto: *Siegfried Idyll*, 297
  Venusberg Music, 299
  influence on Debussy, 303
  Debussy's revulsion against, 303
  Lohengrin Vorspiel, 322
  Power to create 'seed'-motives, 323
  use of Bass Trumpet, 331
  synthesis of arts, 350

Index

Wagnerites, 37
Wales
 see under *Welsh Types*
Walk to the Paradise Gardens, The (Delius), 313
Wallace, Edgar, 127
Walter's *Preislied* (Wagner's *Meistersinger*), 119
Walton, William, 277
Waltz
 Valse Triste (*Sibelius*), 128
 from *Rosenkavalier* (Strauss), 129
 by fine composers, 132
 Wein, Weib und Gesang (Johann Strauss), 185
 by Schubert, 234
 Valses nobles et sentimentales (Ravel), 247
 by Sibelius, 319
Wandlungen (Josef Hauer), 56
Waterloo, Battle of
 in Mussolini's play *Napoleon*, 121
Weber
 technique, 30
 the waltz, 132
 studied by Wagner, 194
 mystical inspiration, 199
Webern, Anton von, 253, 272
 name coupled with Berg, 258
Wein, Weib und Gesang Waltzes (Johann Strauss), 185
Weismann
 quoted *re* Berlioz, 223
Wells, H. G.
 Tono-Bungay, 178
Welsh Types
 founding national music on folk-art, 259
Wesendonk, Mathilde
 re Wagner's *Tristan und Isolde*, 197
Wheeler, Dr
 quoted, 31 fn.
Whistler
 'Symphony in White,' 99
 quoted, 271
Whiteman, Paul, 274
Whitman, Walt
 words of Delius' *Sea Drift*, 306 fn.
Whole-tone 'Scale', 303
 discussed, 43
 Debussy addicted to, 43, 303
 used by Mozart as a joke, 43
 an Eastern 'scale,' 43
 Debussy erected into a system the, 303
 foreshadowed, 303

Wieniawski
 as performer and composer, 243
Winter Landscape, A (Delius), 311
Wireless
 see under *Radio*
Wohltemperirte Klavier, Das (Bach)
 stabilized Equal Temperament, 60
 as musicians' 'daily bread,' 176
Wolff, Albert
 and Concerts Lamoureux, 93
Wolf, Hugo
 art-songs, 67
 accentuation and word-stress, 73
 Vignette, 249
 comparison with Schönberg, 250 *et seq.*
Women, 111
 as creative artists, 111 *et seq.*
 polarization of male and female, 111
 as 'inspirers' of creative artists, 112
 response to music, 113
World Requiem, A, 281 fn.
'Worlds'
 see under *Realms of Nature*
Wozzeck (Berg), 272

X

Xylophone
 example of use of, 85, 86

Y

Yeats, William Butler
 quoted *re* wedding of words and music, 69
 failure of musicians to enhance his poems, 69
 often compared with composer Bax, 276
 resemblance with MacDowell's music, 314
 ditto : Keltic influence, 314

Z

Zarathustra (Nietzsche)
 text for Delius' *Mass of Life*, 311
Zarathustra (Strauss)
 see under *Also Sprach Zarathustra*

www.ingramcontent.com/pod-product-compliance
Lightning Source LLC
Chambersburg PA
CBHW071214080526
44587CB00013BA/1376